GUIDE TO INVESTMENT TRUSTS
&
UNIT TRUSTS

Joanna Slaughter

London · Hong Kong · Johannesburg · Melbourne · Singapore · Washington DC

PITMAN PUBLISHING
128 Long Acre, London WC2E 9AN
Tel: +44 (0)171 447 2000
Fax: +44 (0)171 240 5771

A Division of Pearson Professional Limited

First published in Great Britain 1996

ISBN 0 273 62518 7

British Library Cataloguing in Publication Data
A CIP catalogue record for this book can be obtained from the British Library.

10 9 8 7 6 5 4 3 2 1

Typeset by Northern Phototypesetting Co Ltd, Bolton
Printed and bound in Great Britain by Redwood Books, Trowbridge, Wiltshire

The Publishers' policy is to use paper manufactured from sustainable forests.

CONTENTS

The legal position · The tax position · Inheritance tax ·
Getting the child involved

FOREWORD

Today, more than ever, we need to make our savings and investments work hard for us. Changes to the welfare state – and the likelihood of further changes to come – mean that managing our capital properly is a key factor in financing the purchase of our home, our healthcare, our children's education and – perhaps most important – our retirement planning.

De-regulation of the financial services industry, which began in the 1980s, has led to a sometimes bewildering proliferation of financial products. The quantity and complexity of products mean investors need guidance. True, there is a world of information out there – some of it free, a lot of it cheap – but is it any good?

The *Investors Chronicle* series of investment books – like the weekly magazine – has been produced to help answer that question, with objective and authoritative advice, written from the investor's point of view.

The aim is to provide readers with a practical, jargon-free guide to all areas of personal finance and investment. Thus, whether you are a sophisticated investor, keen to learn more about the DIY approach to investing, or are new to investment, the books will arm you with the facts and understanding that you need. As such, they should be the natural complement to the high-quality, independent assessment that the magazine aims to provide every week.

MARK VAN DE WEYER, Publisher, *Investors Chronicle*,
FT Magazines

INTRODUCTION

This book has been written for everyone who would like to know more about investing money in unit and investment trusts.

It can be used as a starter kit by beginners or as a reference book by the experienced, who are looking for more technical information about collective funds. It has something to say to the £50 a month saver as well as the £50,000 investor.

I believe that a well-managed investment trust or unit trust is likely to be the best home for the long-term savings of the majority of investors. But no investment will be profitable – and it is certainly not going to be much fun – unless you understand what you are doing with your money when you invest in one of these funds.

Investment trusts and unit trusts are rather like commercially run investment clubs. They enable even people with modest resources to benefit from the sort of stockmarket portfolio that would be beyond the pocket of private investors without a seven-figure bank balance.

By clubbing together through a collective fund investors secure a number of advantages. They contain some of the risk of being in the stockmarket, because their money is spread over a large number of UK and overseas companies. They secure the services of a professional investment manager at a price they can actually afford. And they eliminate the decision-making and administrative paper mountain of managing their own stockmarket investments.

Despite these benefits, unit trusts and investment trusts continue to be viewed with a little nervousness by some members of the savings public. The funds have never enjoyed the cheap popularity of privatisation issues and 14 times as many savers have money in a building society as in a unit trust.

I suspect, too, that even some existing unit trust and investment trust investors consider that the funds are complex, and that their inherent risks are pretty well unfathomable.

One of the aims of this guide is to dispel such misgivings. Its main purpose, however, is to provide a handbook that will give D-I-Y investors the information they need to become educated and successful users of investment trusts and unit trusts.

How do you invest in a unit trust or investment trust? What's the difference? What choice of investments are there? How do you find the right fund when there are nearly 2,000 to choose between? How do you know what risk you are taking?

You will find the answers to these questions, and many more, in the following pages. There are signposts to related pieces of information and summaries of each chapter to help you along the way. As the investment industry also has a secret language to rival that of professional Internet surfers, unfamiliar terms are explained at the beginning of each section, and in a comprehensive concluding glossary.

ACKNOWLEDGEMENTS

I am very grateful to the stalwarts at the Association of Unit Trusts and Investment Funds (AUTIF) and the Association of Investment Trust Companies (AITC) for patiently answering my endless questions; to Tim Miller of Portfolio Fund Management, Mark Mathias of Henderson Touche Remnant, Peter Smith of Hill Martin plc, and David Aaron of the David Aaron Partnership for their kindness in checking some very raw copy; and to Audrey Jeanneret for all her help and encouragement.

The basic aim of investment trusts and unit trusts is to provide investors with a professionally managed portfolio of shares and bonds, at a reasonable price

COLLECTIVE INVESTMENT: WHAT IS IT ALL ABOUT?

1

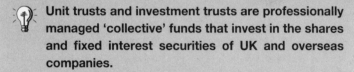

■ THE FUNDAMENTALS

Unit trusts and investment trusts are professionally managed 'collective' funds that invest in the shares and fixed interest securities of UK and overseas companies.

The funds give private investors access to professional investment management at a reasonable cost.

By investing in a unit trust or investment trust, private investors reduce stockmarket risks because they have exposure to a portfolio of shares and are not dependent on the fortunes of just a few companies.

Unit trusts and investment trusts provide access to virtually every stockmarket in the world, so investors are able to diversify risks further by spreading their money across a number of industrial and geographical market sectors.

Unit trust and investment trust holdings can be bought and sold at any time. Investors are not locked in.

Prices of unit trust units and investment trust shares are published in the daily and weekend newspapers, making it easy to keep track of the progress of the investments.

■ TERMINOLOGY

Investment trust: A publicly quoted company with a fixed number of shares which are traded on the London Stock Exchange. The business of an investment trust is to invest in the shares and fixed-interest securities of other companies.

Unit trust: A legal trust that manages a fund of stockmarket securities on behalf of a number of investors. The pool of investments in the trust is divided into equal portions, called units.

Closed-end fund: An investment vehicle like an investment trust that has a fixed capital structure with a fixed number of shares. The share price of a closed-end fund will reflect investor demand for its shares.

Open-ended fund: A fund like a unit trust that increases or decreases in size, depending on the buying and selling demands of investors.

Net asset value (NAV): The total value of an investment trust's assets, at current market values, after all debts and prior charges have been deducted. The NAV is usually quoted in pence per ordinary share. This figure is calculated by dividing the net assets by the number of ordinary shares in issue.

Discount: An investment trust trades at a discount when its share price is lower than its net asset value (NAV) per share.

Premium: An investment trust trades at a premium when its share price is higher than its net asset value (NAV) per share.

Thursday, 19 March 1868 deserves to be marked by a minute of appreciative silence. It was a momentous date in the history of private investment in this country.

Readers of a brief announcement in the 'Money Market & City Intelligence' column of The Times newspaper learned that a new company had been formed, of a type that bore no resemblance to any other. Its business was not to make paint, or pulp wood or run railways; it was to invest in other companies. The aim was to enable investors of 'moderate means' to put their money into a spread of overseas shares 'without incurring the entire risk, incidental to any one particular stock'.

The new company was Foreign & Colonial, the world's first investment trust, and its innovative terms of business were an almost instant success. Within seven years, 17 more investment trusts were quoted on the Stock Exchange.

Although some turbulent times were to follow, with a number of the new trusts crashing under the weight of managerial incompetence or greed, Foreign & Colonial rode out all the early storms.

Today the original F & C trust has more than £1.8 billion of assets, and at the end of 1995 it qualified for entry into the FTSE 100 Index, as one of the 100 leading companies quoted on the London Stock Exchange. It has also spawned a number of satellite trusts, all bearing the Foreign & Colonial name.

The second milestone for private investors came in April 1931, with the establishment of the first British unit trust by Municipal and General Securities, the present day M & G Group, now a £15 billion investment company, running 35 unit trusts and five investment trusts.

M & G's First British Fixed Trust was launched in the wake of the 1929 stockmarket disaster, a financial crisis which had rattled investors badly. Understandably so. Between 1929 and 1932 the price of industrial shares fell by two-thirds.

Like the existing investment trusts, the new M & G venture also limited risks for investors by providing them with a spread of shares, initially confined to 24 named companies, among them

Boots, Commercial Union, Harrods and Shell. However, the trust's structure was quite different from that of an investment trust because it was an open-ended fund.

This was an important distinction. Unlike a closed-end investment trust, the new unit trust did not have a fixed number of shares. The more investors there were, the more money was available to buy assets and the larger the fund became. The converse was true if there were more sellers than buyers.

The first unit trusts were fixed funds. New money from investors was placed in a predetermined portfolio, and there was almost no flexibility in investment policy or scope for active management. It was not until 1935 that a 'flexible' unit trust – the type of fund now on offer – went on sale to the public.

Clearly both collective fund industries have grown far from their pioneering roots. At the start of 1996 the 161 unit trust companies managed £113 billion of investors' money, while the 340 investment trusts had combined assets of some £51.95 billion. The funds invest on behalf of investors in all the world's stockmarkets, and they cater as effectively for the £25 monthly saver as for the millionaire investor.

WHY INVEST IN THE STOCKMARKET?

Investment trust and unit trust investors put their money into the shares and fixed-interest securities of different companies. Why should they do this, rather than stick to the known and familiar security of an interest-paying bank or building society savings account?

■ INVESTMENT SNAPSHOT

When you put £1,000 into a deposit-based savings account you know exactly what to expect. You will receive either a fixed interest rate, or a rate that will rise and fall in line with general interest rate movements. When you withdraw your capital, it will still be worth £1,000 and you probably will not even notice that its real value has been eroded by inflation.

When you invest in the shares of a company, either directly or through a collective fund, there are no guarantees. Indeed in principle (although not, one hopes in scale of risk) you are in much the same position as investors in the first ever jointstock company in Britain, the Muscovy Company.

> **When you invest in the shares of a company, either directly or through a collective fund, there are no guarantees.**

In 1553 the entrepreneurial Muscovy Company merchants each paid £25 to buy shares in a trading venture with Russia, which was at that time under the heel of Ivan the Terrible. The merchants could have lost all their money – how many of us would choose to invest in an enterprise which depended on the goodwill of Tsar Ivan? – but the investment paid off.

Like the Muscovy merchants, stockmarket investors do not *know* what return to expect on their money. All they know is that by investing in a company they are investing in the right to share in its future growth and prosperity. An investment through a unit trust or investment trust in a number of companies, from all sectors of industry, is therefore an investment in the long-term growth of the economy of the country.

Naturally the fortunes of the economy, and of individual companies and investment sectors, will not always be buoyant, and an investment in shares cannot be divorced from the risk of capital and income loss. Ordinary shares are a company's risk capital. You hope the share price (and therefore the value of your investment) will grow over the years, and you hope that dividends will rise each year too, but there is certainly no guarantee that this will happen.

Share prices are driven by investor demand and this in turn is largely motivated by an objective assessment of a company's past showing – its profits and dividend record, for instance – and a more subjective view of its future prospects. Put simply, when there are more buyers than sellers, a company's share price will rise; when there are more sellers than buyers, the share price will fall.

Events quite unconnected with market sentiment about the ranking of an individual company will also move investor sentiment and therefore share prices. Political and economic news has an impact on share prices; so does news about the sector or industry in which the company conducts its business.

So there will undoubtedly be times when investors will be unnerved by the dreaded headline 'Billions of pounds wiped off the value of shares', and there will certainly be occasions when individual companies experience rough trading conditions, and cut their dividends because their profits have fallen. Direct investors in the stockmarket may even be unlucky enough to have money in the ordinary shares of a company that fails and involves its shareholders in financial losses that they will never recover.

People accept the risks of investing in the shares of companies, however, because over the longer term they hope to increase the value of their capital. They also hope that the income earned from their investment will grow because as companies make more profits they should also increase dividend payments to their shareholders.

> *Political and economic news has an impact on share prices; so does news about the sector or industry in which the company conducts its business.*

Most long-term investors in the stockmarket have not been disappointed. Over the years the average increase in the value of shares has outpaced inflation and investments in property, gilt-edged securities and bank and building society deposits. And the wider the range of industries and economies in which you invest, the smaller the risk that you could be badly damaged by the collapse of one company.

This is the central appeal of unit trusts and investment trusts. You are buying a stake in a portfolio of investments, which is being run for you by professional fund managers. These managers have access to the latest information on all sectors of industry, on individual companies and on the economies of this country and on what is happening in international stockmarkets.

No collective fund manager would claim that a large portfolio of investments eliminates the risk of stockmarket investment, but such a spread undoubtedly provides a greater security of capital and income than any investment in the shares of a single company.

The other advantage of collective investment funds is cost. The dealing expenses involved in trading small holdings of individual shares can make a formidable dent in investment profits.

Unit trusts and investment trusts must not be viewed as an investment panacea, however. They are not suitable investments for short-term savings, nor for those who do not want, or cannot afford, an investment that puts their capital at risk.

Investment trusts and unit trusts are both collective investment funds, and there is no difference between their basic *raison d'être*, which is to provide private investors with a professionally managed portfolio of shares and bonds, at a reasonable price.

But while the funds share a common philosophy, they have preserved their original and quite distinct legal structures. The mechanics of investment trusts and unit trusts are discussed in greater detail in Chapters Two and Three. The following section discusses and contrasts their fundamental differences.

INVESTMENT TRUSTS: WHAT ARE THEY?

■ DEFINITION

Investment trusts are publicly quoted companies with a fixed number of shares which are traded on the London Stock Exchange. The business of an investment trust is to invest in the shares and fixed-interest securities of other companies.

The name 'investment trust' is a misleading one. Investment trusts are not legal trusts. They are publicly quoted companies, whose shares and other securities are bought and sold through the Stock Exchange. In structure, investment trust companies are no different from Sainsbury, Marks & Spencer or British Gas. They are unique only in that their business is to invest in the shares and bonds of other companies, rather than to run supermarkets, or sell goods, or supply central heating.

Investment trust shares are traded on the Stock Exchange and they must be bought and sold directly through a stockbroker or indirectly through one of the savings and investment schemes run by most of the trusts (see Chapter Four, pages 77–79).

So why are investment trust called trusts at all? Although the company structure rapidly became ubiquitous the first investment trust was set up as a legal trust and was called the Foreign & Colonial Government Trust. It was not re-organised as a public company until 1879.

There were good pragmatic reasons why the F & C founders favoured the trust structure. Nineteenth-century investors were punchdrunk with a spate of stockmarket scandals, as any reader familiar with the works of the great Victorian novelists such as Dickens, Thackeray, Trollope and Wilkie Collins will know. Many people had lost money by investing in badly, and more often fraudulently, run companies. So to reassure investors, and to avoid what at that time had become an unpopular concept, F & C initially decided not to adopt the company structure.

It seems likely that no-one knew quite what to make of this. According to the official history of the birth of Foreign & Colonial (by Neil McKendrick), the *Economist* commented at the time: 'The shape of it (i.e., the Foreign & Colonial Trust) is very peculiar; it is not a company, and yet it is to do things like a company.'

The business of investment trust companies is to invest in the shares and securities of other companies and they employ professional fund managers to run their portfolio of investments.

These managers are given very considerable freedom as to the type of investment they can buy, but they are not uncontrolled mavericks. They are accountable to the independent directors of the company, and in turn these independent directors are accountable to their shareholders. By law, investment trusts must publish audited annual results and an annual report, and they must hold an Annual General Meeting.

As investment trusts are 'closed-end funds' the amount of capital in issue is determined when the trust is formed, and there are a fixed number of shares. When you sell investment trust shares the transaction takes place on the open market and the fund's manager does not have to sell any of the trust's holdings, in order to buy these shares back.

As companies, investment trusts can borrow money on fixed terms to buy other assets, and they are able to have different share structures. For instance, some trusts have one class of share for income seekers and one class of share for those who want capital growth. There are also trusts that have a fixed winding-up date when they will repay investors' capital.

The value of an investment trust's assets is the total value, after borrowings, of the shares and other assets in which it has invested. The price of the investment trust's shares is driven by investor demand, however. As a result, an investment trust's share price does not directly reflect its net asset value (NAV), the total value of all the assets it holds at current market prices, after the deduction of liabilities.

The NAV per share is calculated by dividing the NAV by the number of shares in issue. Very often the price of an investment trust's shares is lower than the value per share of all the assets it holds. In this case the share price is said to be trading at a 'discount'. This benefits buyers of the shares, as they are effectively acquiring a share in the trust's assets at a bargain price.

If investor demand is high, on the other hand, the trust's own share price may exceed the NAV per share, and the trust will be trading at a premium. In this case buyers of the shares are actually paying more for the underlying assets than these are worth. Sellers benefit from this if they had bought at a discount, however. They are receiving a bit of extra profit, on top of any increases in the value of the trust's portfolio of investments.

UNIT TRUSTS: WHAT ARE THEY?

In many respects a unit trust is a simpler vehicle than an investment trust. It is a pooled fund of investments which is divided into equal portions, called units. Investors buy and sell these units from the unit trust management company, either by completing an application form, or by telephone or fax, or by filling in a coupon on an advertisement, or through a financial adviser. They do not have to deal through the Stock Exchange.

As a unit trust is an 'open-ended' fund, there is no fixed number of units, so supply and demand does not affect the price of the units, it simply dictates the size of the unit trust.

> **■ DEFINITION**
>
> **Unit trusts** are legal trusts that manage funds of stockmarket securities on behalf of their investors. The pool of investments in the trust is divided into equal portions, called units.

When there are more buyers than sellers of a unit trust, the new money buys more assets, and the fund increases in size. Conversely, when there are consistently more sellers than buyers, the managers will have to sell some of the trust's assets in order to repay the sellers. Managers invariably retain some cash in the trust, in case they need to meet a spate of redemptions.

Prices of units directly reflect the value of the shares and bonds in the unit trust's underlying portfolio. This has the advantage of making it a relatively straightforward matter to see how well or how badly the investment is performing.

Unlike an investment trust, a unit trust is a genuine trust constituted by a trust deed. A trustee, usually one of the large banks or leading insurance companies, acts as custodian of the trust's cash and securities and polices the managers, making sure that they manage the fund in accordance with the terms of the deed. (For more information on trustees, see Chapter Three, pages 46–48.)

It is a system that works. There is absolutely no guarantee that a unit trust investor will not lose money because of poor investment management or investment conditions, but no unitholder has ever lost his investment as a result of fraud.

Generally a unit trust is only allowed to put up to 10 per cent of its money into unquoted shares (shares in very small companies or new ventures which are traded on the Stock Exchange but are not officially recognised) or into shares that are traded on emerging markets not officially recognised by the UK authorities. This is in contrast to an investment trust which as a company has virtually no restrictions placed on its investments.

UNIT TRUSTS AND INVESTMENT TRUSTS: WHAT THEY OFFER

The unit trust and investment trust industries would be unrecognisable to their founding fathers, not least because of the sheer number and size of the funds on the market. At the end of 1995 there were 1,633 unit trusts (recently the number has been increasing by around five a month) and 340 investment trusts. Assets of some of the largest funds are well in excess of £1 billion.

The industries would also be unrecognisable to their founders because of the diversity of the investment opportunities they provide for investors, and because of the proliferation of additional investment services they now offer.

Both the unit trust and the investment trust industries classify their funds into broad investment groupings or sectors. Funds in a specific sector may be very different in management style, and in risk profile, but they will share the common characteristic of investing in the same markets. If a trust ceases to share this characteristic – perhaps because it no longer produces the target yield or because it has widened or narrowed its investment parameters – it is reclassified.

At the start of 1996, the unit trust industry divided its funds into 24 sectors, while the investment trust industry had 19 different categories. These broad classifications help investors to identify the funds most suited to their own particular needs – there is little point in looking through the growth trusts if you want income, for instance – but they give little indication of the truly comprehensive range of investment opportunities on offer.

Through these collective investment schemes you can invest in government and corporate bonds and cash at one end of the risk spectrum, and in volatile venture capital and emerging market funds at the other. In other words everyone has an opportunity to tailor their investment risk to their pocket and their temperament.

An additional bonus is that you do not have to have substantial capital to invest in a unit trust or investment trust.

■ INVESTMENT SNAPSHOT

Flexible, low-cost investment schemes, to help the monthly saver build up a managed portfolio of shares, are offered by most unit trust groups and investment trust companies. And there are share exchange schemes to enable investors with existing share stakes to convert these inexpensively into unit trust holdings or investment trust shares.

There are also packaged products, which provide opportunities to use the money invested in a unit trust and investment trust to repay a mortgage or provide you with a pension. Most important, virtually every fund that invests in eligible shares provides the means to ring-fence holdings in the tax shelter of a personal equity plan (see Chapter Nine).

Such services demonstrate how sure-footed many unit trusts and investment trusts have been over the past 15 years in responding to investor needs and demands. It will be interesting to see how these traditional funds face the challenge of a new type of collective investment vehicle, the open-ended investment company or OEIC.

The acronym 'OEIC' may not win many votes for elegance, but these funds are the normal form of collective investment in Europe. The forecast is that they are likely to attract many UK investors, and that some of the unit trust groups will in future launch new OEICs, rather than new unit trusts. A few managers may even decide to convert their existing unit trusts into OEICS (see Chapter Three, pages 61–62).

UNIT TRUSTS AND INVESTMENT TRUSTS: HOW THEY COMPARE

- **Fundamental aim.** Identical. To spread the risks of stock-market investment for individuals by providing them with a stake in a professionally managed portfolio of securities.

- **Structure.** Quite different. Unit trusts are open-ended funds and the number of units in issue will expand or contract, according to investor demand. All the trust's money and assets are held by an independent trustee. Investment trusts are listed public companies and closed-end funds and have a fixed number of shares. Shareholders are protected by a board of independent directors and company law.

- **Prices.** The price of units will directly reflect the value of the unit trust's portfolio of investments. The price of an investment trust's shares will be driven by investor demand. It may therefore be greater or smaller than the value of the trust's underlying investments.

- **Investment areas covered.** Very similar, but investment trusts have greater freedom to invest in unquoted shares and shares traded on stockmarkets that are not recognised by the UK authorities. Unit trusts provide a much wider range of funds investing in fixed-interest securities such as gilts and corporate bonds.

- **Costs.** Unit trusts charge an initial fee and an annual management fee. Investment trusts have an annual management fee but very few have any initial charge, although you will have to pay commission and expenses to buy and sell investment trust shares. On balance, the cost of putting money into an investment trust and the cost of investing in a unit trust will be quite similar, but investment trust management charges are generally lower.

- **Ease of buying and selling.** Investment trust shares have to be bought and sold through a stockbroker, either directly or indirectly through the management company. With unit trusts you can deal by applying directly to the company, and you can also buy units by filling in an advertisement coupon.

- **Risk.** Investment trusts are slightly more risky. Unlike unit trusts they are able to borrow to buy more investments for the fund. This 'gearing' will accelerate a trust's performance in a rising stockmarket, but it will depress it when share prices are falling. Investors could also be caught by a widening of the discount when they want to sell investment trust shares.

- **Public image.** Unit trusts can and do advertise widely. As companies, investment trusts cannot advertise their shares except at the time of issue, although they can advertise packaged products such as savings schemes and personal equity plans.

The unique character of invest-ment trust companies comes from the fact that their business is to make money by investing in the shares and securities of other companies

INSIDE AN INVESTMENT TRUST

2

■ THE FUNDAMENTALS

 An investment trust is a publicly quoted company whose business is to invest in the shares of other companies.

 The shares of investment trusts are traded on the Stock Exchange.

 The price of an investment trust's shares will be driven by investor demand. It will not directly reflect the value of the fund's investments.

 As public companies, investment trusts may issue more than one class of share.

 Investment trusts are allowed to borrow money on fixed terms, to buy other investments for the portfolio. This can enhance performance in a rising market.

 There are virtually no restrictions on the shares and securities that an investment trust can buy.

■ TERMINOLOGY

Ordinary shares: The main type of the share capital of a company. Ordinary shares are traded on the Stock Exchange and earn a proportion of the profits of a company in the form of dividends. They are the risk capital of a company.

Split capital trust: An investment trust with a fixed life that has more than one main class of share to meet the different investment priorities of its shareholders.

'Annuity' income shares: The shares of a split capital investment trust that offer a very high income, but which repay only a nominal amount of capital.

Zero dividend preference shares (zeros): Shares that provide no income but offer a fixed return, which is paid to investors when a split capital investment trust is wound up.

Income and residual capital shares: Shares that are entitled to a split capital trust's income, and any surplus capital left when the trust is wound up.

Stepped preference shares: A share with a fixed redemption value which provides dividends that rise each year by a known amount.

Hurdle rate: The annual rate of growth in the assets of an investment trust that is needed if a class of shareholder is to be repaid at redemption.

Warrants: A type of stockmarket security that gives holders the right to purchase shares at a specified price, at a specified date or dates in the future.

Convertible loan stock: A fixed interest security that gives holders the right, at a specific date or dates, to convert into the shares of the company that has issued the stock.

Gearing: The effect on the capital growth and income of an investment trust of borrowing money on fixed terms to buy more assets.

Venture capital trusts: Companies similar to investment trusts that invest in unquoted companies and provide generous tax incentives for investors.

The activities of an investment trust may be undertaken by professional investment managers, but don't let that confuse you. Investment trusts are quoted companies and they have exactly the same structure as any other public company. Their unique character comes from the fact that their 'business' is to make money by investing in the shares and securities of other companies.

WHAT DOES IT MEAN TO BE A PUBLIC LIMITED COMPANY?

When investment trusts are first launched, like all public companies, they issue shares and these shares are then traded on the London Stock Exchange. When you want to invest in an investment trust, therefore, you buy its shares on the stockmarket. You don't hand cash directly to the fund manager, as you do with a unit trust.

An investment trust is controlled by the Companies Acts and is constituted by its own rules, which are the contract that it has with its shareholders. These rules are contained in what are known as its 'Memorandum and Articles of Association'. With an investment trust, these are likely to contain powers to invest the funds of the company in securities and property, to borrow, and to prohibit the distribution of capital profits as dividends.

The key pieces of information in the Memorandum set out the objectives for which the company has been formed and the structure of its share capital. The Articles of Association outline the internal operating regulations which determine how the trust must conduct its business.

An investment trust is a closed-end fund which means it has a fixed number of shares. It can increase the number of shares in issue only with the consent of its shareholders. It is allowed to borrow money, however, and dealing profits also provide new capital for investment.

The price of an investment trust company's shares is driven by whether people want to buy them. The more enthusiastically investors chase after the shares, the higher the share price will go. If no-one is buying, the share price will not move. And if people are tripping over their feet to off-load the shares, the price will fall.

An investment trust cannot advertise its shares, although the managers are always ready to answer queries from the public, and investment trust companies are able to promote packaged investments and services, such as their savings schemes, personal equity plans (Peps), personal pensions and share exchange schemes.

As with all public companies, investment trusts have an independent board of directors and are obliged to publish audited results each year and to hold an Annual General Meeting (AGM).

The right to attend an investment trust's AGM is an important one for shareholders, and too few investors take advantage of it. This is your opportunity to question the directors about the management of the fund. What are the credentials of any new directors? Why has the investment policy of the trust changed? Why has the dividend been cut?

Don't be shy about voicing your concerns or asking for more information. AGMs are the forum where shareholders can, and should, make their views heard.

SAFEGUARDS FOR INVESTMENT TRUST INVESTORS

As far as the security of their money is concerned investment trust shareholders are in no better and no worse position than shareholders in, say, ICI. They have the protection of company law and Stock Exchange regulations and it is the duty of the Board of Directors to look after their interests.

The assets of an investment trust are registered in the name of the trust, and are not owned by its shareholders. The assets are held by a custodian. It is normal practice for stock to be kept with a major bank, for instance.

Although investment trust shares are a risk investment, and there is no guarantee that investors will not lose some of their money, there is only one way in which investors can actually be defrauded. This is for the managers themselves to behave dishonestly with the trust's portfolio. It is the responsibility of the Board of Directors to ensure that there are sufficient internal checks to ensure that this does not happen.

WHO MANAGES AN INVESTMENT TRUST?

When you buy shares in an investment trust, you are buying the services of professional fund managers. The investment trust company will either have its own managers, or – which is more common – it will employ an independent management company to run the fund for it. The Board of Directors will lay down the investment policy it wants these managers to implement. (The world of professional investment managers is examined in Chapter Five, pages 118–120).

THE DIFFERENT TYPES OF INVESTMENT TRUST SHARE

Although every investment trust runs one portfolio of shares, as public companies, they are able to have a number of different share structures. This can be a considerable advantage for investors who want to use investment trusts for financial planning.

> *The investment trust company will either have its own managers, or – which is more common – it will employ an independent management company to run the fund for it.*

For example, there are investment trust shares that produce only income, investment trust shares that only provide capital growth and investment trusts that have a fixed wind-up date. With these trusts, investors can assume that, barring some managerial or stock-market disaster, they will get their money back on a predetermined date, and they can organise their financial planning accordingly.

Ordinary shares are the main type of share capital of conventional investment trusts and they are likely to suit the needs of many investors. These shares pay out income, usually in the form of a twice-yearly dividend (some trusts distribute income annually or quarterly), and they offer the hope of a capital gain when investors come to sell. All ordinary shareholders have equal rights to the trust's income and capital (see Chapter Five, pages 94–96).

The situation is not nearly as simple with the different shareholders of split capital investment trusts, however.

■ Split capital investment trusts

There are more than 50 split capital trusts, investment trust companies that are distinguished by having more than one main class of share capital. They could be described as offering 'bespoke', rather than 'off the peg', investment opportunities.

At first glance, split capital trusts look formidably complicated but the fundamentals are very simple. All you need to bear in mind is that every split capital trust will have at least two classes of share, and that these are designed to meet the needs of different investors. Essentially what the trusts do, in other words, is 'split' capital from income, just as their name suggests.

All split capital investment trusts have a specified life span. Shareholders know that, on a certain date, the trust will be wound up, according to its Articles of Association, and that all the various shares will be repaid, providing that there are sufficient assets in the fund. Until the winding-up date, the right to dividends and to capital growth are laid down according to a strict order of priority between each class of share.

The first split capital investment trust, Dualvest, was launched more than 30 years ago, in 1965. It was a relatively simple trust, with just two kinds of share. During the trust's life, all the income earned by its investments went to holders of the income shares, while holders of the capital shares received the surplus capital when the trust was wound up.

For many years, split capital trusts concentrated on this straightforward division between capital and income shares, but then they began to become more innovative and to add some frills in the form of other classes of share. Today investors can find as many as six different types of shares offered by the split capital investment trust sector.

This is more straightforward than perhaps it sounds – some investors like to construct portfolios of different classes of investment trust share – but it is important to remember that each main class of split capital share has a very different risk profile.

When the trust is wound up, and the proceeds are used to pay off shareholders, there are strict rules about the order in which the different shareholders will receive their money. Zero dividend preference shareholders come first, for instance, while capital shareholders are the tail-end Charlies.

Investors at the end of the queue are therefore banking on the ability of the managers to manage the split capital trust's assets and to increase their value, so that at the end of the day every class of share can be repaid, with extra jam for the main risk-takers.

■ Income shares

Take a deep breath. Three types of income share are available from different split capital investment trusts, and it is essential that investors understand which sort of income share they are buying.

▩ 'Traditional' income shares

Generally these income shares receive all a split trust's net income and have a fixed redemption price when the split capital trust is wound up. During the lifetime of the trust, however, the market price of the shares will fluctuate. Investors are assured of capital gain only if they buy the income shares at a price below their redemption, or subscription, value and then hold them until the trust is wound up.

▩ 'Annuity' income shares

These shares are known as annuity income shares for the very good reason that in some respects they perform like an annuity.

They offer a very high income, but repay only a nominal sum of capital. For example, the shares could be issued at 100p and repaid at less than 1p. However, the advantage of an annuity income share over a conventional life insurance annuity is that the annuity shares are traded. If you want to get hold of your capital, you can always sell your shares.

▨ 'Income and residual capital' shares

These shares are discussed below.

■ Zero dividend preference shares

These are low-risk investments which are unique to the investment trust industry. 'Zeros' were first issued in October 1987 and they have become an essential component in tax planning kitbags, extensively used by investors who know that they will need a certain sum of money at a specific time.

Zeros are relatively low-risk because investors are promised a fixed return when the trust is wound up, and zeros have first rights over the assets. The only risk to zero shareholders is that at the end of the day there will be insufficient assets in the fund to provide the promised return.

Zero shareholders don't receive any income from their shares during the life of the trust, and this has useful tax implications. As there is no income there is no income tax bill. The only tax due is capital gains tax (CGT) on the capital growth achieved over the period to redemption, and the annual CGT exemptions and indexation take much, if not all, of the sting out of this tax for many investors (see Chapter Eight, pages 170–173).

■ Income and residual capital shares

These shares are also known as 'ordinary' income shares and 'highly geared' ordinary income shares. They are the tail-end Charlies of a split capital structure that typically has zero dividend preference shares or stepped-preference shares.

These shares are income producers with something of a

difference. Holders are entitled to the trust's income, after any prior charges on it, and they will also receive any surplus capital when the trust is wound up, but only after the zero dividend preference shareholders and any other prior charges have received their money. Ordinary income shares are therefore higher risk because there is no fixed repayment value, and there is potential for both capital gain and capital loss.

■ Stepped preference shares

These shares are low risk. Investors receive dividends, which rise at a guaranteed rate, and they also receive a fixed capital repayment when the trust is wound up. There is a predetermined growth in both dividends and capital, and investors have the comfort of knowing exactly where they stand.

■ Capital shares

Now we move up the risk ladder. Holders of capital shares receive no income, but they get all the assets of the trust when it is liquidated. The payout comes *only* after every other class of shareholder has received what is due to them, however. The value of a capital share therefore depends absolutely on the performance of the investments in the trust's portfolio.

The worst-case scenario is that at wind-up there are insufficient assets to pay capital shareholders anything at all. The best-case scenario is that there will be substantial capital gains. And as capital gains are liable to capital gains tax, not income tax, the first £6,300 (plus indexation) of gains will be tax-free if you are not paying CGT on other profits (see Chapter Eight pages 170–172).

■ Hurdle rates

When talking about the risk attached to the different shares of a split capital trust, investment managers will often refer to a share's 'hurdle rate'. This is the obstacle that has to be jumped in order for the investor to get his money back when the trust is wound up. Broadly, the hurdle rate will be the annual rate of growth in the trust's assets until the wind-up date that is needed for a specific class of shareholder to have his capital repaid. The higher the hurdle rate, the riskier the share. With zeros, for instance, it may well be a negative figure.

WARRANTS

Some 130 investment trusts currently have warrants in issue, and many investors find these securities puzzling. A few probably stuff them in the back of a drawer and forget them. 'Is it a share?' 'Is it worth anything?' 'I never asked for warrants,' are all pretty standard responses.

A warrant is not a share, although it can be bought and sold on the Stock Exchange. It is a type of security that gives investors the right to buy shares at a fixed price (called the 'exercise' price) at some date or dates in the future.

You do not have to exercise your warrants unless you want to, and it will clearly be worth doing so only if the exercise price is less than the market price. Generally speaking, the longer the life of a warrant, the greater the chance that this will be the case.

Warrants can be bought and sold just like any other share until the exercise date, although it may not always be easy to find a buyer or a seller. Warrants don't entitle you to any dividends, however, and you don't have rights as a shareholder, which means you cannot attend or vote at company meetings.

If you hold the warrants past their exercise date, they could also become quite worthless. The investment trust company itself might choose to exercise all its outstanding warrants on behalf of its investors, but you would be rash to bank on this.

When a new investment trust issues warrants, it is usual for investors to be offered something like one free warrant for every five shares. A new investment trust usually issues warrants as an extra safeguard, to encourage investors. If the share price of the trust goes down, after its launch, warrants are a little buffer to offset the effect of this, if the investor can sell them at a profit.

Long-established investment trusts use warrants as a sugar lump to sweeten their shareholders. For instance free warrants are often issued as part of a takeover bid or a restructuring, to make the deal more digestible.

Warrants are high-risk investments because warrant prices, which are only a fraction of the share price, move much more dramatically than share prices. If markets go up, you will make more profit on warrants than on shares, but if markets go down, you will lose much more money. Because these securities are so volatile, it is sensible for prospective investors to get the help of a professional adviser with knowledge of the market.

CONVERTIBLE LOAN STOCK

Convertible loan stocks are sometimes called 'deferred equities'. They are a sort of halfway house between a fixed interest bond and an ordinary share.

Convertibles are fixed-interest investments which are issued by companies, including some 12 investment trusts, as part of their borrowing. They provide a fixed-interest payment and have a fixed redemption date. The added twist is that they also give investors the option to convert their holding into a stated number of ordinary shares at a certain date or dates in the future.

When a convertible loan stock is issued, its rate of interest is usually higher than the current yield on the investment trust's ordinary shares. As convertibles are quoted securities, they can be bought and sold on the Stock Exchange, and although they sometimes tend to be difficult to trade they are a comparatively low-risk investment. The price does not fluctuate as much as the price of an ordinary share.

In a rising market, the price of a convertible will be affected by the value of the shares with which it is linked. In a falling market, the convertible's price will be safeguarded to some extent by the fact that it is a loan stock not an equity.

So a convertible loan stock offers you the chance to make a modest capital gain while also giving you some protection during falling stockmarkets. There is a potential bear trap, however. Investors must keep an eye on the conversion date. Up to that point the price of the convertible will have been boosted by the link with the investment trust's ordinary shares. After the conversion date, this extra value will be lost and the convertible will simply be viewed and valued as a straightforward fixed-interest security.

Your income needs will be an important factor in determining whether you use your right to convert. The decision will probably rest on whether the interest you are getting from the convertible is likely to be less than the dividends you can expect from a holding of the trust's ordinary shares.

NET ASSET VALUES, DISCOUNTS AND PREMIUMS

Contrary to rumour, you don't need to be Einstein to understand why investment trust shares trade at either a discount or a premium to the trust's net asset value (invariably shorthanded to NAV). But you do need to understand the implications of this for you, the investor.

The NAV of an investment trust is the total value of all the shares and securities in its portfolio, at their current market value, after preference shares and other borrowings have been deducted (see Chapter One, page 10). In other words, the NAV is the estimated amount of money per share which would be paid out to shareholders if the investment trust was liquidated.

The NAV is usually expressed as an amount of pence per ordinary share, and it is the most useful measure there is of the performance of the trust's underlying portfolio of investments. Investment trusts regularly publish their NAVs – usually once a month – and investors can also check the prices pages, which include NAV estimates in the *Financial Times* every day.

The NAV does not tell you how much your shares in the trust are worth, however. Unlike units in a unit trust, the price of shares in an investment trust do not directly reflect the trust's portfolio of investments.

Of course an investment trust's share price has a link with the value of the trust's investments, because a good performance stimulates investor demand, the oil in the motor that drives the price. If more investors want to buy than sell, this will push up the price of shares. If more want to sell than buy, this will depress the share price.

This means that the share price of an investment trust is seldom exactly the same as the NAV per share. Most frequently the shares change hands at a price below the NAV, and are said to be trading at a discount. Sometimes, however, when a trust has performed very well and investor demand is very buoyant, the share price is greater than the NAV, and the shares are then said to be trading at a premium.

Obviously discounts on investment trusts narrow during bull markets, those heady times when share prices generally are rising and investors are keen to buy. During bear markets, when all is doom and gloom, prices fall, investors go on strike and the investment trust discounts widen. In May 1996, the average investment trust share price was 9 per cent below the market value of the shares in its portfolio.

When you buy an investment trust's shares at a discount, you are effectively buying its assets on the cheap. It may seem tantalising that you can't get hold of the additional value in the trust's portfolio, but you will get the benefit of income earned on assets which you have bought at a discount, and, by law, investment trusts must pay out at least 85 per cent of total net revenue to their shareholders.

Unless the discount has widened still further by the time you come to sell your shares, you will not suffer any direct loss either. And if you bought your shares at a discount, and you sell them at a price much nearer to the NAV, you will probably have done very nicely, thank you.

You need to be aware, though, that by no means every investment trust that is trading at a whacking discount is a bargain. The market may be showing that it has no confidence in its management.

■ INVESTMENT SNAPSHOT

Buying shares at a premium to their NAV raises a different question. Essentially you have paid more for your share of the assets of a trust than these are worth. The premium may suggest that the market has a very high opinion of the trust's managers but, as far as you are concerned, these managers will need to produce a superior performance with the trust's investments in the future to justify the premium that you have paid.

GEARING

As a public company, an investment trust can borrow money on fixed terms and use the loan to buy other investments. This freedom to borrow, and therefore to 'gear' their portfolios, is one of the the fundamental differences between an investment trust and a unit trust.

■ DEFINITION

Gearing is the effect on the capital growth and income of an investment trust of borrowing money on fixed terms to buy more assets.

Gearing (or 'leverage' as the Americans usually call it) is used to enhance a trust's performance when markets are rising. If the assets of the trust grow in value, shareholders will benefit because the cost of the debt (the fixed-rate loan which has bought some of these assets) remains the same. If the income from an asset rises more than the interest paid on the borrowed money, there will be more income left to distribute to the trust's investors.

In a rising market, a geared portfolio is likely to outperform an ungeared portfolio. But the converse is also true. If the assets that have been bought with borrowed money fall, rather than rise, in value, the performance of the trust's portfolio will suffer proportionately more.

Over the years, however, many investment trust managers have managed to achieve very good results by using their ability to borrow in order to increase returns for their shareholders.

If managers anticipate that the market will fall they can de-gear the trust, perhaps by putting some of the trust's assets into cash, or fixed interest securities.

So gearing is a two-edged sword, and requires skilled judgement. It also increases the risk for shareholders because the lenders will have prior rights to the assets of the trust when it is wound up and the proceeds are paid out.

Over the years, however, many investment trust managers have managed to achieve very good results by using their ability to borrow in order to increase returns for their shareholders.

Case Study   **Gearing an investment trust**

Ivor Pound-Sign is trying to explain to his aunt how the facility to gear might affect the performance of her investment trust shares. He hits on the analogy of borrowing money to buy a property.

'Suppose you buy a house for £100,000,' he says. 'You put down £10,000, your equity, and you borrow the remaining £90,000; that is your gearing. If you then sell the house for £110,000, and you pay back £90,000, you will have doubled your equity, your £10,000 deposit, even though the market has only gone up by 10 per cent. Of course, if the value of the house falls by 10 per cent, and you sell it for £90,000, you will have lost your deposit, or 100 per cent of your equity. The effect of gearing an investment trust will not be as extreme as this but the principle is the same. Does that make it clear?'

Ivor's aunt looks worried. 'I think my flat is worth £180,000,' she says timidly.

THE DIFFERENT INVESTMENT TRUST SECTORS

Investment trusts were founded to provide access to international as well as domestic markets, and today the industry offers a huge diversity of investment opportunities, covering a wide spectrum of risk. There are virtually no restrictions on the investments an investment trust may make.

The Association of Investment Trust Companies (AITC) – whose members represent 95 per cent of the industry by value and 92 per cent by number – ranks its trusts according to the sectors in which they principally invest. It has an additional category for split capital trusts.

This categorisation is quite broad brush. Some investment trusts will have an investment policy that qualifies them for a particular category, but will nevertheless invest in highly specialised areas. So trusts grouped together in one sector category may well have very different objectives and a very different risk profile.

These are the different investment trust categories.

Table 2.1

The average performance of the investment trust sectors			
Sector	One year average	Three years' average	Seven years' average
UK general	+10.8%	+50.4%	+147.5%
UK capital growth	+8.4%	+46.1%	+89.2%
UK income growth	+12.1%	+40.3%	+156.6%
International general	+13.1%	+45.8%	+179.5%
International cap.gth	+8.6%	+51.8%	+151.5%
International inc.gth	+8.8%	+25.0%	+127.7%
North America	+26.9%	+64.7%	+136.6%
Far East inc.Japan	+5.2%	+70.7%	+124.0%
Far East excl.Japan	−5.2%	+65.7%	+237.3%
Japan	−6.7%	+58.8%	+53.0%
Closed-ended funds	+4.8%	+45.9%	+113.0%
Continental Europe	+5.4%	+58.8%	+114.2%
Pan Europe	+9.7%	+24.2%	+144.9%
Property	−14.1%	+41.3%	−28.5%
Commodity & energy	−13.7%	+10.3%	–
Emerging markets	−16.9%	+51.1%	+72.8%
Smaller companies	+7.4%	+60.3%	+76.8%
Venture & dev. capital	+11.7%	+84.5%	+161.2%
Split capital trusts	+4.5%	+45.8%	+101.3%
High income	−1.5%	+31.1%	+56.0%

Figures to 1 January 1996 show returns after an allowance for dealing charges, including net re-invested income.

Source: Money Observer/AITC

■ International general trusts

They have less than 80 per cent of their assets in any one geographical area. The international generalist sector contains many of the oldest and best-known industrial giants such as Alliance, Foreign & Colonial, Scottish American, Scottish Investment, Scottish Mortgage and Witan.

■ International capital growth trusts

These trusts also have less than 80 per cent of their assets in one geographical area, and their investment policy is to maximise capital growth. The sector also includes a number of large diversified trusts.

■ International income growth trusts

These trusts have the same asset allocation requirements as their capital growth brothers but are seeking a high and growing income. There are only a handful of overseas income trusts.

■ UK general trusts

These funds invest at least 80 per cent of their assets in UK-registered companies, and they are looking to produce capital growth and a decent yield for investors. The sector includes the Malvern UK Index trust, the only investment trust that tracks the FT All-Share Index (see *Tracker funds*, Chapter Five, pages 110–114).

■ UK capital growth trusts

The yield will be very small on these trusts, which also have at least 80 per cent of their investments in UK companies. The investment policy of the funds is to seek outright capital growth.

■ UK income growth trusts

These trusts are becoming increasingly popular and the sector contains a number of new funds. The investment aim of UK income growth trusts is to provide a high and rising dividend income. Sometimes a trust has a specific target – for example, to achieve long-term growth of capital and income which betters the returns measured by the FT-SE Actuaries All-Share Index.

■ High-income trusts

These trusts have even more ambitious income targets and there have also been a number of new high-income launches recently. The funds are designed to produce a return of more than 125 per cent of the yield on the FT-SE Actuaries All-Share Index and have at least 80 per cent of their assets in equities and convertibles. At the moment the average yield of trusts in this sector is around twice that of the yield on the FT-SE All-Share Index.

■ North America trusts

These funds have at least 80 per cent of their portfolios invested in all countries north of Panama. The sector has produced particularly good results over the past five years, thanks to Wall Street's strong performance and favourable movements in the exchange rate (see Chapter Five, page 102, for the currency factor in overseas investment).

■ Far East (excluding Japan) trusts

The trusts concentrate on Far Eastern securities and have at least 80 per cent of assets invested in this area. Eleven of the trusts in the sector invest in single countries in the region, such as Korea, Singapore, Thailand and New Zealand. None of the trusts invests in Japanese securities.

■ Far East (including Japan) trusts

These trusts do not exclude the Japanese market but the Japanese content of the portfolio will be less than 80 per cent of the trust's assets.

■ Japan trusts

Funds that have at least 80 per cent of their assets invested in

Japanese securities. The sector tends to be split between trusts investing in large companies and those concentrating on smaller ones. Historically there has been a considerable difference in performance between the two.

■ Continental Europe trusts

These have at least 80 per cent of their assets invested in Continental Europe, with a number concentrating on investment in single European countries. 'Continental Europe' embraces the markets of Austria, Belgium, Denmark, Finland, France, Germany, Greece, Ireland, Italy, Luxembourg, The Netherlands, Norway, Portugal, Spain, Sweden and Switzerland.

■ Pan Europe trusts

Britain becomes a member of Europe in this category and trusts in the sector include holdings of UK securities in their portfolios. The trusts have at least 80 per cent of their assets in Europe, with at least 40 per cent in Continental European markets.

■ Commodity and energy trusts

This is a select group of trusts that invest at least 80 per cent of their assets in listed commodity and energy shares.

■ Property trusts

Another tiny sector. These funds have at least 80 per cent of their assets in listed property shares. Not surprisingly, the trusts (and their investors) have had a tough time in recent years.

■ Emerging market trusts

A relatively new but growing sector. The trusts have at least 80 per cent of their assets invested either in a spread of emerging markets or in a single market such as Chile or Turkey. (For more about 'emerging markets', see Chapter Five, pages 100–101.)

■ Closed-end trusts

These are the investment trust equivalent of the unit trust fund of funds. This small group of trusts puts at least 80 per cent of their investments in other investment trusts and closed-end investment companies.

■ Smaller companies trusts

The fastest-growing of all the investment trust sectors. The trusts have at least 50 per cent of their portfolio (by value) invested in the shares of smaller and medium-sized companies. The sector includes three index funds, Hoare Govett Smaller Companies Index, Hoare Govett 1,000 Index and Gartmore Micro Index.

■ Venture and development capital trusts

These trusts have an undefined but significant proportion of their portfolios invested in the securities of unquoted companies. The largest trust is 3i. The sector will also include the new 'venture capital trusts'.

■ Split capital trusts

These have been discussed earlier in this chapter. The funds have a fixed winding-up date and more than one class of share capital. The trusts pursue a variety of investment policies in a variety of geographical areas.

■ Venture capital trusts (VCTs)

Venture capital trusts (VCTs) were launched on 6 April 1995, to encourage investment in the smaller UK unquoted companies by giving very generous tax incentives to people who invest for at least five years. The maximum investment is £100,000.

A VCT could be described as a high-risk investment trust with tax breaks. The trusts invest in a broad spread of unquoted companies including those traded on the Alternative Investment Market (AIM), a secondary share exchange that has been created for smaller and growing companies. The shares of VCTs are listed on the Stock Exchange. The trusts need Inland Revenue approval, which is conditional for three years.

Tax incentives on VCTs include 20 per cent tax relief on investment in new VCT shares; tax-free dividends; no capital gains tax on the disposal of shares; and an ability to defer the tax on existing capital gains. Shares must be held for five years for the investor to qualify for the tax breaks.

Some of the investment management companies that have launched VCTs are also active in the investment trust and unit trust market place, so they can demonstrate a track record and considerable experience. However, a VCT is a high-risk investment (which the Government has recognised by offering tax sweeteners) and you should take professional advice before investing in one.

For more details on the venture capital market contact the British Venture Capital Association (Essex House, 12–13 Essex Street, London WC2R 3AA, telephone 0171-240 3846), which publishes a free guide.

WATCHING THE PROGRESS OF YOUR INVESTMENT TRUST SHARES

Leading newspapers usually give daily information on the prices of shares traded on the Stock Exchange, including those of investment trusts.

■ INVESTMENT SNAPSHOT

You will receive an annual report and accounts from your investment trust, which will disclose what profits have been earned, what dividend the directors are recommending for shareholders and the assets and liabilities of the company. Read it carefully. It is probably your most important source of information.

The annual report will give details of the movement in the net asset value (NAV) over the period. This will show you what performance the investment managers have achieved with the portfolio, against the trust's benchmark index.

■ WHERE TO LEARN MORE ABOUT INVESTMENT TRUSTS

The trade body of the investment trust industry is the Association of Investment Trust Companies (AITC), which was established in 1932 to protect and promote the interests of investment trust companies and their shareholders. Its membership includes the vast majority of investment trust companies.

The AITC publishes monthly performance statistics, with details of investment trust personal equity plans and monthly saving schemes. This Monthly Information Service is available on subscription. In addition the AITC publishes a number of free factsheets and various publications.

Finally, the AITC also has two packages for computer buffs. Its CD-Rom disc on investment trusts costs £22.95 and can be run on IBM compatible computers with CD-Rom drives, and there is also information on the Internet. For details contact the AITC or http://www.iii.co.uk/aitc on the Internet.

Address of AITC: Durrant House, 8-13 Chiswell Street, London EC1Y 4YY. Telephone: 0171-588 5347. Fax: 0171-638 1803.

■ FURTHER READING

'Buying Shares in Investment Trust Companies','A Guide to Investment Trust Companies,' 'The Choice is Yours', 'Shares for Everyone', 'Split Capital Trusts', 'Investment Trust Warrants' (free booklets and fact sheets from the AITC); *The Investment Trust Directory*, which has detailed profiles of all AITC member companies (£15 from the AITC).

Investment Trusts: Private Investor Guide 1996. £15 from the Investment Trust Department, S.B.C. Warburg, 1 Finsbury Avenue, London EC2M 2PP.

'Making Sense of Splits', by Christopher Gilchrist (free guide from Henderson Touche Remnant (telephone: 0171-410 4410).

The quarterly specialist magazine *Investment Trusts* (£3.50) is on sale at leading newsagents or on subscription (subscription inquiries, *Investment Trusts,* PO Box 503, Leicester LE94 OAD; telephone 01858 410 510).

No unit trust investor has ever lost money as a result of fraud in the sense that someone had raided the till and run away with the money

INSIDE A UNIT TRUST

3

■ THE FUNDAMENTALS

 A unit trust is a legal trust which has been formed to manage a portfolio of stockmarket securities for investors.

 All the trust's investments and cash are held on behalf of investors by an independent trustee.

 The investments in the fund are divided into equal portions called units, and an investor's money buys a proportionate share of these.

 Units may be bought directly from the unit trust company, and the managers must buy the units back when the investor wants to sell them.

 The price of the units of a unit trust directly reflects the value of the fund's investments.

 A unit trust may invest in any security quoted on a recognised stock exchange but not more than 10 per cent of the fund can be invested in unquoted securities.

 In order to ensure a spread of risk, a unit trust must have a spread of investments, and not more than 10 per cent of the fund may be invested in the shares of one company.

■ TERMINOLOGY

Units: The equal portions into which the assets of a unit trust are divided. Investors' units are the measure of their share of the fund.

Trust deed: In the context of unit trusts, the legal arrangement between the company that manages the unit trust and the independent financial institution that acts as trustee, holds all the fund's investments and supervises the managers to ensure that they act in accordance with the provision of the deed.

Offer price: The price at which investors buy units (i.e., the price at which units are 'offered' to them).

Bid price: The price at which investors sell units. The bid price is the cash-in value of the investment.

XD: When prices are marked 'XD', this means that the fund or company has gone ex-dividend ahead of the income payment to investors. The XD price no longer includes the dividend or income distribution.

OEICS: Open-ended investment companies. A type of collective investment fund that is widely available in the rest of Europe, but new to the UK. An OEIC is very similar to a unit trust, but it has a company structure, and there is a single price at which its shares are bought and sold.

The words 'unit trust' may not sound particularly exciting, but they define this collective investment vehicle with precision.

The stockmarket investments managed within a unit trust are divided into equal portions, called units. When you invest money into a unit trust, you buy a number of these units, and your purchase entitles you to the income and capital which corresponds to your share of the spread of investments within the unit trust fund.

The actual number of units you receive will depend on the price of the units on the day you invest. All unit trust buying and selling prices are calculated according to rules laid down by the Securities and Investments Board (the SIB), the over-all regulator for the investment industry.

The funds are unit *trusts* precisely because they are legal trusts, set up by a trust deed. This is a legal agreement between the trustees and the managers and it lays down how the unit trust must be run.

WHAT HAPPENS WHEN YOU INVEST MONEY IN A UNIT TRUST?

In January 1996 there were 1,637 unit trusts run by 161 different management companies. Every working day these companies receive telephone and fax orders, and postal instructions with cheques, from members of the public who want to buy or sell units in one of their funds.

Of course, some days will be busier than others. There will be a heavier flow of business if a group has just launched a new fund, or if it has been advertising its trusts in the financial pages of the Press.

Investors are also swayed by various 'feel good' factors. Brighter economic news, or some favourable political event, can prompt a flurry of business. Reports of booming share prices are also notoriously good for unit trust sales, although they are not necessarily quite such a good buying opportunity for investors (see Chapter Four, page 87).

When you send off your cash to buy units in a unit trust, the management group will bank your cheque and transfer the money into the trustee's name. If the trust is among the minority of funds that calculates prices once a week, the managers will hold the money until the price has been calculated.

Much the same process happens if you decide to sign up for a unit trust monthly savings scheme. The agreed amount of savings will be drawn by direct debit from your bank account (the transaction usually takes place on the 1st of the month) and the units are bought for you a few days later.

In exchange for your money, you will be allocated a proportionate number of units in the fund. The managers of the trust will either have created these units for you, or they will have sold units on to you that they have repurchased from other investors. Either way, you will receive a contract note, confirming your purchase, by return of post. If the investment has been made through an independent financial adviser, with whom you do not have a customer agreement, there will also be a piece of paper explaining your cancellation rights. There are no cancellation rights if you approach the unit trust group directly.

> *Investing in a unit trust is rather like pouring a glass of water into a pond.*

In most instances investors will subsequently receive a certificate for their unitholding. However, some groups now have 'non-certificated' units, and no certificates are issued for investments in monthly savings schemes or in personal equity plans (see Chapter Nine).

Investing in a unit trust is rather like pouring a glass of water into a pond. An investor's individual stake is not earmarked for a particular share purchase, and new money into a unit trust will initially appear as an increase in the cash balance in the fund's portfolio. In due course, this cash will be used to buy investments, but the length of time taken to reduce the cash balance depends on the investment managers.

Most unit trusts keep between 1 and 5 per cent of their portfolio in cash in order to avoid the forced sale of some of their shares if they have to repay investors who want to sell their units. There may be a higher cash balance in the fund if the fund manager is currently pessimistic about the stockmarket.

The regulations covering the amount of liquidity held in a unit trust allow cash to be held for the potential redemption of units or for the efficient management of the scheme in accordance with its objectives, but the interpretation of this is a matter for individual investment managers. Within the unit trust industry there appear to be two opposing views about cash management.

Some managers believe that the management of a trust's liquidity is an important investment tool. They point out that if they correctly anticipate a downturn in share prices, and move the portfolio substantially into cash ahead of the event, they will be protecting their investors against market losses. Managers who actively manage a fund's liquidity in this way may occasionally have as much as 30 or 40 per cent of the portfolio in cash.

In contrast, other investment managers argue that investors have bought units in a unit trust because they want to have that portion of their capital in the stockmarket – and they may well consider that paying a 5 to 6 per cent initial charge for converting cash into cash is not much of a bargain! Managers holding these views will keep their funds almost fully invested through fair and foul stockmarket weather.

THE ROLE OF THE TRUSTEE

Every unit trust is required to have a separate and independent financial institution as trustee, and the name and address of this trustee will be given in each fund's reports, scheme particulars and other literature.

So investors in a unit trust have a unique protection. Most usually the trustee is a large bank, but sometimes it is a leading insurance company. Currently 12 banks and three insurance companies provide trustee services. Some unit trust companies have one trustee for all their funds; others have a selection, although few groups have more than three different trustees.

Although investors are unlikely to come into personal contact with these Olympian beings, trustees perform a central role in safeguarding the assets (the fund's investments), and policing the management of a unit trust.

The trustee acts as custodian of all the cash and securities in the unit trust and all these assets are held in its name. In addition, the trustee issues the unit trust certificates; repays investors when cancelled units have been received; oversees the register of unitholders; settles all a fund's investment transactions; and, as the legal owner of the underlying assets for the unitholders, collects and distributes the income earned from the investments. Not surprisingly it gets paid for its work and these fees are charged to the fund.

Because of the central position of the trustee, you, as a unit trust investor, have the ultimate comfort of knowing that even if the unit trust management company gets into financial difficulties, the money invested in the group's funds is quite separate, and could not be touched. It is a system that has withstood the test of time very well. No unit trust investor has ever lost money as a result of fraud in the sense that someone has raided the till and run away with the money.

Trustees are not only custodians. They also act in the role of policeman, or at least special constable, as far as the fund managers are concerned.

The trust deed sets out the agreement made between the managers and the trustee. Its terms will include a formula for valuing the fund to determine the price of units, and the scope of the managers' investment and borrowing powers. If the managers want to vary the provisions in the trust deed – perhaps to change its investment philosophy or to merge the trust with another fund – they must first secure the approval of the unitholders at a general meeting.

It is the duty of the trustee to make sure that the fund is managed according to the terms of the deed. For example, a trustee has powers to veto an investment, if it contravenes the trust deed. It is also the duty of the trustee to monitor a trust's advertisements, to make sure that they are not misleading and that they contain the appropriate risk warnings.

Trustees are not omnipotent, however, and their central limitation is that they cannot influence a manager's judgement in buying individual investments for the fund. Trustees ensure that a trust is run according to the trust deed but they do not, and cannot, protect investors against poor investment management.

So don't assume that every unit trust is well-run because an independent (and usually well-known) bank or insurer is policing its activities. Trustees are custodians. They have nothing to do with the selection and management of the shares and securities in a unit trust's portfolio.

Table 3.1 gives a list of trustee companies.

Table 3.1

Trustee companies	
Company	Number of groups
Royal Bank of Scotland	47
Lloyds Bank	28
Bank of Scotland	28
Midland Bank	23
Chase Manhattan Bank	14
Citicorp Bank	11
Clydesdale Bank	8
National Westminster Bank	12
General Accident	4
Coutts Bank	9
Royal Exchange	3
Bankers Trustee	6
Sun Alliance	1
SG Warburg	1
Barclays Bank	3

Source: AUTIF

FURTHER PROTECTION FOR INVESTORS

All unit trusts operate under the provisions of the 1986 Financial Services Act. The FSA's primary aim is to ensure that investors are properly protected, and it is fundamental that only people authorised under this legislation may conduct investment business. Built into the FSA is an investor compensation scheme which protects the money of savers up to a limit of £48,000, if something goes wrong.

The working of the FSA is overseen by the Securities and Investments Board and, under the SIB, by a system of self-regulatory organisations (SROs). The Investment Management Regulatory Organisation (IMRO) authorises and monitors the activities of most unit trust companies (and the activities of trustees), while the Personal Investment Authority (PIA) oversees the selling and advertising of the trusts and polices the activities of financial advisers.

If you have a complaint about a unit trust investment that cannot be resolved with the fund management company you may be able to pursue the matter with the PIA, with IMRO, or with the trustee of the fund.

WHERE DO UNIT TRUSTS INVEST?

Unit trust investment managers are able to invest in any security quoted on a recognised Stock Exchange, although not more than 10 per cent of a fund can be placed in the more risky unquoted securities. Funds of funds also invest in other unit trusts (see page 55).

Most unit trusts concentrate on investment in the shares, or equities, of UK and international companies. However, a number also invest in Government stocks (gilts) and in the fixed-interest bonds issued by companies. There is also freedom, hardly exploited as yet, to invest in property and to use options, warrants and futures, which are financial instruments

There are legal constraints to ensure that each unit trust provides its investors with a spread of risk from a reasonably diversified portfolio.

that give investors the right to buy or sell at a known price at a future date. The currency exposure of an overseas trust may be hedged by using forward currency contracts (see Chapter Five for details about the different investment markets).

These parameters give unit trust companies considerable investment freedom, but there are legal constraints to ensure that each unit trust provides its investors with a spread of risk from a reasonably diversified portfolio.

Perhaps most importantly a unit trust must not have fewer than 16 holdings (most funds have between 50 and 100); the largest holding must not exceed 10 per cent of the fund; and the trust must not hold more than 10 per cent of the share capital of any one company.

THE UNIT TRUST MANAGERS

Unit trusts may be run by specialist unit trust managers, or by institutions that are also engaged in many other financial activities. These include life insurance companies, banks, building societies, stockbrokers and financial advisers.

Some unit trust management companies run just one or two different trusts, but the largest may well provide a range of 20 or 30 funds.

The overwhelming majority of trusts invest directly in a portfolio of shares and fixed interest securities, which are selected and actively run by professional fund managers. There is also an increasing number of 'passive' tracker, or index funds, however, which are designed to mirror the performance of a stockmarket index, either by investing in all the shares that make up the index, or by investing in a representative sample, or by using futures and options to 'track' an index (see Chapter Five, pages 110–114).

At first glance prospective investors might be forgiven for feeling daunted by the diversity of choice on offer, but they can preserve their sanity by grasping one fundamental. *All unit trusts are designed to provide either income, or capital growth or a mix of the two.*

■ **INVESTMENT SNAPSHOT**

The first step to choosing a unit trust, therefore, is to decide which of these objectives suits your particular financial circumstances, which should not be too taxing.

The next move is to identify a suitable type of fund, one that meets your investment aims and carries the level of market risk that you can comfortably tolerate. You may be looking for long-term capital growth, but that does not mean that you want to find yourself having a roller-coaster ride in an emerging markets fund.

3

The final and most difficult decision is the selection of the actual trust. How to choose the right investment fund is discussed in detail in Chapter Seven, but the foundations of the selection process have been laid for investors by The Association of Unit Trusts and Investment Funds (AUTIF).

AUTIF places every unit trust into a specific sector category. This eases the selection pain because it clarifies the range of underlying investments held by different groups of trusts. This in turn provides pointers to the risk rating and likely volatility of individual trusts.

Within each sector there will be trusts with very different risk profiles, but the categorisation nevertheless enables investors to make some sensible comparisons between the performances of funds which invest in the same markets. This is important. A comparison of the relative performance of, say, a UK, Japanese and North American fund, each of which invests in totally different markets and economies, is about as useful as a judgement on the respective merits of an overcoat, a bikini and a necktie.

The different sectors are listed below and their specific characteristics are described in more detail in Chapter Five. The average performance of the unit trust sectors over one, three and seven years is given in Table 3.2.

Table 3.2

The average performance of the unit trust sectors			
Sector	One year average	Three years' average	Seven years' average
UK growth & income	+12.1%	+32.5%	+97.3%
UK equity income	+10.2%	+36.2%	+89.7%
UK growth	+14.4%	+38.0%	+89.4%
UK smaller companies	+11.6%	+54.6%	+63.8%
Gilt & fixed interest	+7.6%	+16.7%	+61.6%
UK balanced	+9.4%	+33.9%	+84.0%
International equity income	+9.0%	+36.1%	+94.3%
International growth	+6.6%	+38.6%	+111.6%
International fixed interest	+11.3%	+16.2%	+73.1%
International equity & bond	+9.8%	+28.6%	+104.5%
Fund of funds	+7.3%	+35.6%	+89.8%
Japan	−8.6%	+34.3%	+24.2%
Far East inc. Japan	−4.3%	+48.7%	+107.9%
Far East ex. Japan	−0.2%	+61.0%	+221.8%
Australasia	+4.5%	+51.1%	+79.8%
North America	+25.4%	+37.8%	+187.6%
Europe	+12.0%	+54.8%	+129.1%
Commodity & energy	−3.4%	+103.1%	÷116.9%
Financial & property	+12.7%	+50.4%	+143.8%
Investment trust units	+3.1%	+50.5%	+120.6%
Money market	+3.6%	+11.8%	+52.8%
Convertibles	+3.7%	+20.5%	+49.3%

Figures to 1 January 1996 are on an offer to bid price basis, with net income re-invested.

Source: Money Observer/Investment Intelligence

THE DIFFERENT TYPES OF UNIT TRUST

■ Money market or cash trusts

At least 80 per cent of the assets of these trusts are invested either in bank deposits or in short-term fixed interest holdings. There is no capital growth with cash unit trusts. Their function is to enable ordinary investors to get access to money market interest rates which are usually available only to larger institutions.

Cash trusts are therefore an alternative to a bank or building society savings account and can be a useful 'resting home' for investors who are waiting for some recovery in the stockmarket before placing money into shares.

■ UK gilt and fixed-interest trusts
(also known as UK bond funds)

These trusts have at least 80 per cent of their assets in UK fixed-interest securities. These may be Government securities (gilts), fixed-interest securities such as corporate bonds and preference shares or a mix of the two. Bond funds offer a high initial income but limited prospects of future capital or income growth.

■ Convertible unit trusts

A small group of trusts that invest at least 60 per cent of their assets in UK and international convertible shares. Convertibles are fixed-interest loan stock, with relatively high yields. They are usually issued by large or medium-sized companies. Convertibles give investors the right to convert to the issuing company's ordinary shares or preference shares (shares which pay dividends at a fixed rate) at some predetermined time in the future.

■ International fixed-interest trusts

With these funds, at least 80 per cent of the portfolio is in fixed-interest securities, but there is an international spread of investments. This enables the managers to profit from varying interest rates in different countries and from currency movements.

■ UK equity and bond trusts (previously UK balanced)

These funds offer some of the relative capital security and higher income payments of fixed-interest trusts, whilst also providing an exposure to shares. At least 80 per cent of the portfolio will be invested in the UK but less than 80 per cent will be either in UK gilts and fixed-interest securities or in UK equities. The trusts aim to provide a yield of up to 120 per cent of the yield on the FT-SE All Share Index. The All Share is the stockmarket index that reflects the share price movements of the

UK's quoted companies as a whole. It includes 900 companies in its calculations.

■ UK equity and bond income trusts
(previously UK balanced)

These trusts have the same investment parameters as funds in the UK equity and bond sector but they are more income-orientated. They aim to produce a yield of more than 120 per cent of the FT-SE All Share Index.

■ International equity and bond trusts

These funds have the same mix of equities and fixed-interest securities as their UK-based equivalents. The difference is that they are free to invest in world stockmarkets.

■ UK equity income trusts

UK equity income funds invest at least 80 per cent of their portfolio in UK shares with above average yields. The target for a UK equity income trust is a yield of more than 110 per cent of the FT-SE All Share Index. On 31 December 1995, that meant a yield of 4.18 per cent. One of the most persuasive arguments for putting money into shares is the opportunity this gives for securing a growing income from your investments over the years, and dividend growth is the paramount aim of equity income trusts

■ UK growth and income trusts
(also known as 'general trusts')

These are 'middle ground' funds for those who want a combination of income and capital growth. The trusts provide a yield of around 80 to 110 per cent of the FT-SE All-Share Index, and have at least 80 per cent of their investments in the shares of UK companies.

■ UK growth trusts

These funds will also have at least 80 per cent of their assets in UK equities but the primary objective is to invest in those companies that are likely to produce a strong growth in their share price. Income is a secondary consideration.

■ UK smaller companies trusts

The argument for investing in the shares of smaller companies is that, historically, these have shown more exciting price rises than the shares of larger, well-established companies. The counter-argument is that these shares are more risky, because smaller companies are generally less resilient during adverse economic and financial circumstances. Trusts in this category have at least 80 per cent of their portfolios invested in companies which form part of the Hoare Govett UK Smaller Companies Extended Index.

■ International equity income trusts

Generally speaking overseas companies pay lower dividends than UK companies, However, there are around a dozen trusts specialising in high-yield international equities. The target is a yield of more than 110 per cent of the FTA World Index.

■ International growth trusts

This is the largest unit trust sector. It includes not only funds that invest in mainstream international blue-chip companies but also, at the moment, those that provide an exposure to the world's emerging economies. The risk profile of individual trusts in this sector therefore varies enormously. The common factors are that all international growth trusts have at least 80 per cent of their assets in equities, and that all of them put the investment emphasis on capital growth, not income.

■ Fund of funds trusts

All unit trusts try to spread the risk of stockmarket investment. Fund of funds trusts, or mastertrusts, also limit the risk of choosing a dog, or poorly performing, fund because they invest not in shares but in a range of other unit trusts. Some stick to the trusts offered by their own group; others run a fund consisting of an actively managed selection of trusts run by different companies.

■ Investment trust unit trusts

These funds also spread the collective fund risk. They invest only in the shares of investment trust companies.

■ North America trusts

For 'North America' read 'Canada' as well as 'US'. All these funds have at least 80 per cent of their portfolio in North American securities, but there is a wide choice of investments (and risk/reward ratings) on offer. There are trusts concentrating on larger companies, smaller companies, and recovery and special situations.

■ Europe trusts

At least 80 per cent of the assets of these trusts are invested in European securities, but the investments can include UK as well as Continental European shares. However, a handful of European unit trusts concentrate on the shares of single countries, such as France or Germany.

■ Japan trusts

A Japan trust has at least 80 per cent of its portfolio in Japanese securities. As with the North America sector, investment may be in large or small companies, so within the category there will be funds offering different degrees of risk and providing different performance returns.

■ Far East (including Japan) trusts

These trusts provide an exposure to Japan (still the world's second largest stockmarket) but Japanese securities account for less than 80 per cent of their assets. The balance is invested in other Far Eastern securities.

■ Far East (excluding Japan) trusts

At least 80 per cent of the assets of these trusts is in Far Eastern securities, but there is no exposure to the Japanese market. Unit trusts specialising in single economies such as Hong Kong, Korea and Singapore are included in this category.

■ Australasia trusts

A tiny category of fewer than half-a-dozen trusts. All the funds have at least 80 per cent of their portfolios invested in Australia or New Zealand.

■ Commodity and energy trusts

Unit trusts cannot buy and sell physical commodities such as gold and silver, but they can invest in the shares of mining, oil and other commodity companies. These trusts have at least 80 per cent of their assets in such shares.

■ Financial and property trusts

Few, if any, unit trusts are likely to invest directly in property. Instead they provide an exposure to this investment sector through the shares of property companies. Trusts in this category must have at least 80 per cent of their assets in property shares or the shares of financial institutions such as banks and insurance companies.

■ Personal pension and FSAVC trusts

Funds in this sector are available only to investors in unit trust personal pension or free standing additional voluntary contribution (FSAVC) schemes (see Chapter Ten, pages 227–232). Under the present legislation pension providers have to set up separate pension unit trusts, and these funds then invest in a company's equivalent mainstream trust. The performance of a pension trust will always beat its parallel unit trust fund, because income in the pension fund rolls up free of tax.

■ Emerging markets trusts

A new sector was introduced during 1996 to accommodate funds that have 80 per cent or more of their assets invested directly or indirectly in emerging markets. Indirect investment – for instance, China shares listed in Hong Kong – should not exceed more than 50 per cent of the portfolio.

SELLING YOUR UNITS

Although unit trusts are not suitable investments for cash you may need to get hold of in a hurry, unit trust managers must buy back your units at any time if you want to sell, and you should be able to get hold of some or all of your money very quickly. In periods of extreme stockmarket volatility, such as the great crash of October 1987, investors may have to wait a few days before dealing but such times are very rare.

Details of how to sell your unit trusts will be given to you when you first invest (see Chapter Four, page 73). With some companies, 'sell' instructions can be taken over the telephone. It will probably take less than a week for the cheque to arrive.

SWITCHING BETWEEN TRUSTS

You may want to sell your unit trust holding in order to put money into a different type of fund. At retirement, for instance, it may be appropriate to switch from an emphasis on capital growth to income-producing investments.

■ INVESTMENT SNAPSHOT

There is always a cost in moving from one unit trust to another, because there is a spread between the buying price (which includes the initial charge paid by investors when they first put money into a fund plus dealing costs) and the selling price. However, if you have money invested with a unit management company that runs a large number of funds, it may be possible to reduce these costs by switching between its trusts. (See Switching, *Chapter Four, page 73.)*

HOW THE UNIT TRUST GROUP KEEPS IN CONTACT

Once you have bought units in a unit trust, the managers will usually send you a report twice a year. This will provide details of the fund's investments and its performance over the reporting period, and it will give the manager's views on the prospects for the trust over the next six months.

These managers' reports tend to be workmanlike, rather than glossy in appearance, and some bristle with technical and unfamiliar terms. As a result there is often a strong temptation for busy investors to consign them to the waste paper basket. Resist it. The manager's report contains many nuggets of helpful information. To take an extreme example, if a qualification is attached to the auditors' report, investors should read this as a warning that the trust has some problems.

Each report details the names of the directors, auditors, investment managers – the most useful reports are often those that are signed by a specific investment manager – and trustees of the unit trust company and the relevant self-regulatory organisation.

This may seem arcane information but it is in fact helpful to keep track of any changes in the personnel responsible for the running of the trust. For example, you should make a mental note of any change of investment manager, because this may well affect the fund's future performance, for better or for worse. The listed names will also be needed, of course, if you ever want to make a complaint.

Understandably, most investors will turn first to the performance of the trust over the previous six-month period. The report will show whether the trust has done better or worse than the markets in which it invests (the yardstick will be the relevant index for that market); what the manager's investment strategy has been; and whether there has been an increase in the income payments.

All the shares and securities held by the fund will be listed, as will the changes made to the investments in the portfolio since the last report. The amount of unitholder money that the trust currently holds in cash will also be given.

3

Take a look at how many shares are listed. The more concentrated the portfolio – that is, the fewer the shares in it – the more high-risk the trust will be, because each share will represent such a sizeable proportion of its holdings. On the other hand, a very long portfolio of shares means that the brilliant showing of one or two of the companies listed will have little impact on overall performance. As a general rule if a portfolio has fewer than 40 shares, view it as a concentrated one.

The inevitable drawback of all unit trust reports is that by the time they reach the hands of investors, the information on the trust's performance and the shares in its portfolio will be out of date.

Perhaps of more interest, therefore, is the investment and economic forecast given in the report. No manager can foresee natural catastrophes such as the Kobe earthquake in Japan, on 17 January 1995, but general misjudgements on share price, economic trends and interest rate movements will quickly become apparent.

In addition to the interim and annual reports of individual funds, some unit trust companies send yearly statements to their investors, giving details of any deals the investor has made during the year and listing the number of units they now hold and their current value.

If you have opted for a trust that pays out income, you will also receive this on predetermined dates each year, together with a tax voucher (see Chapter Eight, pages 165–166). The income will either come by cheque or be paid directly into your bank or building society account.

Those who want to monitor the progress of their unit-holding more closely can check daily prices in a number of leading newspapers, such as the *Financial Times*, *The Times*, *The Daily Telegraph* and *The Independent*.

The newspapers will quote two prices. The higher of the two (technically known as the 'offer price') is what you would pay for the units if you were buying them. The lower (the 'bid price') is the cash-in price, and represents what you would get for your units if you sold them.

To work out the current value of your investment, simply multiply the number of units you have – this is listed on your contract note – by the bid price in the newspaper. Remember unit trust prices are expressed in pence, so you will need to divide by 100 to get an answer in pounds sterling! (Unit trust pricing is discussed in more detail in Chapter Four, pages 71–72.)

When prices are accompanied by the letters 'XD' this indicates that a fund has gone 'ex-distribution'. This is a shorthand way of saying that the accumulated income has been put aside so that it can be paid to investors in a few weeks time. The unit price of a fund that goes 'XD' usually falls slightly, simply because accumulated income is no longer included in it.

Share prices of investment trusts and other companies are also quoted XD, or without the dividend, before each distribution and again the price will fall slightly.

A number of unit trust management groups now operate a telephone helpline service, for existing and prospective customers who have a query or want more information on the current house view about markets. For instance the Market Commentary Helpline, run by Perpetual, the Henley-based group, gives the company's views on developments in all the major stockmarkets. It is updated at the beginning of each month and is available to all investors with a touch-tone phone.

LOOKING TO THE FUTURE: OPEN-ENDED INVESTMENT COMPANIES (OEICs)

Many unit trust groups may soon be marketing a different type of collective investment fund, the open-ended investment company or OEIC for short.

OEICs are very similar to unit trusts. The money of individual investors is pooled and managed for them by professional fund managers; it is easy to get cash in and out of the fund; and all assets of the fund are in the safekeeping of an independent financial institution.

Where OEICs differ from unit trusts is in their structure. Like

■ **DEFINITION**

OEICs (open-ended investment companies) are a type of collective investment fund that is widely available in the rest of Europe, but new to the UK. An OEIC is very similar to a unit trust, but it has a company structure, and there is a single price at which its shares are bought and sold.

investment trusts they are companies, which means that some of the terminology is different. Investors buy shares instead of units, for example, and the assets of a fund are looked after by a depository not a trustee.

Perhaps pricing is the most obvious difference between an OEIC and a unit trust, however. An OEIC has a much simpler pricing system than the unit trust's double act of a higher 'offer' or buying price (which includes initial charges for the investment) and a lower 'bid' or selling price.

An OEIC has one price which will be the same whether you are buying or selling your shares. That does not mean OEICs are much cheaper investments than unit trusts. You will almost certainly have to pay a separate initial management charge when you buy shares in an OEIC. (And, indeed, it may well be that unit trust regulations will change, so that unit trusts will have 'single pricing' just like OEICs.)

Although an OEIC is a company it is really more like a unit trust than an investment trust. It can be marketed directly to the public; it will not always be quoted on the Stock Exchange; and the number of shares in issue will vary from day to day, just like the number of units in a unit trust. Importantly, too, the price of an OEIC, like the prices of a unit trust, directly reflects the value of the holdings in the fund's portfolio.

OEICs rather than unit trusts are the familiar form of collective investment in Europe, and as unit trust managers want to sell their funds to investors in European countries, as well as to investors in the UK, it may well be that many existing unit trusts will be converted eventually to OEICs.

Investors with money in unit trusts that do convert have no need to worry. It will make no difference to the security of their investment or to how their money is managed. An OEIC is just another way to organise a collective investment fund.

OFFSHORE UNIT TRUSTS

Some UK investors will already be quite at home with the OEIC structure. Many of the best-known UK financial institutions have established offshore subsidiary companies, to provide investment vehicles for people at home, and for expatriates and foreign nationals, and very often the offshore collective funds that they manage are OEICs rather than unit trusts.

Why should UK investors choose to put money into an offshore fund rather than a domestic fund? The only good reason is if the offshore version offers an investment facility that is not available in the UK.

For instance, offshore funds, unlike UK unit trusts, can be denominated in foreign currencies, and no offshore fund deducts UK income tax at source. This does not mean that these funds miraculously protect you from interference in your affairs by the Inland Revenue, but it does present some tax planning opportunities.

Suppose you choose a 'roll-up' offshore fund, for example, where all the income earned by the underlying assets is accumulated (i.e., rolled up) and reflected in the share price. Tax is due only when shares are sold or switched to another fund. So it is possible to defer (though not to duck) your tax liability.

Popular locations for the offshore operations of UK investment companies are Luxembourg, the Channel Islands, Dublin and the Isle of Man. A number of funds are also based outside the European Union in financial centres such as Bermuda.

Each offshore centre will have its own investor protection rules in place, but if you have understandable fears about security, you can also check whether a fund is described as 'SIB recognised'. If it is, this means that the Securities and Investments Board believes that the regulatory standards the fund is operating under are on par with those in the UK.

However, the best safety net if you do want to go offshore is to stick to the offshore subsidiaries of large and well-known UK companies with reputable blue-chip names – and to take sensible professional advice.

■ WHERE TO LEARN MORE ABOUT UNIT TRUSTS

The Association of Unit Trusts and Investment Funds (AUTIF) was founded nearly 40 years ago, to bring the benefits of unit trusts and other collective investment schemes to the notice of a wider public. It also lobbies Government on legal and taxation matters that affect unit trust management companies. The names and addresses of its members are listed in Appendix One on page 235. These members represent 96 per cent of the unit trust industry by asset value.

AUTIF's Unit Trust Information Service publishes a number of free explanatory leaflets and will answer general telephone queries from the public (0181-207 1361) although it cannot offer investment advice. Written requests for more details and information packs about unit trusts should be sent to:

The Unit Trust Information Service,
AUTIF, 65 Kingsway, London WC2B 6TD.

All unit trust companies have literature available for inquirers. Their brochures are obviously of variable quality, but the best give a clear picture of the company's background and investment style and of the funds and services it provides.

■ FURTHER READING

'Unit Trusts and You'; 'Unit Trusts: A User's Handbook', and 'Unit Trusts: The Directory' (the latter lists all unit trusts managed by AUTIF members). These booklets are free from the Unit Trust Information Service.

You don't need an economics degree or experience in a street market to deal in unit trusts or investment trusts

BUYING AND
SELLING

4

■ THE FUNDAMENTALS

 Unit trust units can be bought directly from the management company, either by writing, telephoning or filling in an advertisement coupon. Units can be sold in the same way.

 Investment trust shares can be bought directly through a stockbroker, or indirectly by using the savings and investment scheme of a management company. Shares can be sold in the same way.

 The buying price of unit trust units includes the trust's initial charge and dealing expenses.

 The share price of an investment trust does not include any expenses, but there will be separate dealing charges for buying and selling.

 The initial management charge on most unit trusts is 5 to 6 per cent.

 There is generally no initial management charge on an investment trust.

 Unit trust and investment trust savings schemes accept investments of £20 to £25 a month upwards.

■ TERMINOLOGY

Accumulation units: Unit trust units that provide for any interest or dividends earned to be automatically re-invested, so that the value of the units is increased.

Forward pricing: The pricing of unit trust units after the sale and purchase orders of the day have been received, and the fund has been revalued.

Historic pricing: The pricing of unit trust units according to the last valuation of the fund.

Execution-only dealing: A facility to buy and sell shares without the provision of any investment advice.

Certificated savings scheme: Scheme where the investor receives a certificate as proof of individual ownership of the investment.

Nominee savings scheme: Scheme where all investments are held in a nominee account to reduce paperwork and simplify administration.

Share exchange scheme: Scheme to enable investors with existing shareholdings to convert these at modest cost into unit trust units or investment trust shares.

Pound-cost averaging: Investing a fixed sum on a regular basis, which results in acquiring shares or units at an averagely lower price than the average of their prices on the days when the purchases were made.

4

Even those who regularly read the financial pages of newspapers are sometimes put off by what they imagine will be the complicated mechanics of investing money in a unit trust or investment trust. Perhaps even more important, they are somewhat nervous of the hoops that they may have to leap through in order to get their cash out again, when they want it.

Well, it may be slightly quicker and simpler to go into one of the building societies in your local high street and open a savings account. But if you have decided that the time has come to put some money where it has a chance to grow over the years, do not be deterred by unfamiliar buying and selling practices. You don't need an economics degree, or experience in a street market, to deal in unit trusts and investment trusts.

HOW TO BUY UNITS IN A UNIT TRUST

You have £1,000 to invest, you have chosen a unit trust, what do you do next?

■ You can ask the management company to send you a brochure and application form, which you can then complete, and return with your cheque.

■ You may be able to place your order over the telephone. You will then be sent a contract note and a request for payment, which must be made within the next few days. This is the most straightforward way to buy units.

You have £1,000 to invest, you have chosen a unit trust, what do you do next?

■ Unit trusts, particularly new unit trusts, are often advertised in the Press. If there is a coupon attached to the advertisement, you can fill that in and send it to the company with your cheque (but beware hasty impulse investing, see Chapter Seven).

■ You can instruct your financial adviser to buy the units for you or you can use the services of a company representative.

Once you have placed your order, the unit trust company will send you a contract note within a day or two. You may find that, under the Financial Services Act, you have the right to cancel the deal within 14 days if you change your mind. If you do cancel, you would still have to accept any investment risk, however. You would get back your original investment adjusted by the appropriate change in value.

Cancellation rights are not given to investors who buy over the telephone, or to those who clip an advertisement, or who make the purchase of units through a broker with whom they have a client agreement.

The unit trust may offer you a choice of income units or accumulation units. If you buy income units you will receive regular payments of any income earned by your share of the trust's investments. If you buy accumulation units the income will be reinvested for you and reflected in the price of the units. You can also choose to have the payments from income units re-invested in extra units. (But you don't avoid an income tax bill by having accumulation units, see Chapter Eight, page 164.)

The contract note you receive from the unit trust company will confirm your investment, and will tell you the price at which you bought the units and the type and number of units you have bought with your money. For instance if the buying price of the units was 25p, you would receive 4,000 units for your £1,000.

Unit trusts have a buying (offer) price and a selling (bid) price (see Chapter Three, pages 60–61). Usually there is a difference of between 5.5 and 7.5 per cent between the two prices, although the gap could be wider.

The buying price of units will always be higher than the selling price because it includes the trust's initial charge (usually 5 to 6 per cent) and dealing costs such as brokers' commission and stamp duty. In other words the offer price – so-called because it is the price which the unit trust company is offering units for sale – reflects the notional price that you would have to pay to acquire your share of the investments, plus the unit trust company's initial charge.

The difference between the offer price and the bid price of a unit trust is known as the spread, and absolutely no mathematical skills are needed to work out that your investment will have to earn the same amount as the spread in order for you to cover your dealing costs and be back to where you were before you wrote the cheque to the unit trust company. Initial buying costs are one reason why you should never put short-term money in a unit trust.

Not all unit trust companies operate the same pricing systems. Some units use 'historic' pricing; others prefer 'forward' pricing. This divergence is a slightly irritating extra 'something' for investors to get their brains around but it should not make any material difference to them.

Companies that opt for historic pricing will sell you units at the price that was calculated when the fund was last valued. Companies that use 'forward' pricing will calculate a unit price only after all the day's orders have been collected and the fund has been valued again. 'Forward' pricing is really the fairer system, but of course it does mean that you will not know the exact price of the units you have bought until you receive your contract note.

Newspapers that publish unit trust prices often show whether a company uses forward or historic pricing. Those companies that use historic pricing must use forward pricing if the investor requests it, or if any revaluation of the units would prompt a shift in price of more than 2 per cent.

The debate between forward and historic pricing may be academic if you invest in a new unit trust by filling in an advertisement coupon. New funds have a fixed unit price during their launch periods, so investors know exactly how many units their money will buy.

Within three weeks of buying your units you will usually receive a unit trust certificate, although, in an effort to reduce the costs of processing pieces of paper, some companies no longer issue certificates. This does not matter – your contract note is a perfectly adequate confirmation of your investment – but the selling process is slightly different for certificated and non-certificated units.

HOW TO SELL UNITS IN A UNIT TRUST

You can sell all or part of your unit trust holding at any time and you should receive your money within a few days, and certainly within five days.

If you have a unit trust certificate this will have a withdrawal form on the back to fill in. If you don't have a certificate, you can still sell your units at any time by contacting the management company in writing or by telephone. If the holding is in joint names, the company will need both signatures. If you bought the units through a company salesman or a financial adviser, they can organise the sale. You will get a contract note recording the transaction.

4

SWITCHING

It may be that you want to sell your units, not to visit China or buy a car, but in order to re-invest in another unit trust that provides a different type of investment.

If so, don't simply sell up and then start to investigate other trusts. Remember the process of buying and selling units is going to cost you money every time you do it.

■ INVESTMENT SNAPSHOT

Before selling and re-investing, check what other funds your existing unit trust company offers. If it has a fund that fits your new investment needs – and appears to be well-managed and has a good performance track record – consider switching your investment to this rather than moving to another unit trust company.

Most unit trust managers will give investors in this position a discount on the offer price of the units of their new trust. This can reduce the buying price of the new units by anything from 1 to 4 per cent.

UNIT TRUST CHARGES

When you invest in a unit trust, you are buying a number of professional services. You are securing the expertise of a professional fund manager, who is running a portfolio of investments for you and for the other contributors to the pool. You are also paying for the technology of administrators who will organise all the investment paperwork. And you are securing an institutional trustee, to look after the safe running of the trust on your behalf. Naturally enough, these services cost money.

Unit trusts usually levy two management charges, an initial charge and an annual charge. The initial charge is factored into the offer price and is typically 5 to 6 per cent. The annual charge will be around 0.75 to 1.75 per cent.

The annual fee is usually taken out of the income the trust earns, but recently there has been a trend for income trusts to use a new freedom to take their charges out of capital. This increases the amount of income that can be paid out to the investor. If the yield is 5 per cent, and the annual management charge is 1 per cent, for instance, taking the annual charge from capital will push up the quoted yield to 6 per cent.

However, there is a potential disadvantage of this charging method. Over time the deduction of annual fees will erode your initial investment if the trust is not managing to grow your capital. This is likely to be a real concern only with a fund that invests in fixed interest bonds, where capital growth will at best be modest (see Chapter Nine, pages 198–199).

There are no fixed rules about how much a trust may charge, although there will be a clause in the trust deed setting a maximum level. These 'maximum permitted' fees are usually considerably higher than the prevailing level of charges, as companies like to reserve elbow room for themselves against an unknown future. If they want to raise charges beyond the ceiling mentioned in the trust deed, they will have the expense and inconvenience of calling a meeting of unitholders to allow them to vote on the proposed change.

The range of charges outlined above are typical, but there are many variations, and there is now increasing competition on price within the unit trust industry. The battle is cutting costs to investors quite dramatically on some unit trusts. For example there are now trusts – particularly those investing in fixed-interest bonds and funds that track the performance of a stockmarket index – that have no initial charge.

Other unit trust companies have cut initial charges but introduced exit fees for investors who cash in their units within five years. Obviously companies can afford to cut initial charges to the bone if they are able to attract a very large number of investors into a fund and to ensure, through a penalty system, that the majority of them will leave their money invested for a number of years.

One reason for the outbreak of price competition is that new disclosure rules are to be introduced which will make it much easier for investors to compare the effect of the build up of different charges. These rules will apply to OEICs (see Chapter Three, pages 61–62) and investment trust savings schemes (see pages 77–79) as well as to unit trusts.

Charges are always important because high management fees can make a considerable dent in the value of an investment.

■ INVESTMENT SNAPSHOT

You should never choose a unit trust simply because it is cheap. If the investment performance of a trust with a 6 per cent initial charge is twice as good as the performance of a trust which charges 3 per cent, the latter fund is not much of a bargain.

Don't ignore charges, though. If you have compiled a shortlist of, say, three trusts, and you can't make up your mind which to choose, the respective charges of the funds will be a very sensible tie-breaker (see Chapter Seven).

All unit trust companies require a minimum investment for their funds. Typical figures are £500 or £1,000, although there are trusts that set the entry level as high as £10,000. Don't let these figures deter you. There are regular savings schemes, which enable people with only £25 to £50 to invest in a unit trust or investment trust (see pages 77–79).

HOW TO BUY AND SELL INVESTMENT TRUST SHARES

Investors tend to view the purchase and sale of investment trust shares as a much more daunting process than the purchase of units in a unit trust. This is the perception rather than the reality, however.

Investment trust companies cannot sell shares directly to the public unless there is a new issue. All investment trust shares must be bought through the stockmarket. The question for investors is whether they do this by a direct or an indirect approach.

■ The direct approach

You can buy investment trust shares through a stockbroker, a financial adviser, a bank or large building society or one of the 'execution-only' share dealing services, such as Sharelink. Execution-only services will not offer you any advice on which share to buy but they may well be cheaper, particularly for relatively modest investments.

When you check the price of an investment trust's shares in the newspapers, there will be no allowance there for your transaction costs. Unlike a unit trust, the expense of buying the investment is not built in to the share price. And as investment trusts must be bought and sold on the stockmarket, the dealing expenses will vary from one deal to another. The cost will depend on the amount of money involved and how and where you buy the shares.

While there is normally no initial charge to pay to the managers when you buy investment trust shares you will have to pay stockbroking commission. This may be a flat fee, but it is more likely to be a percentage of the money you are investing. Typically this will be in the range of 1 to 1.65 per cent and there is usually a minimum fee, which can make it expensive to buy small numbers of shares. There will also be stamp duty on the shares you buy.

You will need the services of a stockbroker again when you sell the shares, so there will be more brokerage to pay, but no more stamp duty.

At this point, novice investors may well be throwing up their hands in bewilderment. Don't worry. There is an another way to buy investment trust shares and it is probably one of the most cost-effective ways of investing in the stock market that has yet been devised. All D-I-Y investment trust investors should make full use of it.

INVESTMENT TRUST SAVINGS AND INVESTMENT SCHEMES

In the past, the fact that shares could be bought only through a stockbroker certainly deterred some private investors from putting money into investment trust shares. Happily, the management companies went to their drawing-boards, and in 1984 the first investment trust savings scheme – which enabled shares to be bought and sold through the company that managed the investment trust – was born. Fittingly, the scheme's parent was Foreign & Colonial, the industry's founding father.

Investment trust savings schemes can provide a means of buying investment trust shares at a bargain basement cost ...

The savings scheme mechanism has proved to be a huge break-through in helping the investment trust industry in its efforts to attract more private investors. Today some 46 fund managers offer savings schemes on 207 different trusts. They will accept occasional lump sums (a minimum of £250 or £500 is common) or regular monthly savings.

Investment trust savings schemes can provide a means of buying investment trust shares at a bargain basement cost, and it is no sur-prise to discover that very large investors use them regularly.

Savings schemes are so cost-effective because the investment trust management groups have muscle on their side, and they use this to cut costs for investors. They amalgamate all the buying orders from investors into one large deal, negotiate bulk-buy rates with their stockbrokers and pass on the discounts to their investors. As a result, less of an investor's money goes in initial costs and more into shares.

Most investment trust companies are to some extent subsidising their savings schemes, but they are not doing so entirely through altruism. Successful savings schemes stimulate demand for a trust's shares, and the more demand there is, the narrower the discount on the shares will be.

Typical charges for buying shares through a savings scheme, excluding stamp duty, range from nothing at all to around 1 per cent. If investors have come through a financial adviser, some managers will offer to deduct up to 3 per cent from their investment, to pay commission to this intermediary, but the money will only be handed over with the agreement of the investor.

Investment trust savings schemes are not only very cheap. They also make the purchase and sale of shares remarkably simple. The manager will provide you with all the necessary forms and many schemes allow you to re-invest your dividends if you wish.

One potential disadvantage of buying investment trust shares through a savings scheme is that of timing. As the managers quite often put through their bulk order only once a week (it may even be once a month) there will be a time-lag between the signing of your cheque and the investment of your money. This means that you won't know beforehand the price at which you are buying your shares.

At the moment an investment trust savings scheme will be either a 'certificated' or 'nominee' arrangement. If it is certificated, you will receive a share certificate and will be treated just like any other shareholder in the company. You will be able to attend the annual meeting, and you will be sent a copy of the report and accounts.

Nominee arrangements are becoming much more widespread, however, because they are cheaper to run. The advent of CREST (the new computerised settlement system for UK equities) heralded the end to certificated savings schemes.

With a nominee arrangement, a firm of registrars holds all the shares bought for investors in a nominee account, and you will receive an advice note, not a share certificate, as proof of ownership. You will often (but not always) still be entitled to all the usual benefits of being a shareholder.

Most investment trust savings schemes offer low-cost selling as well as buying facilities. Selling charges often mirror buying charges.

The sales process can be put in train simply by contacting the managers, and you will get the price prevailing at the next dealing day. Again this means you will be left in the dark as to price, so you won't know how much the sale will raise until the deal has been struck. One or two management companies even require one month's notice for selling, so avoid these schemes if you think you would find this constraint too restrictive.

If you have shares in a nominee account, you will also have to have these transferred to your own name before you can sell them. There may be a small charge for this.

Investment trusts seldom charge investors an initial management charge, and their annual management charges also tend to be lower than those on unit trusts. A typical annual fee would be 0.5 per cent. Investors in savings schemes are not usually charged for the on-going administration services of stockholding.

SHARE EXCHANGE SCHEMES

Perhaps you already own some shares. Many people have various small holdings of privatisation issues, for example; or they have inherited a few shareholdings or bought shares through a share option scheme run by their company.

These holdings may not fit into your overall financial planning. Alternatively you may feel that you have not the time or the expertise to run a portfolio of direct shareholdings. So you decide to spread your risks and buy some professional management for your investments from a unit trust or investment trust.

Pause for a moment before you contact a stockbroker to arrange the sale of the shares. Currently 88 unit trust groups and 16 investment trust management companies (running 136 individual investment trusts) offer share exchange arrangements, and these provide a much simpler and generally more cost-effective way to swap the shares of individual companies for units or investment trust shares.

Case Study

Using a share exchange scheme

Frank Pound-Sign is an impulse buyer. Over the years he has selected his stockmarket investments about as carefully as other people pick blackberries. He now has more than £50,000 tied up in a ragbag of small holdings.

Victoria, his wife, is not amused. She persuades Frank that it could be more profitable to have his shares professionally managed in collective funds. As a bonus, this would reduce the number of pieces of paper littering Frank's office floor.

Frank picks some unit trusts, and then discovers that the group whose funds he has chosen runs a share exchange scheme. This seems to provide a slightly cheaper way to sell his shareholdings, and re-invest the proceeds in unit trusts, but he complains to Victoria that there will still be a liability to capital gains tax when he disposes of the shares. Victoria points out that there aren't any capital gains.

The unit trust company has a list of almost 100 shares that it will accept currently into its funds. Where Frank's shares match this list he will receive the market buying price for them. This is usually 1 to 2 per cent higher than selling price. There will also be no broker's commission to pay. However, four of Frank's holdings are not on the wanted list. These shares will be sold at the normal bid or selling price and broker's commission will be deducted from the proceeds before re-investment.

Frank completes the Authority for Share Exchange form from the unit trust company, listing all the shares he is offering for exchange. He signs this in front of a witness, who also signs. Frank then returns the form, with the share certificates and an investment application form for the unit trusts he has chosen.

Frank's shares are sold on one day, and the cash is re-invested on the next. He is impressed to find that the share exchange transaction is so speedy, that he is only out of the market for 24 hours.

Unit trust and investment trust companies run their share exchange schemes very largely as a customer service. They don't make much profit out of them and they can seldom afford to advertise them.

With a share exchange scheme, the managers take over your shares, and either sell them or put them into the portfolios of one of their trusts. In exchange, you will get the value of the shares to invest in units or investment trust shares. You will be offered cut-price dealing terms by the managers, and you will save yourself a great deal of administrative hassle.

Costs do vary quite considerably, however, as do the terms and conditions of the schemes and individual management views on the securities they are prepared to accept. You will always be welcome with a parcel of gilts and blue chips, but your unquoted shares may well receive a dusty reception. Managers also impose different minima for the size of share portfolios that they will take in. The figure could be as low as £250 or as high as £5,000, or there could be no minimum.

One word of warning. When you dispose of shares through a share exchange scheme, the taxman views this as a disposal, as if you had sold them in the normal way. This means that any profits could be liable to capital gains tax (see Chapter Eight, pages 170–173).

REGULAR SAVINGS SCHEMES

One of the great virtues of unit trusts and investment trusts is that they offer a regular savings facility to enable those who do not have capital to build up a stake in stockmarket assets.

Many funds will accept a £25 or £50 monthly contribution, and a handful are even happy to take £10 or £20. It is also possible to make monthly contributions to a unit trust or investment trust through a Personal Equity Plan (Pep), and pay no tax on the profits and income you earn from your investment (see Chapter Nine).

Unit trust savings schemes have been around considerably longer than their investment trust counterparts, and managers now offer a choice of some 400 plans. Monthly payments are collected by standing order or direct debit, and virtually every plan has a facility to enable you to make an additional contribution at any time.

All the income earned from your investment is re-invested to buy more units, and although you will not receive a unit trust certificate, you will be sent regular statements showing how your plan is progressing and how many additional units you have acquired.

The investment trust savings schemes work in a very similar way. Again, your money is collected through standing order or direct debit and the managers then buy shares in the market with the cash. This transaction usually takes place once a month, but sometimes managers buy more frequently. You will then be allocated the number of shares your monthly payment has paid for.

If the shares are registered in the name of a nominee company, you won't get a share certificate, but as with unit trusts, regular statements are sent out, so it is not difficult to monitor the progress of your investment.

Unit trust and investment trust savings schemes provide the most cost-effective gateway into the stock market that is available to the regular saver. Unit trusts make no extra charge for the extra administration involved, and most investment trust savings schemes are extraordinarily good value for money.

Savings schemes are also extremely flexible, so that payments can be tailored to financial circumstances that may well change without warning. You can add to your investment at any time, and you can stop investing when it suits you to do so, without any surrender penalty. You can then either take the proceeds of your plan or leave your money invested. If you wish to resume saving at a later date, you can do so, without paying any fee to re-activate the plan.

Because you are investing a fixed amount of money, too, you will buy the shares or units at a lower average price than the average of the prices on the days when you actually invested, as the figures in Table 4.1 illustrate. This averaging effect is technically known as pound-cost averaging.

The more volatile the share price or unit price of a fund, the more cost-effective pound-cost averaging becomes. Regular savings schemes are therefore the ideal mechanism for building up a

Table 4.1

Fund-cost averaging		
Month	Offer Price	Units bought for £10 each month
1	50p	20
2	25p	40
3	10p	100
4	25p	40
Average price of units: 27.5p		
Price paid for units by saver: 20p		
Total units bought: 200		

Source: AUTIF

4

stake in a commodity fund, or in a fund investing in emerging economies.

Over the years savings schemes have proved themselves to be most efficient accumulators of capital.

For example, if you had invested £50 a month for 20 years into a

■ **DEFINITION**

Pound-cost averaging is investing a fixed sum on a regular basis, which results in acquiring shares or units at an averagely lower price than the average of their prices on the days when the purchases were made.

high-yielding building society account from 1 March 1976, and had re-invested your net interest, your £12,000 savings would have grown to £24,589.87 by 1 March 1996, according to figures calculated by Micropal.

Not bad, you might think. But if you had made the same investment into the average (not the best) performing UK growth and income unit trust, and re-invested your net income, your investment would have been worth £67,190.88, well over double the building society figure. This despite some quite extreme stockmarket conditions along the way, not the least of which was the stockmarket crash of 1987.

Which brings us neatly to the second great virtue of buying units or investment trust shares through a savings scheme. These vehicles enable investors to rise above that most thorny of problems, finding the right moment to buy a share or a unit trust.

Is the stockmarket too frothy and speculative? Are share prices about to start falling? As a regular saver you don't have to agonise. If the stockmarket is depressed you will simply buy more units or shares with your monthly payment.

Suppose you had wanted to give your largely UK investment portfolio an exposure to the US, the world's largest stockmarket at the start of 1996. You are reasonably confident that the US market will grow over the years, and you are picking a North American investment fund with a view to being a long-term investor.

But you are also aware that the American market rose nearly 40 per cent in 1995, and you can't help wondering whether now is a very sensible time to put money into it. If you start to invest through a monthly savings scheme, you can stop biting your nails.

We all tend to be suckers, only too willing to invest at the wrong time, when the stockmarket is full of good news, and share prices are nearing a peak. Savings schemes provide the discipline of investing regularly through good times and bad. The only benefit they cannot provide is advice on the best moment to sell.

Savings plans also provide plenty of choice for investors who want to diversify their investments overseas. Plans can be linked to funds that concentrate on European, American or Japanese companies. There are even schemes that provide access to the volatile emerging economies of the world. (For more about investment markets and choosing an investment trust and unit trust, see Chapters Five and Seven.)

INVESTING THROUGH AN INDEPENDENT FINANCIAL ADVISER

There are close on 2,000 unit trusts and investment trusts. What to look for when selecting a trust is discussed later (Chapter Seven), but you may feel that, in this uncertain world, you would prefer to take advice about your investment selections. So, how do you choose an investment adviser?

Nothing in life is free, say the cynics, and certainly the people who are officially authorised to offer you investment advice quite rightly expect to be paid for their services. Different financial advisers choose to receive their remuneration in different ways but they certainly don't earn a living by giving free advice.

First you must be quite clear whether the adviser is 'tied' or 'independent'. Tied advisers or agents have an arrangement with one company, or group of companies. They earn their income by advising on – and selling – this company's products. Banks and most building societies are tied advisers, although they may be linked to their own in-house companies.

Independent advisers are not acting for one company. They should act for you and advise on a wide range of financial products from a wide range of companies. But most still need to sell to you, their client, in order to earn commission. One way the unscrupulous adviser can generate more income is to 'churn' a client's investments – needlessly changing one unit trust or investment trust for another, simply to collect another dollop of commission.

Of course, there may be very good arguments for moving out of one investment sector and into another but the reasons do need to be compelling. Each time you change funds, it will cost you money and you won't start to benefit from any profits from your new investments until you have recouped these costs.

Commission-earning advisers tend to recommend more unit trusts than investment trusts, because more unit trust groups build commission payments into their pricing. However, some financial advisers – including accountants and solicitors – do not live off the commission they can earn from financial organisations for selling their products. They charge fees (usually based on how much time they have spent on the affairs of a client) and they then rebate any commission they receive to their clients.

Clearly fee-charging advisers are under much less financial pressure to sell investment products to their clients. But the snag is that fee-based advice is expensive; it can cost up to £200 an hour. No one has yet found a way to bring truly impartial advice, at an affordable price, to smaller savers and investors.

Money Management magazine keeps a National Register of Fee-Based Advisers. Its service includes a public hotline to help consumers through the adviser selection process (Telephone: 01179 769444).

Of course how advisers are paid – and how much they earn – is not as important as the quality of the advice they give. By taking professional advice on which unit trust or investment trust to buy you are hoping to add value to the investment decision.

Personal recommendation from a satisfied client is probably the most valuable pointer to an adviser's competence. If you don't have this, see if the firm can provide some clear statistics about the investment performance it has achieved for other clients as a result of its advice. And check how long they have been in business. Longevity and experience are assets in the investment advice business.

THE TIMING CONUNDRUM: WHEN TO BUY AND WHEN TO SELL

It is easy to say when you should buy and sell an investment. Any fool knows that. You buy when prices have bottomed, just before they start to rise again; and you sell when prices are at their peak, just before they start to slide downwards.

Unfortunately no-one – whether professional fund manager or enthusiastic amateur – has ever discovered the magic formula that will enable them to identify with pinpoint accuracy the top or the bottom of a market. What they can do (and if they are professionals, it is what they should be doing) is to make informed decisions by looking at the economic, social, sector and currency factors which affect different markets. Even so they may be bowled a googly.

Investment markets are dynamic, and can be unpredictable however well they are researched. No-one can forecast a major earthquake or the social unrest following an unexpected election victory, yet these events may have a sharp, although possibly short-term, effect on unit trust or investment trust investors who live on the other side of the world.

The most successful investment managers go against the herd.

They are not slaves to fashion. For instance, when share prices slumped during the Gulf War, Michael Hart, investment manager of the Foreign & Colonial trust, borrowed £50 million to buy stock, including £3 million worth of ICI shares.

But timing can still prove difficult, even for the most inspired fund manager. And for private investors, it is an even tougher challenge, not least because at heart we want to believe that good news will last for ever.

You will help yourself as an investor if you bear in mind two things:

■ The herd instinct is seldom a good one. Try not to put a lump sum into a unit trust or investment trust at a time of investor euphoria, when television, radio and newspapers are awash with headlines about share prices reaching new heights. If it is practicable, wait until share prices have had their inevitable correction.

■ No-one ever lost money by taking a profit, so don't give in to fruitless regret if you sell your unit trust or investment trust holdings and the prices then go a few pence higher.

And all investors would do well to engrave on their hearts the following maxim of Sir John Templeton, the great investment guru:

'Bull markets are born on pessimism, grow on scepticism, mature on optimism and die on euphoria. The time of maximum pessimism is the best time to buy, and the time of maximum optimism is the best time to sell.'

In later chapters, the need both to clarify what you want from your unit trusts and investment trusts holdings, and to establish investment time frames for yourself, are discussed in more detail.

KEEPING TRACK OF YOUR INVESTMENT

Rip Van Winkle went to sleep for 20 years, and it caused no end of bother. Unit trust and investment trust investors shouldn't follow his example. Although you have delegated the day-to-day management of your investments to professional fund managers, you should keep an intelligent eye on how your holdings are progressing.

This does not mean obsessive price-watching. Indeed daily price checks can prompt even experienced investors to become unduly cast down or elated by the vagaries and volatility of share and unit prices. But you should keep a watching brief on all your investments.

Try to be methodical about it. Keep a list of every unit trust and investment trust holding you have, with the purchase date and the price at purchase. Update the information with the latest valuation and the gross income that you have received to date.

And, at regular intervals, look at your list and ask yourself three questions: Are your unit trusts or investment trusts performing broadly in line with other trusts in their particular investment sector and with the stockmarket index that is the benchmark of that sector? Are they fulfilling their investment objectives? And, crucially, are these investment objectives still suited to your particular financial needs?

If the answer to any of these questions is 'No' it is probably time to take corrective action.

Finding the right company in the right sector may sound almost as daunting as finding that proverbial needle.
A central advantage of investment trusts and unit trusts is that someone else will conduct the search for you

THE INVESTMENT MARKETS

5

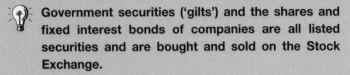

■ THE FUNDAMENTALS

Government securities ('gilts') and the shares and fixed interest bonds of companies are all listed securities and are bought and sold on the Stock Exchange.

Not every industrial sector will be booming at the same time. A professionally managed portfolio of shares helps investors to avoid being in the wrong company, in the wrong place at the wrong time.

An exposure to overseas investments enables investors to avoid having all their money tied to the fortunes of one country's economy.

Investment in emerging markets provides an opportunity to participate in young economies which have the potential to grow faster than mature economies.

Returns from an overseas investment will depend not only on the performance of the shares of the companies selected, but also on the performance of the pound against the currency of the country concerned.

■ TERMINOLOGY

Rights issue: The issue of new shares by a company in order to raise additional capital.

Debentures: Loan capital which is secured on a company's assets. Debentures pay a fixed rate of interest and have a fixed repayment value.

Preference shares: Part of the share capital of a company. Preference shares pay dividends at a fixed rate, and if the company is wound up holders of preference shares are paid out before ordinary shareholders.

Convertible loan stocks: Fixed-interest securities that give holders the right to convert into the ordinary shares of the company at a future date.

Eurobonds: International bonds issued outside the domestic market of the issuer.

Market capitalisation: A measure of the value of a company, calculated by multiplying the number of shares it has in issue by their current market price.

Tracker funds: Unit trusts or investment trusts that mirror the performance of a specific stockmarket index.

Bottom-up investment: An investment approach that concentrates on stock selection and an analysis of the balance sheet strength and prospects of individual companies.

Top-down investment: An investment approach that assesses investments by taking into account broad macro-economic and political circumstances and market trends.

5

Before getting down to the nitty-gritty of risk assessment and the selection decision (see Chapters Six and Seven), it is worth looking in rather more depth at the UK and world investment markets, and at what is involved when you put your money into funds that invest in a portfolio of shares, bonds and other stockmarket securities.

MORE ABOUT SHARES

When you buy ordinary shares, the main type of equity capital of a company, you become a member of the company and one of its proprietors. In other words, you have bought a share in the company and a stake in its fortunes.

All companies listed on the Stock Exchange are limited liability companies, so shareholders do not normally have any liability to creditors if the company defaults. If the company is wound up the shareholders own its residual assets (its equity), if there is anything left after meeting all prior claims, such as debts and the payment of preference shareholders.

> *... any view of a company's future can be no more than an educated assessment, based on available knowledge.*

The only investment 'guarantee' of share ownership is that share prices will fluctuate from day to day, and that in some circumstances these fluctuations will be violent. In the October 1987 crash, share prices fell 20 per cent in a matter of days.

Movements in a company's share price are triggered by a number of factors. First the market will be making a judgement on the company itself, how it is running its business, how efficiently it is managed, its record of making profits and increasing dividends, and – crucially if subjectively – what its future prospects are.

Naturally any view of a company's future can be no more than an educated assessment, based on available knowledge. The unexpected can always happen. A successful takeover, a spectacular export order or the development of a revolutionary new product will boost its share price. The resignation of a high-profile chief executive could shake the market's valuation of the company, or an expensive legal case could dent its ability to pay dividends.

Companies do not operate in splendid isolation, either. Share prices will also reflect the fortunes of the industry sector in which a company does business. If there is an oil glut, you can't expect much growth from companies in the oil sector; if the construction industry is going through a rough patch, this will affect the share prices of companies that are involved in the production of building materials.

For example, 1995 was a very good year for the UK pharmaceuticals sector, which was up 57.09 per cent, but in 1993 and 1994 shares in drugs companies had been very depressed, largely because of fears of the likely effects of healthcare reform in the US. Similarly shares in the banking sector did well in 1995, as the banks at last began to put behind them the bad-debt problems of the late 1980s and early 1990s.

A third trigger that moves share prices has little to do with the value of an individual company or the position in the trading cycle of the industry in which it does business. Share prices are affected by economic conditions in the country and by both domestic and international political factors.

The amount of new money institutional investors are putting into company shares also has an effect on share prices. Obviously if these institutions feel that shares are more attractive than, say, gilts and property, they will want to invest more money in them.

In the light of so many external factors, over which investors have absolutely no control, finding the right company in the right sector may sound almost as daunting as finding the proverbial needle in a haystack. A central advantage of investing in unit trusts and investment trusts is that someone else will conduct the search for you.

Professional fund managers have access to the latest company research and economic forecasts. They should have much more information than the rest of us on which to make an informed decision about whether to buy, sell or continue to hold the shares of a company, and whether to take up a company's rights issue (the issue of new shares) and what action to take on a takeover offer.

They are also running portfolios of perhaps 100 shares. This spread reduces the risk of having all your money in a company that runs into trouble, or that operates in a sector of industry that is currently languishing in the doldrums.

MORE ABOUT BONDS

Ordinary shares are not the only securities that are listed and traded on the Stock Exchange. The Government and individual companies also issue fixed-interest securities.

In the UK fixed-interest securities are known either as stocks or bonds. This sometimes prompts a slight confusion, because in America stocks are ordinary shares. As the advent of corporate bond Peps (see Chapter Nine, pages 192–196) has made the word 'bond' increasingly familiar to UK investors, therefore, that is the term that will be used throughout this chapter.

Bonds are basically a form of borrowing, or IOU, and they are issued by governments or by public companies to raise money. A bond promises to pay interest on the money borrowed normally at a fixed rate, and to repay the capital in full after a fixed period of time. If you buy a bond at issue and hold it to redemption, all you need to worry about is whether the borrower will default.

Bonds have two attractions for investors. They provide a high fixed income and there is a guaranteed repayment date when you will get your money back. However, bonds are traded on the stockmarket, and prices will fluctuate. You are secure from capital loss only if you buy a bond when it is first issued and hold it until its maturity date.

Of course bond prices will be less volatile than share prices, but then bonds have far less potential to grow your capital or income.

GILT-EDGED BONDS

Gilt-edged securities ('gilts' for short) are probably the best-known fixed-interest bonds. Gilts are issued by the Government and, most importantly, they are also guaranteed by HMG. They are used to fund Government borrowing and they form a large part of the National Debt.

Gilts have a long history. British Governments have been raising money from public subscribers by issuing fixed interest securities since 1694, when a little matter of a war with France was proving expensive. The Government of William III had to raise £1.2 million at 8 per cent in perpetuity, in order to finance it.

Each issue of gilt-edged stock has a name, a nominal interest rate and a redemption date. In newspapers you will read listings such as Treasury 8.75% 1997 or Funding 3.5% 1999–2004, for instance. The name doesn't mean a lot nowadays (it is just a way of distinguishing one bond from another), but the other two pieces of information do.

5

■ Coupon rate

The nominal rate of interest (the coupon rate) shows the amount of interest paid each year on every £100 of nominal stock. Of course the investor will have paid the market price for the gilt, which may be more or less than its par value.

Gilts are traded on the stockmarket and can be bought and sold at any time. Prices will be affected by any political, economic or industrial news that changes expectations on future interest rates, inflation, or the amount of money the Government is going to need to borrow. If general interest rates rise, and there is gloom about inflationary prospects, gilt prices are likely to fall. If interest rates fall, gilt prices will probably rise.

■ Redemption date

The redemption date is the date on which (or the range of dates between which) the Government will repay the issue. A very small number of gilts are undated, which means that they will be repaid only when the Government feels like it. In the notorious case of War Loan, that looks suspiciously like never.

When gilts are redeemed, repayment will be at par, which means that £100 will be paid out for every £100 nominal of stock. The only exceptions to this are index-linked gilts. With these gilts, redemption values are linked to changes in the retail prices index (which measures price inflation) over the investment period. Income payments are indexed in the same way, rising every six months in line with RPI.

CORPORATE BONDS

Gilts are not the only fixed-interest securities available to UK investors. Like the Government, UK companies also raise money by offering various types of fixed-interest security, such as debentures (which are secured on the company's assets) and loan stocks (which are unsecured). In addition a company may issue preference shares, which are shares that pay dividends at a fixed rate; and 'convertibles', which are bonds that pay a fixed rate of interest and can be converted into shares at a predetermined price on a predetermined date in the future.

Companies must pay the holders of their fixed-interest secuities each year before they pay anything to their shareholders. Holders of corporate bonds will also be paid out before ordinary shareholders in the event of the liquidation of the company.

Nevertheless, there is clearly more risk attached to an investment in corporate bonds than to an investment in gilts. You *know* if you lend money to the Government you will get it back. In contrast, bonds issued by companies are only as secure as the company itself.

'Eurosterling bonds' are issued in sterling through the international Eurobond market by UK companies and foreign companies and governments. They are similar in structure to domestic corporate bonds, and many are listed on the London Stock Exchange. Bulldog bonds are issued by foreign governments and corporations, in sterling, and they are either settled like gilts through the Central Gilt Office or through the Stock Exchange.

THE WORLD IS YOUR OYSTER: THE OVERSEAS MARKETS

October 1979 was a significant month for UK investors. UK exchange controls – which had placed restrictions on the freedom of investors to move their capital abroad – were scrapped. Suddenly the world investment markets really were on our doorstep and all at once life became much easier for investors who wanted to spread their risks and avoid having all their money dependent on the fortunes of a single country's economy.

Investing money in more than one country spreads risk because world stockmarkets do not perform in step, like trained drum majorettes. Individual countries will be at different stages of their economic cycles and they will be moved by different social and political forces. These factors will be reflected in their stockmarket performances.

For example, in 1995 the US stockmarket was the world's star, with the Dow Jones Industrial Index rising by 33.4 per cent; Switzerland's market was the best performer in Europe, with a rise in the index of leading shares of 27.9 per cent; and the UK market also reached new heights, with the FT-SE All-Share Index up by 18.5 per cent. In the Far East the Hang Seng Index (a weighted index based on a parcel of shares on the Hong Kong Stock Exchange) was up 23 per cent.

But the other main countries in Continental Europe had a disappointing time. Returns from the German equity market were 5.3 per cent; the French market was down 0.5 per cent while Italy's market was down 6.8 per cent. In Japan, the world's second largest stockmarket after the US, stockmarket returns as measured by the Nikkei Dow (an index of 225 Japanese companies) averaged just 0.8 per cent. The worst-performing market, Taiwan, was down 27.5 per cent.

But consider what happened in 1994. The picture for the world stockmarkets looks very different. In 1994 Hong Kong was the worst-performing market, falling 31.1 per cent (it had doubled in 1993!) and our own market was down 9.5 per cent. South Africa was the stockmarket of the year, with a rise of 25.2 per cent and Taiwan, 1995's laggard, was up 17.1 per cent.

EMERGING MARKETS

Investing abroad also enables you to put money in the small stockmarkets of young 'emerging' economies which have the potential to grow much faster than the mature economies of Western Europe and North America. It is hard to remember now, but 20 years ago investors would have viewed Japan as an emerging economy.

Emerging markets are not sitting on the fringes of the world. They include 18 of the world's 30 largest economies and 71 per cent of the world's population. They are not necessarily Third World countries, either. There are emerging markets in the Pacific Basin and the Far East; in the former Communist-controlled countries of Eastern Europe; in South America; in Africa; in India; and in Israel, Turkey, Greece, Cyprus and Portugal. China, where roughly one-fifth of the world's population live, is the pre-eminent emerging economy.

In stockmarket terms, however, emerging markets are the minnows. They account for something like 8 per cent of the total value of world stockmarkets and it can be very difficult to deal in the shares of emerging market companies.

Developing economies grow faster than mature economies for a number of reasons. The rate of population increase and adult literacy provide a progressively better-educated, better-trained and therefore more productive workforce. The introduction of more liberal economic and political policies tends to encourage growth, and emerging economies are able to benefit from technological advances that have been developed in other countries.

Unit trusts and investment trusts offer exposure to many of the world's fledgling markets, usually through a general 'emerging markets' fund, which covers several different economies, thus limiting the political and currency risks of concentrating on one area. However, there are trusts (particularly within the investment trust industry) that take the even more speculative high risk/high reward route of concentrating on the economy of a single emerging market. For example there are funds that invest exclusively in Turkey, Chile, India and Israel.

Investors who put money into emerging markets obviously do so in the hope that rapid economic growth rates will bring high investment returns in their wake. However, it is axiomatic that high growth potential also means high risk, and investing in emerging markets is a very high-risk business indeed.

You should not put more than a small proportion of your capital (say, 5 per cent maximum) into a unit trust or investment trust that concentrates on the emerging markets. Alternatively, buy yourself some protection against market fluctuations by investing through a monthly savings plan (see Chapter Four, pages 81–84).

5

Stockmarket falls in emerging markets can be as spectacular as stockmarket rises, as investors know from recent experience. A crisis was triggered by Mexico's devaluation of the peso on 20 December 1994 which sent shock waves throughout the South American region. These waves (known in the US as the 'tequila effect') rocked the world's other emerging economies, causing sharp falls in prices. As one investment analyst commented: '1995 will be remembered as the year when emerging markets were almost submerged'.

In the space of a few months, people with money in emerging markets collective funds found that the value of their investment had dropped by around a third. And in the 12 months after the devaluation of the peso the market capitalisation of the companies on the Mexican stockmarket had shrunk by 52 per cent, from $176 billion to $84.5 billion.

Funds investing in the financial markets of developing countries are therefore among the most highly specialised and risky investments. Economic events, and the fall-out from political instability, can send an emerging market into a tailspin, and investment returns are also likely to be heavily affected by currency movements.

CURRENCIES

An investment in the shares of foreign companies is also investment in the fortunes of their currencies. When you sell your overseas shares, the proceeds will have to be converted back to sterling.

This adds an additional element to the risk/reward equation, as clearly the value of your investment will depend not only on the performance of the underlying shares, but also on the relationship between the pound and the currency of the country in which you are investing.

You will benefit if the foreign currency is stronger than sterling, as this will enhance your returns. For instance, 1995's 27.9 per cent return, in local terms, from the index of leading Swiss shares became a huge 46.6 per cent when translated back into sterling. On the other hand if the pound rises against the currency, this will reduce your investment profits – it might even turn gains into losses.

Sometimes unit trust and investment trust fund managers decide to 'hedge' to reduce the currency risk to the fund. They buy financial instruments such as futures, options and forward currency contracts to protect their portfolios against currency movements.

Some investment managers dislike – even disapprove of – hedging, however. They prefer to concentrate on stock selection, arguing that investors put money into an overseas fund because they have chosen to take the risk of both foreign investment and currency exposure. Hedging also carries costs and risks itself, so it is a difficult decision for a fund manager.

WIDENING INVESTMENT CHOICE BY GOING OVERSEAS

At the end of January 1996 there were 2,149 companies listed on the UK Stock Exchange, and you might think that provided quite enough choice and spread of risk, in all conscience. But not only is it a good idea to ensure that all your stockmarket investments are not linked to the economy of one country; perhaps surprisingly, there are also some investment opportunities that are not available in the UK.

To take three examples: if you want to invest in a major car maker or computer manufacturer you will have to go overseas; internationally, there are many more opportunities to invest in new privatisation issues than in the UK, where the privatisation programme is grinding to its end; and the US indisputably leads the world as far as the information technology sector is concerned.

And it is worth bearing in mind that the world's largest companies are not UK owned. According to the FT 500 Survey 1996 of the world's largest quoted companies, only one of the companies in the top 10 – Royal Dutch/Shell – is not American or Japanese. The UK's largest company – Glaxo Wellcome – is ranked 25th in the world; British Petroleum is 27th.

The ability to offer professional investment management of foreign shares is one of the great strengths of unit trusts and investment trusts.

It is difficult and expensive for a private individual to invest directly overseas and in some markets it may be next to impossible. There are costs, time differences, currency exchange and tax requirements and you will need access to research. It is also hard to deal in some of the smaller markets.

MORE ABOUT THE DIFFERENT INVESTMENT SECTORS

Individual unit trust and investment trust management companies will often have their own investment house style, which imposes an overall discipline on their fund managers. This does not prevent the companies from offering a wide range of funds, providing access to a diverse selection of investment markets.

The investment trust and unit trust industries classify funds according to the markets in which they principally invest (see Chapters Two, pages 32–38, and Three, pages 51–58), and these sector categories are useful signposts for investors. If your primary aim is put money into smaller companies, you certainly don't want to have to investigate nearly 2,000 unit trusts and investment trusts in order to weed out the funds that will provide the exposure that you want.

Nevertheless the categories *are* broad ones and there is a considerable diversity of investment strategy and share selection among the funds in each sector.

(The task of choosing a unit trust or investment trust is discussed in Chapter Seven.)

■ The income producers

There are literally hundreds of unit trusts and investment trusts that give some degree of priority to the provision of income for investors, but this is where their general similarity ends. The investments within the portfolios of these funds vary enormously.

> *...there is a considerable diversity of investment strategy and share selection among the funds in each sector ...*

Most income-seekers will probably stick to the UK market because this is where the majority of income funds invest. However, there is a handful of international equity income trusts for those who want an international exposure.

The fundamental thing to bear in mind about income funds is that there is a perfectly straightforward trade-off between growth and income. If you want a high immediate yield, you will inevitably sacrifice some – perhaps most – of your prospects for future income and capital growth. If you want an income that will grow with your capital over the years, you will have to settle for a more modest initial yield. Your choice will inevitably be dictated by your personal circumstances, and it is most important to understand whether you are buying a high distribution or a growing income fund.

The yield quoted by a unit trust and an investment trust should not be confused with the interest rate paid on a bank or building society savings account. A yield shows the size of the income you are likely to receive on your investment, relative to its price. Yields are usually quoted gross, but income will be paid after the deduction of income tax (see Chapter Eight, pages 164–166).

There is no guarantee that any dividend will be paid, however. Companies can and do cut their payments to shareholders if trading conditions demand this; and unit trusts may therefore cut their income distributions. There is no guarantee that unit trusts and investment trusts will meet the yield targets set out in their sector definition (see Chapters Two and Three).

The funds that provide the highest immediate income are those that invest in gilts and corporate bonds, followed by those that have fixed-interest securities, like convertible shares and preference shares, in their portfolios.

A corporate bond fund is a useful investment bridge between a building society account and an equity fund. It is more risky than the former, but less so than the latter. Investors can expect little if any income growth from corporate bond funds over the years and the potential for capital growth is also modest.

Investors must also understand the limited capital performance they are likely to have from the income shares of some split capital investment trusts (see Chapter Two, page 24). With the 'annuity' type share from a split capital trust the redemption price will be negligible.

While the trade-off between a high immediate income and future growth is pretty unambiguous with, say, a corporate bond unit trust or a split capital investment trust income share, assessing the suitability of an equity income collective fund is perhaps rather less straightforward. Investment trust and unit trust income funds are a mixed bag, and you will need to look at the latest report to understand what investment strategy an individual trust pursues.

For example, some equity income funds enhance returns by having convertible shares in the portfolio or by buying shares that have a high yield because they are out of favour or have poor growth prospects.

Never forget the general rule, the higher the yield, the greater the risk. Equity income investment trusts and unit trusts that offer particularly high yields will struggle to produce much growth in income or capital value over the long-term.

Income growth funds with more modest yields have demonstrated over the years that they have a good chance of doing so. The snag is that you will not receive your rewards immediately, and there is always the temptation to be dazzled by short-term prospects, and to opt for a fund that offers a higher immediate yield.

For example 'high-income' funds often quote almost twice the yield of funds that eschew fixed-interest securities. At the start of March 1996, the average gross yield on a UK income growth investment trust (a fund that does not invest in convertibles) was 4.6 per cent. In contrast, the average gross yield on a UK high-income investment trust was 8.7 per cent.

What you are buying with an equity income growth fund is a reasonable income now and the prospect of the managers being able to grow that income over the years and to increase the value of the capital you have invested.

Example | A tale of two investments

This 'jam tomorrow' argument can be illustrated by looking at the capital and income performance of the £1.1 billion M & G Dividend Fund, which was launched in May 1964 and is the largest equity income unit trust in the UK. The figures are given in Table 5.1.

As you can see, if you had put £1,000 into this fund at launch in 1964, you would have received £40 of net income by the end of 1965. A £1,000 deposit in a building society account would have earned you £61 over the same period, and you might well have thought that the building society was going to be the better bet. By the end of 1974, when the value of your £1,000 unit trust investment had dropped to £770, you were probably sure of it!

But the managers of the Dividend Fund have stuck to their knitting. They have increased the fund's annual income distributions slowly and steadily over the years; indeed they have never cut a distribution. After 15 years, the results of concentrating on growing the income were really starting to show. As an initial investor, your net annual income had become £140 and the capital value of your original £1,000 investment had more than doubled to £2,278.

And the income has continued to increase. For the year ending December 1995, you would have received £609 of income, a current yield on your original investment of 60.9 per cent. The value of your unit holding, on 31 August 1995, was £17,280.

And what about your building society savings account? Well, over the years, returns would have followed interest rate movements, peaking at an annual net income of £105, in 1990. Since 1990 your income would have more than halved, and in the year to December 1995 you would have received just £40 – almost exactly what you were getting 30 years previously. And of course your £1,000 would still be worth £1,000.

■ The growth producers

The number of unit trusts and investment trusts that are looking to produce growth of capital for their investors is even greater than the number of income trusts.

There are conservatively run funds looking for profits from large and medium-sized UK companies, and funds that concentrate on a similar investment strategy in North American, Japanese, Far Eastern and Continental European companies.

There are also many more specialist, and therefore more speculative, funds. For instance, there are trusts that crank up the potential for profit – and the potential for loss – by looking at what are known as recovery shares. These are the shares of companies that have gone – or are going – through hard times but which the managers believe will start to perform again. Some do; some don't.

There are funds, too, that concentrate on 'special situations', seeking out companies that have above average growth potential because of a prospective change in their fortunes.

Such companies might be takeover targets, for instance, or be due for a revaluation of their assets, or have had sweeping management changes which have artificially depressed their share price. Or they might have developed a potentially valuable, but still unrecognised, new product.

Table 5.1

What happened to £1,000 invested in the M & G Dividend Fund at the trust's launch in May 1964, and to £1,000 deposited in a building society account at the same time.

Year to end-December	Building Society Income	Building Society Capital	M & G Dividend Fund Income	M & G Dividend Fund Capital
1964	£23	£1,000	£0	£ 950
1965	£38	£1,000	£40	£1,020
1966	£40	£1,000	£41	£ 920
1967	£42	£1,000	£43	£1,046
1968	£44	£1,000	£43	£1,384
1969	£48	£1,000	£44	£1,108
1970	£49	£1,000	£46	£1,076
1971	£50	£1,000	£49	£1,566
1972	£49	£1,000	£52	£1,682
1973	£65	£1,000	£61	£1,362
1974	£75	£1,000	£73	£ 770
1975	£72	£1,000	£83	£1,630
1976	£70	£1,000	£91	£1,474
1977	£70	£1,000	£103	£2,220
1978	£65	£1,000	£120	£2,334
1979	£85	£1,000	£140	£2,278
1980	£103	£1,000	£166	£2,428
1981	£92	£1,000	£184	£2,524
1982	£88	£1,000	£186	£3,004
1983	£73	£1,000	£190	£4,128
1984	£77	£1,000	£202	£5,430
1985	£87	£1,000	£228	£6,516
1986	£78	£1,000	£268	£8,482
1987	£76	£1,000	£320	£9,908
1988	£70	£1,000	£368	£10,506
1989	£92	£1,000	£444	£12,780
1990	£105	£1,000	£522	£10,320
1991	£83	£1,000	£562	£10,160
1992	£63	£1,000	£564	£12,160
1993	£43	£1,000	£564	£16,840
1994	£40	£1,000	£568	£15,040
1995	£40	£1,000	£609	£17,280

Sources: M & G; Central Statistical Office, Financial Statistics. All income figures shown are net of UK income tax for basic rate taxpayers. The building society income figures are based on the average rate of a building society share account Capital figures for M & G dividend fund are realisation values.

Some companies, too, are trapped in a depressed or unfashionable sector. With others the fund managers may simply feel that their shares are wrongly priced. The market is not always perfect. Sometimes a share price and the true value of the underlying business can get out of kilter.

■ Smaller companies

There is a wide selection of funds that concentrate on seeking out value among smaller companies, both in the UK and overseas. Why should you want to invest in a small company, when you can buy shares in ICI or Marks & Spencer? No prizes for guessing. You think that you will make more money by backing the world's up and coming entrepreneurs.

Historically, the share prices of small companies have grown faster than those of large ones, although in the UK this long-term record has been somewhat dented by the difficult business environment in the first half of the 1990s.

Smaller companies generally have greater growth potential than large ones, because it is easier to double earnings when you are starting from a low base. The converse is that smaller companies also experience sharper falls when there is a downturn in the market, and of course there is a greater risk that they will founder altogether, because they have lower reserves to cushion them.

Generally speaking, you can expect smaller companies to outperform larger ones during periods when there is a pick-up in economic growth, and to underperform when there is a growth pause or a recession.

■ The generalists

UK and international general (or growth and income) investment trusts and unit trusts may lack marketing glamour, but they are ideal long-term core investments.

These funds tend to concentrate on the larger household name companies, although they certainly don't have an exclusion policy on smaller companies. Their object is to provide both capital growth and reasonable prospects of rising income payments, although their target yield is more modest than that of the equity income funds.

The unit trust industry does not have a separate sector for international general funds, but the investment trust industry does, and many of the trusts in it represent the heart of the investment trust movement. Here you will find many of the oldest and largest funds, and these 'flagship' trusts tend to be run by particularly experienced investment managers.

■ The highly specialised

Unit trusts and investment trusts provide private investors with an efficient means to invest in highly specialised (and therefore highly volatile) world markets.

Both types of collective fund run commodity and energy funds, for instance. Naturally the managers of these funds do not have gold bars, sacks of coffee, barrels of oil and stockpiles of uranium tucked away in their cellars. What they offer investors is access to the listed shares of UK and overseas commodity, energy and mining companies.

There are also some 20 investment trusts which are categorised as 'venture and development capital' funds and which have a significant portion of their assets invested in the securities of unquoted companies. It is quite common for a 'start up' company to fail completely. An investment trust spreads this very real risk.

■ Tracker or index funds

It is only comparatively recently that private investors have been able to put money into index or tracker funds, although pension fund managers have been doing so for a number of years.

These funds mirror the performance of a chosen stock market index. They are designed to perform no better and no worse than the stockmarket average.

There is at least one representative stockmarket index that can be used as a yardstick to measure the performance of every unit trust and investment trust.

The performance barometers for the UK are the indices produced under the auspices of the *Financial Times*.

The best-known measures of the performance of the UK stockmarket are the FT-SE Actuaries All-Share Index, which covers around 900 companies and 95 per cent of the market, and is perhaps the most useful yardstick to use when assessing portfolio performance; the FT-SE 100 Index or the Footsie, a weighted index of the shares of the 100 largest companies by market capitalisation; and the FT-SE Mid 250 Index, which covers the next 250 companies in the pecking order after the top 100 and represents around 22 per cent of UK stock market capitalisation.

The *Financial Times* also publishes the FTA World Index, which is used to measure the performance of overseas stockmarkets and is based on more than 2,000 share prices from more than 20 countries. The FT-SE Eurotrack 100 index is a weighted average of 100 stocks in Europe.

In America two of the best known indices are the Dow Jones Industrial Average (an index of 30 companies on the New York Stock Exchange) and the Standard and Poor's 500, a wide general index of shares. The Tokyo Stock Exchange has the Nikkei Dow index.

Such indices are becoming increasingly familiar to private investors, not only as performance yardsticks for individual funds, but also because of the recent proliferation and popularity of tracker funds.

The aim of a tracker fund is not to beat a specific index, but to mirror its performance. The fund's success is measured by the fidelity of its performance to that of its chosen stockmarket index.

> ■ **DEFINITION**
>
> **Tracker funds** are unit trusts or investment trusts that mirror the performance of a specific stockmarket index.

To achieve this tracking performance, the fund does not invest in an actively managed portfolio of shares, run by a hands-on investment manager. Instead, tracker funds use one or more of four investment systems. They either buy every one of the securities in an index ('full replication'); or they invest in a representative sample of the shares ('sampling'): or they use a sophisticated statistical model to select shares ('optimisation'); or they buy index futures.

Obviously, investors with tracker funds have some of the risk of investing in shares removed or at least limited because, for better or worse, they know exactly what they are going to get – the index performance, less the costs of investing. They have also eliminated the risk of choosing a duff investment manager as, in theory, there should be little performance deviation among tracker funds. However, they will not have any protection against the market risk of, say, a 30 per cent fall in the index.

Management charges on tracker funds are usually low. After all you are not buying active management, but a computer system. This combination of a limitation of risk and lower management charges means that tracker funds can also be very useful core equity investments.

The funds received much publicity when Virgin Direct Financial Services entered the market with a tracker fund Pep in 1995 and they have become increasingly popular recently. There are now trusts tracking virtually all the main stockmarket indices and one innovation is designed to provide investment returns that *either* match the FT-SE 100 Index *or* the retail prices index, whichever is the greater after six years.

Critics of tracker funds argue that these funds do not provide investors with the benefit of the active investment management skills of professional fund managers. This is quite true and the upside potential of an investment in a tracker fund is inevitably limited, as there is no intention or ambition to add value.

But it has to be said that, quite frequently, tracker funds produce better performance than their actively managed competitors.

This is not something that active investment managers like to dwell on, but it is the case that it is quite difficult to beat the stockmarket index of a mature and well-researched market like the UK. In a market such as Japan, where information about individual companies is everything, actively managed funds have a much better record against their tracker rivals.

■ UNIT TRUST AND INVESTMENT TRUST TRACKER FUNDS (at March 1996)

Investment trusts

Abtrust European Index (Managers, Abtrust Fund Managers; contact number: 0171-490 4466).

Fairbairn Euro Smaller Companies Index (Managers, Old Mutual Portfolio Managers; contact number: 01256 743361).

Gartmore Micro Index (Managers, Gartmore; contact number: 0171-623 1212).

Hoare Govett Smaller Companies Index Trust, and **Hoare Govett 1,000 Index Trust** (Managers, Broadgate Investment Management; contact number: 0171-374 1942);

Malvern UK Index Trust (Managers, Edinburgh Fund Managers; contact number: 0131-313 1000).

Unit trusts

Direct Line FT-SE 100 Tracker (Direct Line Unit Trusts; contact number, 0181-253 7738); **Fidelity Moneybuilder Index** (Managers, Fidelity Investment Services; contact number: 0800 414161).

Foreign & Colonial Target Index (Managers, Foreign & Colonial Unit Managers; contact number: 0171-628 8000).

Gartmore UK Index (Managers, Gartmore; contact number: 0800 289336).

Govett FT-SE Mid 250 Index Trust, Govett UK Index Trust, Govett US Index Trust, Govett Hong Kong Index Trust, Govett Japan Index Trust, Govett French Index Trust, Govett German Index Trust (Managers, John Govett Unit Trust Management; contact number: 0171-378 7979).

HSBC UK Index Trust, HSBC Trixie Index Trust, HSBC American Index Trust, HSBC Japan Index Trust, HSBC Tiger Index Trust, HSBC Eurotrack 100 Trust (Managers, HSBC Unit Trust Management; contact number: 0171-955 5050).

Legal & General UK Index Trust, Legal & General US Index Trust, Legal & General Japan Index Trust, Legal & General Euro Index Trust (Managers, Legal & General (UT Managers); contact number: 01277 227300).

Lloyds FT-SE 100 (Managers, Lloyds Bank Unit Trust Managers; contact number: 01634 834000).

Midland FT-SE 100 Index (Managers, Midland Unit Trust Management; contact number: 0345 456123).

Morgan Grenfell UK Index Tracker Trust, Morgan Grenfell US Index Trust, Morgan Grenfell Japan Tracker Trust (Managers, Morgan Grenfell Investment Funds; contact number: 0171-588 7171).

Norwich Union UK Index Tracking Trust, Norwich Union International Index Tracking Trust (Managers, Norwich Union Trust Managers; contact number: 01603 680231).

Old Mutual UK All-Share (Managers, Old Mutual Fund Managers; contact number: 01256 768888).

River & Mercantile Top 100 (Managers, River & Mercantile Investment Funds; contact number: 0171-405 3240).

Royal Life UK Index Tracking (Managers, Royal Life Fund Management; contact number: 01733 390000).

Sovereign FT-SE 100 (Managers, Sovereign Unit Trust Managers; contact number: 01202 435400).

Virgin UK Index Tracking (Managers, Virgin Direct PFS; contact number: 0345 959595).

■ A double spread of risk

A number of unit trust groups, and financial advisers, manage unit trusts that invest only in other unit trusts. These trusts are usually either described as funds of funds or mastertrusts.

The idea is to provide a managed portfolio of unit trusts, so that investors do not have to worry about whether they are in the right trust in the right sector of the market at any one time. The managers – in theory at least – will provide the correct exposure for them.

Some mastertrusts invest only in the parent company's unit trusts, while others run a portfolio of trusts from a selection of management groups. One inevitable problem with the funds is that there can be an element of double-charging, because you are paying charges on the master fund and on the other funds in which it invests.

Closed-end funds are the investment trust industry's version of mastertrusts or funds of funds. They invest only in the shares of other investment trusts or closed-end funds. As with unit trust mastertrusts, this additional diversification of risk comes with a price tag, because double management charges are involved.

■ Ethical funds: Embracing the good and avoiding the bad and the ugly

Would you want to invest money in a company whose business was the production of arms? Do you have strong views about tobacco or pornography, alcohol or environmental issues?

According to a recent survey, 94 per cent of people would like to invest in companies that are helping, rather than harming the world, and 92 per cent would like to make a profit, but without anyone suffering in the process.

When you invest directly in shares, you can at least avoid the companies of whom you disapprove, even though it is sometimes difficult to discover just what activities and interests a very large multinational company has.

But how do you start to monitor your investment in a collective fund, which may have more than 100 different shares in its portfolio, all chosen not by you but by the fund manager?

Twelve years ago Friends' Provident, a life company that was founded by Quakers, launched the Stewardship Unit Trust, the first UK collective fund to screen companies to ensure that the managers only made investments in those businesses that were concentrating on products or services that were of long-term benefit to the community.

This was the first 'ethical' unit trust. Today there are more than 20 unit trusts and investment trusts, with some £1 billion of funds under management, that have either an ethical or a 'green' investment policy. They include UK growth and UK income funds, and funds that invest internationally.

Obviously, there is a limited number of companies in which these funds are prepared to invest, but over the years, there has been no evidence that their performance has materially suffered because of their self-imposed investment restrictions. Indeed a company that concentrates on energy efficiency, and takes pains not to waste resources may well have a competitive advantage over a more prodigal rival.

The fund manager of an ethical or green trust will screen companies using both negative and positive criteria. Many trusts use the Ethical Investment Research Service (EIRIS), which was established in 1983 by a group of churches and charities.

The managers of ethical and environmental funds will differ in their investment views, but all use a set of criteria which will exclude certain businesses, such as companies with interests in gambling, or arms, or tobacco or pornography, or those that have interests in oppressive regimes. For example the Stewardship fund will not invest in British Telecom because it has defence contracts.

In addition, positive screening is often used to ensure that the investments are also made in companies that are doing something to improve the environment, or have progressive employment policies or produce products that benefit the community.

If you have strong views about the type of business in which you want to invest, get hold of the reports of two or three ethical or green trusts, to check where different managers are putting their money.

ETHICAL AND GREEN UNIT TRUSTS AND INVESTMENT TRUSTS

Unit Trusts

Abbey Life Ethical;
Abtrust Ethical;
Allchurches Amity;
CIS Environmental;
City Financial Acorn Ethical;
Clerical Medical Evergreen;
Co-operative Bank Ethical;
Credit Suisse Fellowship;
Eagle Star Environmental Opportunities;
Equitable Ethical;
Framlington Health;
Friends Provident Stewardship;
Friends Provident Stewardship Income;

Friends Provident Stewardship North America;
Henderson Touche Remnant Ethical;
Jupiter Ecology;
NPI Global Care;
Scottish Equitable Ethical;
Sovereign Ethical;
TSB Environmental Investor.

Investment trusts

Commercial Union Environmental Trust;
Friends' Provident Ethical Split Capital Trust;
Jupiter International Green Investment Trust.

■ Split capital investment trusts

The ability of split capital investment trusts to provide investors with a choice of income returns or capital returns has already been discussed (see Chapter Two). In addition it is worth bearing in mind that while the 50 or so split capital trusts have similar share structures, they certainly do not have similar portfolios. Splits offer access to a wide range of investments markets in the UK and overseas.

■ Guaranteed funds

Some unit trust groups have started to look at a new type of vehicle for the industry, a fund that enables investors to strip some of the volatility out of stockmarket investment by locking in a percentage of their investment profits and limiting falls in unit prices.

The insurance companies have been offering similar investments for a number of years, but unlike unit trusts insurance guaranteed equity bonds have a limited life, you can only buy them on original issue and you cannot normally sell them during the investment period.

It is important to remember with any guaranteed fund that all safeguards have a price tag. You may limit any stockmarket losses but you will also lessen any potential stockmarket profits.

THE INVESTMENT MANAGERS

When you put money into an investment trust or unit trust, you do so having first made two decisions. Some, at least, of your future financial comfort may well depend on whether you have decided wisely.

In the first instance you will have decided what type of fund to choose, a selection which will be determined by your investment aims, your financial position and your attitude towards stockmarket risk (see Chapters Six and Seven).

The second decision is just as important. You will have selected a specific fund and put your investments in the hands of an investment manager or investment management team. These managers cannot be held accountable for whether the fund in question fits your needs, but they are solely responsible for ensuring that it performs well within its market sector.

There is no typical investment manager and very few bear much, if any, resemblance to the two popular stereotypes – the old Etonian with more connections than brains, and the brash young risk-taker in red braces.

Most fund managers these days are probably graduates – a mathematics degree seems to be a popular first step to life in investment management, although virtually all academic faculties are represented – but their route to fund management may be a direct one from university or an indirect one, via actuarial, accountancy or business studies qualifications or through other areas of business. Men still tend to dominate the top positions, but the number of women fund managers is growing steadily.

There is no essential difference between an investment trust manager and a unit trust manager, either, or even between those who manage collective funds and those who look after private clients. In companies that run both types of collective fund, and have a private client department, there may be something like a 90 per cent overlap between the managers.

All fund managers need, and thrive on, information. They get it from external research, from their own research departments, from in-house or external economic teams, and by visiting different companies and different investment areas themselves. In 1995, managers at Schroder, the largest unit trust company with £9.9 billion under management, made 900 company visits in the UK and 3,000 worldwide.

The latitude allowed to individual managers in determining asset allocation and stock selection within a trust varies from company to company. Some companies impose a tight discipline, running white lists of shares that managers may invest in, and black lists of those that they must avoid. Others give their fund managers almost complete freedom to run their funds as they think fit.

There are companies that adhere to an essentially income-driven house style and have particular expertise in the UK market. Others may have built their reputations by specialising in smaller companies or in recovery situations or in markets in a specific geographical region.

5

■ INVESTMENT SNAPSHOT

Investment styles vary. Look at the report of a trust, or at the literature produced by the management company, to assess the approach taken by a specific company or manager. It is usually made clear in these pieces of paper.

Some managers may emphasise 'value investing' for instance, concentrating on shares that are unloved and which therefore look cheap when compared to a company's assets and earnings. Others are growth investors, backing companies that are likely to increase profits year after year.

Views on the optimum portfolio size also vary. Some manage funds that invest in 150 or more companies. Others run a tight ship, concentrating on a limited number of shares, an approach that entails knowing each company in the trust's portfolio very well indeed.

There is also some division between those managers who adopt a 'top-down' approach and those who prefer a 'bottom-up' investment style. Managers of mainstream funds, that concentrate on larger markets and larger companies, tend to be 'top-down' investors. They assess investments by looking at the broad economic and political circumstances – and at market trends – rather than by concentrating on the strengths of individual companies.

The 'bottom-up' managers do the opposite. Their emphasis is not on the broad picture but on stock selection and on the analysis of a company's balance sheet strength, prospects and management.

Just to confuse matters, not a few managers also combine the two stances, marrying a top-down asset allocation strategy to a bottom-up share selection process!

While different houses and different managers adopt different styles, however, it is important to bear in mind that no one style can be identified as the 'right' way to manage investments. The proof must be in the performance each manager achieves.

■ **THE WORLD'S TOP 20 COMPANIES BY MARKET CAPITALISATION at end-September 1996**

Nippon Telegraph & Telephone (Japanese)
General Electric (US)
Royal Dutch/Shell (Netherlands/UK)
AT & T (US)
Exxon (US)
Coca-Cola (US)
Merck (US)
Philip Morris (US)
Toyota Motor (Japanese)
Industrial Bank of Japan (Japanese)
Roche Holding (Swiss)
Fuji Bank (Japanese)
Sumitomo Bank (Japanese)
Microsoft (US)
Intel (US)
Mitsubishi Bank (Japanese)
Dai Ichi Kangyo Bank (Japanese)
Procter & Gamble (US)
Intl Business Machines (US)
Sanwa Bank (Japanese)

Source: FT 500 Survey 1996

FURTHER READING

'An Independent Guide to Ethical and Green Investment Funds' (sixth edition, free from independent financial advisers Holden Meehan, telephone: 0117-925 2874/0171-404 6442).

Money and Ethics (£12.50 from EIRIS, the Ethical Investment and Research Service, 504 Bondway Business Centre, 71 Bondway, London SW8 1SQ)

'Emerging Markets' (free leaflet from The Unit Trust Information Service, 65 Kingsway, London WC2B)

'Investing for Income' (free leaflet from The Association of Investment Trust Companies, Durrant House, 8-13 Chiswell Street, London EC1Y 4YY)

'Investing in Gilts: A guide for the small investor' (free from the Bank of England, Threadneedle Street, London EC2R 8AH; telephone number for public inquiries, 0171-601 4878).

The Merrill Lynch Guide to the Gilt-Edged and Sterling Bond Markets, by Patrick Phillips (£45, The Book Guild)

A Guide to Saving and Investment, by James Rowlatt (Pan). Published in the 1980s and now out-of-print, but available at some public libraries. Parts are completely outdated, but there are excellent timeless chapters.

5

*There is no such thing as a
completely risk-free investment*

LOOKING AT RISK

6

■ THE FUNDAMENTALS

 Every investment carries some risk, even very low-risk savings deposits.

 Before investing any money, everyone should establish the amount of risk they can afford to take, financially and temperamentally.

 There is always a trade-off between risk and potential reward.

 Sector categories are the first guide to assessing the risks of different unit trusts and investment trusts.

 Within each sector category, individual funds will have a different risk rating.

■ TERMINOLOGY

National savings: The savings arm of the Government, which raises money from the public to help fund the National Debt. National Savings is the only savings institution that can provide investors with complete security from the risk of default.

Retail prices index (RPI): An index of a basket of consumer goods and services in retail shops which is calculated each month to determine the movement of prices. The RPI is the main measure of the rate of inflation.

6

WHAT IS RISK?

Many people, if asked what is meant by a 'risk-free' investment, would probably answer that you take no risk with your money if you put it in a bank or building society savings account.

After all, they would explain, if you had deposited £1,000 with a bank in January 1996, you could be confident that exactly that amount of money will be sitting in the account when you return to recover your cash in January 1999. In the interim you would have earned interest on your deposit. Where is the risk in that?

It would be a risk investment, these same people might explain, if you transferred money from your bank or building society into a stockmarket investment. This would be a move into risk territory because you might lose money and get back less cash than you had invested, and there would be absolutely no guarantee that your income would increase over the years. It might decrease; it could even dry up altogether.

It all sounds quite clear cut. But unfortunately for those who like life to be simple, one of these two widely accepted definitions of 'risk-free' and 'risk investments' tells only half the story.

Bank and building society savings accounts are low risk, they are very low risk, but they are not no risk. Let's repeat that, because it is important. Bank and building society savings accounts are not no risk investments.

There is the risk of default by the financial institution (however remote it might seem to customers of Barclays Bank or the Halifax Building Society), which is why compensation schemes are needed. And there is the more pervasive risk of future inflation. This is the insidious thief that raids the pockets of long-term 'risk-free' savers who put their money into savings accounts.

When you invest in a bank or building society you know that the £1,000 you invest will remain £1,000 even if share prices plummet, house prices go through the floor and tax rates rocket. While financial Armageddon may stare the stockmarket investor in the face your £1,000 is safe. What's more, you have not incurred any buying or selling costs to reduce its value still further.

However, what you cannot know for certain with a bank or building society savings account is whether you will earn enough interest, after tax, to combat the corrosive effect of rising prices on your 'risk-free' income and capital. By the end of 1995 some savers had seen income from their building society savings virtually halve over the past six years. Prices had risen 27 per cent over the same period.

Of course, you might argue that the present level of inflation is so modest that it is no longer a worry to bank and building society savers. Not so. Suppose annual inflation averages 2 per cent a year over the next few years – and it is an optimistic supposition. If you put £1,000 into a savings account today, and withdraw it after 10 years, your £1,000 will have a purchasing power of £820, ignoring any interest you have earned.

If you envisage a rather gloomier, but perhaps more realistic, inflation rate of 5 per cent a year, the value of £1,000 in today's money will have reduced to £614 after 10 years. Be deeply pessimistic, and assume a 10 per cent annual inflation rate, and £1,000 will be worth just £386 in real terms at the end of 10 years.

The nearest approach to an absolutely risk-free investment is probably a National Savings index-linked savings certificate. The provider is absolutely secure (investors with the Government don't need to worry about fraud or whether there is a decent compensation scheme), and capital is inflation-proofed. The value of the certificate increases in line with the retail prices index (RPI) over the investment period.

However, the income is not protected – the interest paid on the certificate is not indexed – and there is no inflation-proofing if you withdraw your cash during the first year.

So even index-linked savings certificates are not *totally* risk-free investments. You cannot have access to your money at any time, secure in the knowledge that both its real value, and the real value of the income you have earned, have been completely protected.

So, what is the conclusion? Unfortunately it is all too clear. *There is no such thing as a completely risk-free investment*!

Every savings and investment scheme known to man and woman has one or more of the following uncertainties:

- the risk of default by the provider;

- the risk that the real value of your capital will not keep pace with rising prices;

- the risk that the real value of your income will not keep pace with rising prices;

- the risk that pounds will be wiped off the value of your initial investment and you will lose money;

- the risk that the income from your investment will decrease or even disappear.

Within this general framework there are dramatically different degrees of risk among the available investment opportunities and it is of the first importance to understand this and to take a cool look at what risk you can actually afford. Would any capital loss seriously damage your financial health?

The next consideration – and it is just as important – is to assess what risk you yourself can absorb temperamentally. No investment is a good investment if it keeps you awake at night.

Think of the market risk position of different savings and investments as rungs on a ladder. The higher up the ladder an investment is positioned, the greater the risk you are taking with your money and the greater the potential rewards. But if any investment is going to be a source of permanent anxiety you must accept that its risk/reward trade-off is just too high for you and you should move your money further down the risk ladder.

ASSESSING THE RISKS OF INDIVIDUAL UNIT TRUSTS AND INVESTMENT TRUSTS

Investment trusts and unit trusts limit some of the risks of stockmarket investment because they spread investors' money over the shares and securities of anything from 50 to 400 different companies.

The value of any capital put into the fund will fluctuate from one day to another but if the shares of any single company in the portfolio do spectacularly badly (or, conversely, spectacularly well) this will not have the dramatic impact on your capital that such a movement would have on the wealth of an investor with half-a-dozen direct share holdings.

All unit trusts and investment trusts therefore share the common characteristic of smoothing out some of the peaks and troughs of stockmarket performance. But this is certainly not the same as saying that one collective fund is just about as chancy as another. There is a very wide spectrum of risk among the funds available.

Your first guide to the broad risk profile of a fund is its sector category (see Chapter Two, pages 32–38 and Chapter Three, pages 52–58). Clearly, the unit or share prices of funds that invest in, say, securities that pay a fixed income and have a fixed redemption date are likely to be less volatile than the prices of funds that invest in the shares of companies, where nothing is guaranteed.

Equally clearly investing in UK shares and bonds avoids one of the risks of putting money into overseas shares and bonds. If a UK investor goes overseas, there is the danger of being hit by a double whammy, adverse share price movements *and* adverse currency movements.

But it is quite wrong to conclude that an international fund is always riskier than a UK fund. The currency risk must be balanced against the risk of pinning all your hopes on the fortunes of one economy and an assessment must also be made of the risk profile of the underlying investments. A big international generalist fund is a comparatively low-risk stockmarket investment; a UK fund investing in unquoted companies is very high-risk indeed.

The initial step, therefore, is to decide which investment sectors best suit your objectives. You can then make assessments of the comparative risks of investing in the sectors you have chosen.

This is still not the complete answer to assessing the inherent risk of individual funds, however. Within each sector, there will be trusts which invest in the same markets, but have totally dissimilar investment management styles and strategies. As a result, the funds that comprise an investment sector demonstrate very different price volatility.

For example, there is a move among unit trust companies to launch funds that put guaranteed limits on the amount of stock-market risk an investor will be exposed to. So the risk profile of a trust such as the Govett UK Safeguard Fund, the first 'protected' unit trust to be launched, will bear little resemblance to the risk profiles of other unit trusts in the UK Growth and Income sector.

■ **INVESTMENT SNAPSHOT**

The Govett UK Safeguard Fund is specifically designed to limit potential losses. It uses financial instruments such as options to provide investors with a proportion of the gains of the FT-SE 100 Index, while limiting losses to 2 per cent of the unit price at the beginning of each three-month period. So investors who begin their investment at the start of the quarter cannot lose more than 8 per cent of the value of their money in a year, whatever the stockmarket conditions.

Even such seemingly similar trusts as corporate bond funds carry different levels of risks. Investors put money into these funds for income, but it will be the trusts with the lower yields that invest in the highest quality bonds, the bonds of companies where realistically there is no risk of default and which are therefore likely to provide the most stable returns.

Split capital investment trusts involve two risk assessments. There is the risk attached to the investment policy of the under-lying portfolio of the trust, and there is the risk inherent in each of the different classes of share.

With some split capital income shares you are effectively parting for good with your original investment in return for income, and the returns from capital shares depend on the value of the portfolio when the trust is wound up. Certainly capital shares have the potential to produce handsome capital gains, as holders are entitled to all the assets of the trust at the winding-up date, after the other shareholders have been paid. But you cannot know when you buy capital shares what, if any, increase there will be in the trust's assets by the wind-up date.

Neither the unit trust nor the investment trust industry has as yet made any concerted effort to help investors identify a fund's likely volatility by flagging the risk rating of specific trusts, but some experts are not so coy. The Investment Trust Department of SBC Warburg, for one, risk-rates every sector, and every individual investment trust within each sector, in their 1996 guide for the private investor.

For instance, they give the emerging market *sector* a high-risk rating, but within this category they classify the Genesis Emerging Markets trust and the Kleinwort Emerging Markets trust as low-risk.

All the Warburg judgements clearly reflect their current views on the risk profile of individual trusts. As the writers of the guide point out, these could change if, for instance, there was an unexpected event, such as the loss of a successful fund manager.

6

Nevertheless, the Warburg rating system illustrates the importance investors should place on selecting both the investment sector that best meets their needs, and provides a level of risk with which they are comfortable, and a trust within that sector that fulfils the same requirements.

LIMITING RISK THROUGH SECTOR DIVERSIFICATION

'My ventures are not in one bottom trusted,
Nor to one place; nor is my whole estate,
Upon the fortune of this present year;
Therefore, my merchandise makes me not sad.'

Antonio, the merchant, in Shakespeare's *The Merchant of Venice*, Act 1, Scene 1.

Shakespeare's merchant may have been a somewhat gloomy fellow, but his strategy for limiting his investment risk is as valid today as it was in Elizabethan times. Spread your market risks. Never have all your investment eggs crunched together in one basket.

Each sector categorisation is a signpost to risk but, unfortunately, it is not a route map, and not just because of the different risk profiles of individual funds within the sector.

No single country's economy or stockmarket, and no single sector of industry, performs well year after year after year. A great advantage of unit trusts and investment trusts is that they enable you to diversify this geographical and industrial sector risk by providing you with low-cost access to a number of different markets.

Once you have built up a central holding of UK investments you have the ability to add specialist UK funds and international trusts, to protect your capital when the UK market is in the doldrums.

> **No single country's economy or stockmarket, and no single sector of industry, performs well year after year after year.**

You can pretty well tailor this international exposure to your means and to your temperament. At the low end of the risk spectrum, an international general or growth fund will provide market spread, and is also an excellent core investment. Somewhat more volatile are funds that invest in North America and Japan (the world's two largest stockmarkets) and in Europe and the Far East, while at the top of the risk ladder there are the immature emerging market economies.

Here price performance will be very volatile, because the markets are hard to deal in, vulnerable to political instability and present a high currency risk. Potential investors must balance these risks against the fact that emerging markets are also capable of expanding their economies and their corporate earnings much more rapidly than the mature economies.

A spread of exposure to different industrial sectors also helps to contain risk. Let's take the one example that millions of us have experienced. Suppose you had put all your money into property at the start of 1988. It looked a comfortably secure investment and experienced heads would have nodded their approval to an exposure to bricks and mortar. Indeed, the enthusiasts might even have shouted encouraging exhortations such as 'fill your boots'.

But we all know what happened to the property sector after that and most of us experienced the effects in our personal lives.

The heady over-inflated prices of the late 1980s were succeeded by a recession from which the property market has yet to recover. Never put all your money into one narrow sector of the investment markets.

LOOKING AT THE FUND MANAGERS

Ways to assess the qualities of individual fund management groups are discussed in more detail in the next chapter (Chapter Seven), but clearly consideration of the quality of the fund managers who run an investment trust or unit trust is part of the risk assessment exercise.

It is certainly not the case that a fund can be classified as 'low-risk' if it has performed consistently well within its sector in the past, but it is the case that it presents a better bet than a fund investing in the same market sector which has consistently performed badly.

The most gifted managers cannot buck a market trend, but they can limit its effects for investors. You therefore have a good chance of reducing the risks of putting money into one specific industrial sector or geographical market if you choose a fund that, year in and year out, has performed as well as, if not better than, the average in its sector.

The one way to eliminate the risk of putting money with a poor fund management group, of course, is to choose a tracker fund, where there is no active management.

YOUR OWN ATTITUDE TO RISK

Every choice of investment involves some personal compromise. If you put your money in a higher-risk investment you do so in the hope of making greater profits. Obviously. Why else would you risk losing money?

On the other hand, if you want ready access to your investment, or you are eager to eliminate risk in every way possible, you can achieve your aims only by limiting the returns you will earn on your money. Any low-risk strategy involves sticking to savings accounts with banks, building societies or National Savings, where capital values will not vary.

In the same way there is a cost to investing in new types of stockmarket funds that guarantee some protection from share price falls, and are now offered by some banks, building societies, insurance companies and, increasingly, by unit trust groups.

If share prices slump, you won't lose as much money with these funds as you would with the exposure to the market offered by a conventional unit trust or investment trust. But conversely, if share prices rise, you will only benefit from a proportion of the profits that you could otherwise have made.

The aim of every investor is to look for ways in which they can maximise returns for the amount of risk that they personally can accommodate. This involves first looking at all your resources to see what risk you can actually afford.

The answer will depend on your financial position, your temperament and the length of time you are confident of being able to leave your money invested. The longer you intend to invest, the more you diminish the risk of being wrong-footed by stockmarket cycles.

■ INVESTMENT SNAPSHOT

There are two essential pieces of advice for investors who are putting together an investment strategy:

■ *Never put money into unit trusts or investment trusts before you have built up a fund of cash in a savings account, where it is readily available if you need to get hold of it in a hurry.*

■ *Never put surplus savings into stockmarket investments before you have bought life insurance protection for your family, insurance cover for your possessions, started contributions to a pension plan (which can be linked to an investment trust or unit trust, see Chapter Ten, pages 227–232) and put a first foot on your own personal property ladder (again, investment trusts and unit trusts may be used as mortgage repayment vehicles, see Chapter Nine, pages 207–210).*

PUTTING TOGETHER AN INVESTMENT STRATEGY TO FIT YOUR INVESTMENT PROFILE

Once you are over these hurdles it is time to start to think about long-term investment and asset allocation.

The most fundamental risk of stockmarket investment is that you will need to get hold of your money in a hurry, and that this will be at the very time when share prices are depressed. So, never put short-term money into a unit trust or investment trust or into any other investment where capital values will fluctuate.

It may not be short-term money, but of course you may still have a known point in the future when you will need to realise your investment. The shorter your time frame, the more essential it is that you avoid highly specialist funds.

You should be prepared to leave your money in a collective investment fund for at least five years, in order to give the managers a chance to perform through more than one market cycle.

On the assumption that, over the long-term, most stockmarkets tend to go up, the longer you can be in a market, enjoying the good times and hanging on to your seat belt during the bad, the better the returns you are likely to achieve. The reclusive American investor, Anne Scheiber invested a $5,000 nest-egg in 1944 and turned it into $22 million (£14 million) by the time she died in January 1995, at the age of 101. She bought blue-chip companies, seldom sold any shares and re-invested her dividends.

Frequent dealing in unit trusts and investment trusts adds to, rather than diminishes, risk. The more you buy and sell your holdings, the more dealing costs and charges you will incur, and the more these will erode any investment profits that you have made.

SHOULD YOU BE IN THE STOCKMARKET?

If you cannot afford the risk of a capital loss on any portion of your money you should not invest in the stockmarket. But there are also people who have the means to take the hit, but still should not be in equities.

Think honestly about how you personally would react to a sharp fall in the value of your stockmarket investments. In October 1987, for example, your capital would have lost one-fifth of its value in a few days.

If you fully accept that higher returns can be achieved only by taking risks, consider how best to keep these risks under reasonable control.

If that sort of scenario would worry you into an ulcer, stick to a portfolio of low-risk savings, where capital values will not fluctuate.

If a capital loss would make you uncomfortable – but you understand and appreciate the long-term argument for investing in the stockmarket – look at bond funds, or at the relatively low-risk investment trust zero dividend preference shares, or stick to a broadly based, conservatively managed UK or international general or tracker fund.

If you fully accept that higher returns can be achieved only by taking risks, consider how best to keep these risks under reasonable control. One answer is to diversify. Retain some money in cash deposits, have some assets in fixed-interest securities and make sure that your investment trust and unit trust holdings are not all linked to the fortunes of the same industrial sector, the same economy – or the same management company. And don't be in a hurry. Remember Anne Scheiber!

FURTHER READING

'Making Risk Work For You: An investor's guide to understanding risk and using it' by David Fleming. Free factsheet from the Association of Investment Trust Companies, Durrant House, 8–13 Chiswell Street, London EC1Y 4YY.

Investment Trusts: Private Investor Guide 1996. £15 from the Investment Trust Department, SBC Warburg, 1 Finsbury Avenue, London EC2M 2PP.

The statistical evidence suggests that when a fund is heading the performance tables, this is the time for new investors to avoid it

HOW TO SELECT AN INVESTMENT TRUST OR UNIT TRUST

■ THE FUNDAMENTALS

 There are nearly 2,000 unit trusts and investment trusts; none will meet the requirements of every investor.

 Investors must be quite clear about what they want and expect from a unit trust or investment trust before parting with any money.

 There is no miracle investment. Every investment decision involves some personal trade-off.

 Management charges on a fund are important; the investment competence of the manager is critical.

 Investors should not be influenced by the fact that a fund is new or heavily advertised. The only relevant factor is whether it will meet their specific needs.

 Investors should try to be contrarian, investing when share prices are depressed, not when a bull market is roaring to its peak.

 Constant dealing costs money; every fund manager should be given an opportunity to perform through more than one market cycle.

■ TERMINOLOGY

Total return: The return from a fund taking into account both dividends and interest received, and any capital gains or capital losses. With an investment trust, total return may be calculated either on the NAV performance of the trust or on the share price performance.

Dog funds: Funds that consistently underperform the benchmark index for their sector.

Investing money without first checking that the fund suits your personal objectives is rather like boarding a train without finding out whether it is stopping at your station. You may be lucky but the odds are that you will end up miles away, in the wrong county.

The first step to sieving through the long list of available unit trusts and investment trusts is to identify your objectives and to do so realistically, bearing in mind that every investment decision involves some personal compromise.

If you want to go all out to achieve maximum growth on your money you will have to be prepared for (and to be able to afford) maximum risk. If you want a fund with a very high immediate income, you will inevitably reduce the potential for future capital and income growth.

ESTABLISHING YOUR INVESTMENT PROFILE

You have enough money in a bank or building society account to meet short-term cash calls and you have arranged adequate insurance cover for yourself, your dependants and your property.

You appreciate the balance between risk and return and you have established how much volatility you can afford to take, both financially and temperamentally. Now you want to put surplus savings and/or free money to work where the capital, and the income earned from it, have a chance to grow over the years.

You look at the unit trusts and investment trusts listed in the newspapers, and your eyes start to bulge. Your arithmetic may be a bit shaky, but a rough check seems to suggest that there are something like 2,000 funds to choose from. Are they all offering something different and special?

Well, no. Within their sectors, most investment funds have much the same aims, although their portfolios will be markedly different. Investors should view this diversity of choice as a buying opportunity rather than an obstacle race, however. With such a variety of funds, there is no need to put money in a trust that either produces poor performance or charges high fees or does both. And there is no need to adopt a high-risk strategy if you do not have the stomach for it.

Ask yourself what you want from an investment fund. Are you looking for a core investment that will provide a wide spread of UK, or UK and international equities, and the potential to grow your income and capital steadily over the years? Or do you have your core investments in place and now wish to widen your geographical and sector diversification? Or are you ready to do something rather more adventurous with part of your capital and to put together a satellite portfolio of specialist funds?

The answer to these questions will be dictated to some extent by your reasons for investing and your time frame. For example, a relatively cautious investment approach will be needed if you are putting money aside for a specific purpose such as the payment of future school fees.

Trusts that qualify as core investments are those that provide diversified, relatively low-risk, income or growth portfolios which either concentrate on the UK or provide a broadly based international spread of investments. The general advice to first-time investors is to stick to a large general fund, such as the flagship international generalist investment trusts.

A UK tracker fund is another example of a suitable core investment, providing a broadly based exposure to the stockmarket, generally with the added benefits of lower management charges and lower transaction costs within the fund.

One or two unit trust companies, with private client departments, also offer funds that essentially mirror the firm's current asset allocation for these clients. For instance, Cazenove, the Queen's stockbroker, has a Portfolio Fund unit trust which is designed to replicate the portfolio of a typical Cazenove private client.

Income-seekers will probably be the most specific in their investment requirements. Broadly, they will divide into two groups, those that they are looking for a flow of increasing dividends and some capital growth, and those whose circumstances require them to look for a high initial yield, even if this is at the sacrifice of future income and capital growth.

The unit trust and investment trust industries have a wide range of income-producing funds for those who need to live off the returns from their invested capital and the different characteristics of the funds grouped under the equity income, balanced and fixed-interest sectors have already been discussed (see Chapter Five).

Even if you do not need to take income from your investment fund at the moment, don't cross trusts that offer a decent yield off your shopping list without a second thought. The special characteristic of equity investment is the 'total return' from re-invested dividends and capital growth that it can produce. By looking at total return figures, you can compare funds with different dividend policies.

While there are undoubtedly periods when capital returns will dominate – this has largely been the case in recent years – over the long haul, income may prove to be the most important component in the total return from an investment.

The 1996 edition of the *BZW Equity-Gilt Study*, which tracks back to 1918, demonstrates that over that 78-year period, around two-thirds of the total real return from equities – adjusted for inflation – comes from income rather than capital gain, although in the short-term capital gains or losses are often more important. For instance, UK company dividends fell overall in 1992, while share prices rose.

THE TRACK RECORD OF THE MANAGEMENT COMPANY AND THE FUND MANAGERS

It is a chicken and egg situation. Do you select an investment trust or unit trust first, and then look at the pedigree of the investment managers? Or do you choose a superior investment management company and then pick one of the funds it manages?

There is no right or wrong answer to the order in which a selection process should be made, but it is certainly the case that you need to be satisfied with both the investment aims of a fund, and the credentials of the managers behind it.

Be wary of investing in a fund that is the only one in that particular management stable that has ever produced any performance. This could mean either that the fund in question has been lucky or that its fortunes are inextricably linked with those of one manager. If the latter is the case, what happens if this manager takes his services elsewhere?

Conversely never choose a fund that does not really suit your needs, simply because you like the sound of the managers. Remember that there are more than 200 investment trust and unit trust management companies. One of them is bound to run a fund that actually meets your requirements.

Although only a few of the men and women managing unit trusts and investment trusts have a high public profile – the likes of Michael Hart of Foreign & Colonial, Mark Mobius of Templeton, Anthony Bolton of Fidelity and Michael Moule of Henderson Touche Remnant spring to mind – the past fortunes of a trust may well be linked to those of one fund manager. So take the trouble to find out who manages a fund now, and how long they have been in charge.

A recent change of fund manager should be fed into your selection criteria. If a fund with a poor track record has had a bout of managerial musical chairs this may well presage better performance in the future, although this is not axiomatic. Conversely, if there has been a managerial reshuffle at one of the investment industry's star funds, it may be prudent to suspend judgement (and investment) until the new supremo has had an opportunity to show his or her paces.

In general the stability of a fund management team within a unit trust or investment trust company encourages good performance. When there is a high turnover of fund managers (particularly when a number leave as a group) or when there are Press rumours about a company (perhaps of an impending sale or merger) there must always be a risk that these factors will distract the attentions of those whose job it is to look after and grow the money of investors.

A change of ownership or management may also impact on the general showing of an investment fund. It does not always follow that the change will produce an improved performance, particularly if it is a question of merging two opposing investment styles.

The Association of Unit Trusts and Investment Trusts (AUTIF) and the Association of Investment Trust Companies (AITC), whose contact addresses are repeated at the end of this chapter (see page 158), will supply inquirers with details of the available funds and of the management companies behind them. Measured by value of assets, AUTIF membership covers 96 per cent of the unit trust industry, and AITC membership accounts for 95 per cent of the investment trust industry.

Appendix One and Appendix Two at the end of the book give the names and addresses of the AUTIF member companies, and the names and address of the management companies that run the 317 trusts that make up the AITC membership.

FINDING OUT MORE ABOUT THE MANAGERS

It is one thing to know where to contact an investment company. But how do you learn about the investment strategies and capabilities of different companies and different fund managers?

Ask for any printed material that the companies produce. Corporate literature is often helpful, while the annual report and accounts of individual funds contain a wealth of selection indicators for those who can be bothered to read them. Indeed, many would argue that these are among the most important sources of information available to investors.

The more you can read about the fund or sector in which you plan to invest the better, and the financial pages of the weekend Press, in particular, devote many column inches to the unit trust and investment trust industries.

The former is particularly well-covered, probably because unit trusts are the richer source of advertising revenue to newspapers. Much of the comment is well-informed and helpful and it will give you a good insight into what has happened, is happening and may happen in the wider investment world and within individual management companies.

PERFORMANCE RECORDS

'The light which experience gives is a lantern on the stern, which shines only on the waves behind us!'
Samuel Taylor Coleridge

Past performance is one selection tool commended to investors, but it is a tool that needs to be used with discretion and intelligence if you are to avoid chopping your fingers off.

The weakness of past performance as a guide to fund selection is that it illustrates history. The challenge for the investor is to establish whether history is likely to repeat itself. This involves attempting to assess whether a trust's strategy for past success will stand it in equally good stead in tomorrow's economic and political environment.

The Press is the best source of comparative performance figures, but as the purveyor of the latest news has an understandable tendency to concentrate on the latest short-term performance stars. There is a similar and distracting concentration on the stars of today by the marketing departments of collective funds.

So the first thing to bear in mind is that if a unit trust or investment trust is among the top ten performers this year, it is very unlikely to be in the same position the following year.

■ INVESTMENT SNAPSHOT

Never pick a trust simply on the strength of one year's good performance, without first asking yourself if this is the type of fund you actually want to invest in, and without checking the trust's past consistency through all market conditions.

A star trust may be up in lights partly because of the skills (or luck) of its fund manager, but it may also be there because it is invested in a sector of the stockmarket that happens to be producing above-average returns at that particular time.

No stockmarket sector outperforms all other sectors year after year, and all the statistical evidence suggests that when a fund is heading the performance tables this is the time for new investors to avoid it.

An analysis by Fund Research Ltd, the independent qualitative research company on open-ended and closed-end funds, found that on average only 20 per cent, or one in five, of the top quartile funds over six separate five-year periods turned in a top quartile performance over the subsequent five years. Random choice, says Fund Research, would have given the funds a one in four chance of being in the top quartile.

> *The bottom line is whether income payments have outperformed, or at least kept pace with, inflation as measured by the retail prices index.*

You should always look at the performance of an investment fund over a number of periods, scrutinising the three-, five-, ten- and 15-year track records if it has them. This will provide evidence of the fund's consistency and of the skill of the managers through a number of market cycles.

Consistency – the achievement of a good performance year in and year out, relative to the market – is a much better indicator of successful investment management than sporadic bursts of growth. Compare a fund's record to the average performance of the trusts in its sector and to the stockmarket index that provides the sector's yardstick, and do your comparisons over a number of years.

Long-term performance tables can also be useful in providing evidence of the overall investment competence of a fund management company as well as an individual fund manager. You are unlikely to go far wrong by backing managers who achieve consistent above-average performance across the range of funds that they run.

Although past-performance tables must be treated with caution, however, they are one of the most readily accessible statistical guides available to private investors. Used with intelligence, they can provide valuable selection pointers on a trust's consistency and on the overall competence of the managers.

■ Income records

Income-seekers who are looking at equity rather than fixed-interest trusts should pay close attention to a fund's record of increasing its dividends or income distributions. The bottom line is whether income payments have outperformed, or at least kept pace with, inflation as measured by the retail prices index.

Watch out for any sudden increase in the yield of an income fund. The change may represent fool's gold if you are looking for a progressive increase in dividends over the years. Managers sometimes push up yields on equity income funds by increasing the weighting of convertibles and bonds in the portfolio. That's fine if this happens to be the sort of investment portfolio you are looking for, but the strategy necessarily puts some constraint on the fund's future income and capital growth.

PRESS ADVERTISEMENTS

As as been already noted, investment trusts are public companies and direct 'off the page' advertising of investment trust shares is prohibited, other than with new issues, although management companies may advertise packaged services such as Peps, savings schemes and personal pensions.

In contrast, unit trust groups can and do advertise both new and existing funds directly to the public in newspapers and magazines and, much more rarely, on television.

Many people have invested in a unit trust by clipping a coupon from an advertisement and have done so to their own benefit and without subsequent regrets. But investors who are tempted to respond to advertisements should keep their wits about them.

> *Unit trust advertising is invariably heaviest during booming stockmarkets, when share prices are high and investors are feeling optimistic.*

Unit trust advertising is invariably heaviest during booming stockmarkets, when share prices are high and investors are feeling optimistic. From the unit trust company's perspective, this makes commercial sense. Response to financial advertising at these times is much greater than when share prices are depressed and investor confidence is fragile.

Unfortunately commercial commonsense does not always work in the interests of investors. The tendency of some unit trust groups to advertise funds that are current sector leaders means that investors run the risk of being sucked into the market, just as share prices are about to peak. As a result they may have to sit out a market cycle before they even recoup their initial investment, let alone make any profits.

If you want to put money into an advertised unit trust, and stock-markets are booming, either wait until prices have dipped or con-sider dripfeeding your investment in through a savings scheme.

Don't suspend normal rules of judgement, either. Do the proper checks on the track record of the management group and the individual fund manager (see pages 144–146) before sending off any cheques.

OLD WIVES' TALES OR INVESTMENT POINTERS?

Three of the most persistent selection theories are that first, new trusts perform better than established ones because they don't have the ball and chain of past investment bloomers to drag them down; second, small trusts will have a performance edge because the larger the fund the more conservative and closer to the aver-age its investment performance will be; third, investors should take the contrarian approach, and invest each year in the funds that are at the bottom of the performance tables.

Skilled counsels for both prosecution and defence would have little difficulty in arguing for or against any of these theories. A look at the statistics shows that there is a germ of truth in all three statements, but that the evidence is not sufficiently conclusive to make them investment mantras.

A small fund can be nimbler than a large one, and the success of one of its investments is likely to have more impact on the fund's performance (but then the converse is true if there is a duff investment).

On the other hand many of the collective fund industry's largest and most illustrious funds – such as the M & G Recovery and Perpetual High Income unit trusts and the Foreign & Colonial and Alliance investment trusts – continue to produce enviable returns for investors. Moreover, there are some rotten performance apples to be found in the basket of smaller funds.

There is also some validity in the 'new trust' argument in that investment management companies have an added incentive to make a new trust perform, particularly if it has become a highly visible 'shop window' fund because of heavy promotion or Press coverage. And if a new fund can perform 15 or 20 per cent better than its benchmark index for the first six months of its life, this relative good performance will probably stay with it for two or three years.

In addition new funds may be launched with sweeteners, such as discounted charges or warrants, which provide a one-off benefit for investors who come in on the ground floor.

However, new funds do not automatically perform well. They certainly will not do so if the launch is badly timed to coincide with a market peak, nor will they do so over any length of time unless they are run by competent investment managers. New trusts are unknown quantities, in fact, and investors should always check whether the managers have a proven track record with other funds.

Example | ### Worst-performing *versus* average-performing

Table 7.1 shows the results of investing £100 in the worst performing unit trust at the end of the previous calendar year for 10 years, starting in February 1986. As a comparison, it also shows what would have happened if a similar investment had been made every year for 10 years into the average-performing UK equity growth trust.

The results are generally inconclusive. Over five of the periods, you would have scored by backing the laggard; over the other five you would have done better with the average growth fund. That said, in at least one instance – backing 1987's laggard, INVESCO Hong Kong & China Growth – the 'last year's loser' strategy would have succeeded triumphantly.

As to the counter-cyclical argument, yes, investors who are trying to add value to their core holdings should look for funds that invest in market sectors that are ripe for recovery. A mechanical selection of last year's laggards is far too chancy, however. Investment sectors do not perform in neat 12-month cycles, and a trust may well be lurking in the lower reaches of the performance league tables for no better reason than the fact that it is very poorly managed.

Table 7.1

The results of investing £100 for ten successive years in the worst-performing unit trust at the previous calendar year-end		
(The results of investing the same amount, on the same date, in the average UK Equity Growth unit trust appear in brackets)		
Unit trust	Date of investment	Value at 1 February 1996
Waverley Pacific Basin	3 February 1986	£278.52 (£301.90)
Abbey US Emerging Companies	2 February 1987	£307.71 (£217.45)
INVESCO Hong Kong & China Gth	1 February 1988	£575.96 (£199.59)
S & P Gold & Exploration	1 February 1989	£225.67 (£173.54)
BG UK Smaller Companies	1 February 1990	£196.78 (£161.15)
Barclays Unicorn Japan & Gen.	1 February 1991	£118.84 (£189.48)
MGM Special Situations Growth	3 February 1992	£156.02 (£157.53)
Friends Provident Jap. Sm. Cos.	1 February 1993	£127.49 (£137.80)
Govett Gilt Bear	1 February 1994	£92.25 (£104.82)
Beckman Bio Tech	1 February 1995	£186.54 (£121.65)

Source: Micropal Ltd. All figures are taken to 1 February 1996. They are calculated on an offer to bid price basis, with net income re-invested.

REDUCING THE SELECTION SHORTLIST

Once you have made a shortlist of two or three funds you can apply some simple tie-breakers to whittle the number down to one.

■ Charges

Over the long-term a fund's investment performance is far more important than the fees its managers charge to run your investments, pay their salaries and the office rent, and provide themselves with a profit.

Nevertheless, don't ignore management fees. The charges on respective funds are probably the most straightforward differentiator there is. Not only are the figures clearly spelled out; you also know that charges will have some impact on the returns you will get from the fund.

7

■ INVESTMENT SNAPSHOT

While the initial charge on a unit trust is the most visible fee – and the one that managers will discount for promotional purposes – it is the annual charge that will have most effect on your investment returns over the longer-term.

Overseas trusts are somewhat more expensive to manage and may have slightly higher annual charges. As an overall guide for unit trust investors, an initial charge of 6 per cent and an annual charge of 1.5 per cent are at the top end of the fee structure, but some funds will charge even more. Funds that load this sort of cost structure on to investors, therefore, need to offer very good investment performance to justify it.

Investment trusts tend to have lower management charges than unit trusts and, specifically, there is seldom any initial fee on the purchase of the shares. Some of the large, long-established investment trusts, the flagships of their management companies, have particularly low management fees. Also, while there are dealing costs on both purchases and sales of investment trust holdings these are greatly reduced by some of the competitive investment trust savings schemes that are available.

Of course, a fund with low management charges is not necessarily a fund with good investment performance, so never make your choice on price alone. On the other hand, if you have narrowed your fund selections down to two or three, the comparative charges are the obvious and sensible tie-breaker.

This is particularly the case when selecting either a corporate bond fund, which is a relatively low-cost fund to manage, or a tracker fund, which is even cheaper to run.

Many tracker funds are very competitively priced, having no initial charge and an annual fee of 0.5 per cent to 1 per cent. It always makes sense to choose one of the cheaper, rather than one of the more expensive, versions – there is at least one UK tracker unit trust with a 6 per cent initial charge – because funds tracking the same index are not striving for outperformance. If they are doing their jobs properly, their comparative performances should be identical within one or two percentage points.

There has been a move recently by some unit trust companies to take their annual management fees out of capital rather than the income. This has the effect of enhancing income returns for investors. For instance a unit trust with a 1.5 per cent management charge and a 7.5 per cent yield could increase the advertised yield from 6 per cent yield to 7.5 per cent, if it decided to take this management fee out of capital instead of income. Unit trusts that take charges from capital are highlighted with the letter 'C' in the *Financial Times* listings.

If your priority is the highest possible income this charging practice is perfectly acceptable, but you should be aware that it does involve a compromise, particularly with a unit trust such as a corporate bond fund, where there is little potential for capital growth.

You could find that the capital that is generating income is being progressively eroded by charges. The net result might well be that, over the long-term, you were actually receiving smaller income payments (see Table 9.1, page 199).

■ Other factors

Your final choice of fund may well be determined by practical considerations. For example, if you wish to sell existing shareholdings in order to place the proceeds in a collective investment fund, you will probably save on dealing costs if you choose an investment trust or unit trust that offers a share exchange facility. Similarly, you can eliminate funds, if they do not offer other services that you want, such as savings plans or monthly or quarterly income distributions.

WHEN TO SELL

Don't put money into an investment fund and forget about it. Ideally, you should have decided on an investment period of at least five years for an equity fund – stick to cash or fixed interest trusts for shorter-term investments – but the unexpected may happen and you should ensure that you know, more or less, what is happening to your money.

There will be times, too, when it will be right to sell a unit trust or investment trust holding. A particular fund's investment aims may no longer suit your financial needs or you may require cash to pay school fees, celebrate your retirement in style or pay off a mortgage.

Unfortunately, while there is never any shortage of investment professionals urging you to buy a collective fund, precious few round the circle will tell you when to sell it!

In part, this is because selling is often a decision based on personal circumstances, but it is also the case that no investment managers want to encourage any sort of mass exodus from one of their funds. More sellers than buyers drive down investment trust share prices, and managers of unit trusts may be forced to sell holdings they would prefer to keep, in order to repay the departing investors.

When you come to sell, you will obviously endeavour to do so at a time when stockmarkets are buoyant, but don't become neu-

7

rotic about trying to pinpoint the very top of a market. Even professional fund managers seldom pull off that particular feat.

WHAT TO DO ABOUT A DOG INVESTMENT

■ DEFINITION

Dog funds are funds that consistently underperform the benchmark index for their sector.

There may be times when you will be well-advised to sell at a loss, however. Just occasionally, despite their best research endeavours, investors find that they have put their money into that most unappealing of investment animals, a 'dog fund'.

Every trust that loses money is by no means a dog. Some managers are certainly better than others at running portfolios during a bear market, but the most brilliant fund manager cannot make profits when values in the investment sector in which a trust invests are universally depressed.

Even poor fund managers ought to be able to grow their trusts during rising markets, of course, but good fund managers do the double. They capitalise on the good times and limit falls in value during the bad.

You can check whether your fund manager is doing this by comparing the performance of your trust, in rising and falling markets, against the benchmark index for its sector. If a trust underperforms this benchmark – and underperforms the other funds in its sector – over a period of years, you must consider whether to cut your losses and sell your holding.

Before doing so, you may wish to ask the managers what they are doing about this laggard performer. For instance, if the company has re-organised the portfolio or brought in new investment managers for the trust, you may feel like giving the fund one further chance. If, on the other hand, the strategy appears to be to do not very much, if anything, then you should bite the bullet and sell.

PICKING AN INVESTMENT FUND: THE CHECKLIST

■ Don't invest any money unless you are sure that you have understood, and want, the risk/return profile of the type of fund you have chosen.

■ Look at the track record of the fund, the experience of its manager and at the overall performance produced by the fund managers for a number of years across all the funds they manage.

■ Read any literature there is on the specific fund and the investment style of the management company.

■ Don't select a fund simply because you've noticed that it is among the current top ten performers.

■ Never assume that a fund is bound to have a change of fortune because it has performed so badly recently.

■ Do remember to look at a fund's charges but don't choose a fund just because it's cheap.

■ Try not to invest money in the stockmarket when share prices are reaching new heights; wait until prices fall back, to catch their breath.

■ If you are worried about timing, dripfeed your money in through an investment trust or unit trust savings scheme. Remember, the more volatile the fund, the better value the regular savings mechanism is.

■ Avoid an impulse buy on the strength of Press comment or a striking advertisement.

■ Never agree to invest simply because that seems to be the only way to get a financial adviser or salesman off your back, and never proceed with an investment if you know in your heart that you are not really comfortable with it.

7

CONTACT ADDRESSES

AUTIF: 65 Kingsway, London WC2B 6TD
(Telephone: 0181-207 1361)

AITC: Durrant House, 8–13 Chiswell Street, London EC1Y 4YY
(Telephone: 0171-588 5347)

Under self assessment proper records must be kept of the income received from investment trust and unit trust holdings, and the capital gains that are made

TAX AND THE INVESTMENT TRUST AND UNIT TRUST INVESTOR

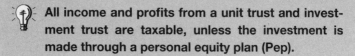

■ THE FUNDAMENTALS

All income and profits from a unit trust and investment trust are taxable, unless the investment is made through a personal equity plan (Pep).

Every man, woman and child in the UK has a personal tax allowance and their own capital gains tax allowance.

Investment trust dividends and unit trust distributions are paid to investors net of 20 per cent tax. Non-taxpayers can reclaim the tax deducted; lower rate and basic rate taxpayers have nothing further to pay; higher rate taxpayers must pay a further 20 per cent.

All tax vouchers sent out with dividends and distributions must now be kept for 22 months after the end of the tax year.

Capital gains on investments are taxable at the investor's highest rate of income tax, but the first £6,300 of gains in a tax year are exempt and an indexation allowance is given to offset the effect of inflation.

■ TERMINOLOGY

Capital gains tax (CGT): A tax on the gains or profits made when an asset is sold or otherwise disposed of. There is no capital gains tax to pay on your home, your household goods or on your assets when you die.

Tax voucher: A tax voucher is sent with each dividend and unit trust distribution. It shows the amount of the income payment and the tax credit, which is the amount of lower rate (20 per cent) income tax that has been deducted.

Foreign income dividends (FIDs): Dividends issued by investment trust companies or unit trusts when they have received income from overseas sources. FIDs are paid net of lower rate income, but there is no tax credit and non taxpayers cannot reclaim the tax deducted.

Scrip dividends: The issue of shares rather than cash dividends to help conserve a company's cash flow and to enable shareholders accumulate more shares.

Equalisation payment: A refund, made with a unit trust investor's first income payment, of that part of the buying price of the units that reflects income accumulated in the fund but not yet distributed. There is no tax credit, and equalisation does not have to be declared on a tax return. The equalisation payment is deducted from the initial investment when calculating CGT.

Bed and breakfasting: The transaction of selling shares or units on one day and buying them back on the next, in order to realise either a capital gain or a capital loss. Bed and breakfasting establishes a new base, or acquisition, cost for future disposals.

8

Unless you invest through a personal equity plan (Pep) income and capital gains earned from your investment trust and unit trust holdings are taxable.

Peps are discussed in detail later (Chapter Nine). This chapter is concerned with the tax position of UK investors who have unit trust and investment trust investments that are not protected by a Pep shelter.

There are two areas of potential tax liability. Your unit trust distributions and investment trust dividends are liable to income tax, and any investment profits from your investment are liable to capital gains tax (CGT). Some tax at 20 per cent on your income will be automatically taken from each dividend or distribution payment, but there will not be a potential CGT bill until you sell your investments and realise the profits on them.

INCOME TAX

This chapter is concerned with the tax position of UK investors who have unit trust and investment trust investments that are not protected by a Pep shelter.

All income from investment trusts and unit trusts is liable to tax, even if you choose accumulation units or opt to have dividends from your shares and your unit trust distributions re-invested in the fund. Whether you will actually have to pay any tax will depend on your annual total income from all sources. Tables 8.1 and 8.2 show the personal allowances and the income tax rates for the 1996 tax year. At the last count, 25.7 million of us were paying some income tax.

Table 8.1

Income tax rates: 1996/7 tax year	
Lower rate on first £3,900 of taxable income	20 per cent
Basic rate on next £21,600 of taxable income	24 per cent
Higher rate over £25,500 of taxable income	40 per cent
Rate on dividends/savings income when not subject to higher rate	20 per cent

Table 8.2

Income tax allowances: 1996/7 tax year	
Personal Allowance	£3,765
Age Allowance (65–74)	£4,910
Age Allowance (75 plus)	£5,090
Blind Person's Allowance	£1,250
Relief restricted to 15%:	
Married Couple's Allowance	£1,790
Age Allowance (Married, elder 65–74)	£3,115
Age Allowance (Married, elder 75 plus)	£3,155
(All age allowances are reduced by £1 for every £2 of income over £15,200, starting with the personal allowances)	

WHAT TO PUT ON YOUR TAX RETURN

When you receive income from your investment trust and unit trust holdings, tax at 20 per cent will already have been deducted from the payments. There is no way round this. Non-taxpayers cannot elect to receive gross income payments from dividends, as they may with bank and building society interest, but they can subsequently reclaim the tax deduction (see pages 166–167).

From 6 April 1996 all income from shares and unit trusts, and all savings income (including interest from gilts and corporate bonds as well as interest from bank and building society accounts) has tax deducted at source at the lower income tax rate of 20 per cent. If you pay income tax at the 20 per cent lower rate, or at the 24 per cent basic rate, you will have no more tax to pay on this type of investment income.

When you receive your investment trust dividends or unit trust distribution cheque, you will also be sent a tax voucher with a tax credit showing how much tax has been deducted.

You will need the information on this tax credit to complete your tax return. The Inland Revenue will want details of the size of the dividend or distribution, the tax credit (or tax deducted) and, with unit trusts, the gross income, which is the amount of the distribution plus the tax credit.

The gross income will be the relevant figure to use in

determining whether you are a non-taxpayer or what rate of income tax you are subject to.

With some investment trust and unit trust income payments you may also be given information about foreign income dividends (FIDs). FIDs may be paid when a fund's income is received from overseas sources, or when the fund itself invests in a UK company and receives a FID.

There is a tax-saving if income is distributed as a FID, and this should result in a higher payment. FIDs are treated as if they have had tax deducted from them at the lower, 20 per cent, rate but they don't carry a tax credit. So a non-taxpayer cannot make any tax reclaim.

FIDs are entered as separate items on your tax return. You will be asked to put the amount of the dividend or distribution and the amount of notional income tax that has been treated as paid.

You will need to keep all your tax vouchers in a safe place, particularly with the advent of self assessment (see pages 169–170). Don't worry if your investment trust or unit trust income is paid straight into your bank; the vouchers will either be sent to you or to the bank.

Dividend payments from unit trusts and investment trusts are usually made every six months, but some funds distribute income on a quarterly and even a monthly basis. This can cause a bit of administrative panic, because when you fill in your tax return you are going to need all the vouchers for all the income payments that have been made. Check the date on all tax vouchers, to make sure the income payment relates to the tax year in question.

NON-TAXPAYERS: HOW TO RECLAIM TAX

Although you will receive all distributions and dividends net of 20 per cent tax, you can claim the money deducted back from Inland Revenue if you are a non-taxpayer, and parents can reclaim the deduction on behalf of their non-taxpaying children (see the section on 'Investing For Children' on pages 177–178, for the position on parental gifts). Don't forget to make a claim. Literally millions of pounds of unclaimed tax is sitting idle in Inland Revenue's coffers.

To recover the tax deducted you will need to get a claim form (R 40) from your tax office and send it back with all the tax vouchers you have received with your dividend and distribution payments. Claim as soon as you have received all your investment income for that tax year; there is no need to wait until 5 April. Inland Revenue leaflet IR 110 ('A guide for people with savings'), which is available at tax offices, includes the relevant claim form.

Non-taxpayers cannot reclaim the deductions on quite all the investment income that is paid to them net of tax, however. When investment trusts and unit trusts issue FIDs, with a notional 20 per cent tax already deducted, there is no tax credit and no facility for non-taxpayers to reclaim the tax. Similarly shareholders on low incomes cannot reclaim tax on any scrip dividends (see page 168).

LOWER-RATE AND BASIC-RATE TAXPAYERS

8

If, after taking account of grossed-up dividends/distributions, you pay income tax at the lower rate of 20 per cent, or at the current basic rate of 24 per cent, your fiscal life as an investment trust or unit trust investor is very straightforward. You will receive net dividends or distributions and you will have no further tax to pay on this income.

The 20p tax rate for investment and savings income has been introduced as a step towards the target of a 20 per cent standard tax rate and it provides a little extra boost for investors who pay income tax at the basic rate.

HIGHER-RATE TAXPAYERS

While non-taxpayers should make sure that they reclaim every £ of tax they can, and lower- and basic-rate taxpayers can relax, those who are liable to income tax at the higher (40 per cent) rate will have to pay a further 20 per cent tax on their investment income.

SCRIP DIVIDENDS

Sometimes investment trusts and other companies decide to conserve cash flow and allow shareholders to take their dividends in the form of shares instead of cash. This is usually known as a scrip or stock dividend. It is relatively unusual for an investment trust to issue a scrip dividend – only around half a dozen have done so – but nevertheless investment trust shareholders should be aware of the tax ramifications.

Case Study   **Taxing work**

Angus Pound-Sign is working out his tax bill for 1996/7. After allowances and reliefs he has £27,000 of taxable income. Of this, £22,000 is earned income and £5,000 is income from Angus' portfolio of investments. The £5,000 is the grossed-up figure, including the tax that has been deducted at source.

Angus will pay 20 per cent on the first £3,900 of his earned income, and 24 per cent on the other £18,100 of earnings. The portion of his savings income that is below the higher rate income tax threshold of £25,500 will be taxed at 20 per cent. This means that Angus will pay 20 per cent tax on the first £3,500 of his savings income, and 40 per cent tax on the remaining £1,500.

If you opt for shares rather than a cash dividend you will save on brokers' costs, but not on tax. The net amount of the dividend will be taken to be either the cash equivalent, or the market value, of the shares and you will receive a tax credit. Those whose incomes are too low to pay income tax cannot reclaim any tax. Higher-rate taxpayers will have more to pay.

EQUALISATION

Unit trust investors may also receive information about an equalisation payment. This distribution causes no end of confusion.

When you invest in a unit trust part of the price you pay for your units represents income that has been received by the fund but has not yet been distributed to investors. The average amount of the income included in the purchase price is then refunded to buyers of the units as an equalisation payment.

The equalisation payment is made with your first distribution after you have bought units, but it is *not* a proper income payment. Inland Revenue takes the view that equalisation payments are a refund of capital and are therefore not taxable. The payments do not need to be declared on tax returns and there is no accompanying tax credit.

■ INVESTMENT SNAPSHOT

Don't ignore equalisation payments completely. When you come to sell your units, the equalisation figure may be needed. As it is a return of capital, it is deducted from the initial cost of the units to establish a base cost, when you calculate any profit or loss to work out your capital gains tax liability (see page 170).

8

THE ARRIVAL OF SELF ASSESSMENT

Like it or loathe it – and many people view the prospect with understandable nervousness – self assessment, the new system of collecting tax, starts to come into effect in the 1996/7 tax year. The first self assessment tax returns will be sent out in April 1997 for the tax year 1996/7.

Some 9 million people will need to get their minds round the new system because everyone who fills in a tax return will be affected.

> *Self assessment puts the onus on you, the taxpayer, to provide the required information so that your tax liability can be assessed.*

Self assessment puts the onus on you, the taxpayer, to provide the required information so that your tax liability can be assessed. One legal requirement under the new system is that you must keep proper records of the income you receive from your investment trust and unit trust holdings, and of the capital gains that you make.

All vouchers relating to income distributions must not only be retained, but safeguarded, for 22 months after the end of the relevant tax year.

The Inland Revenue has a number of free booklets to help taxpayers through the maze of self assessment. You can obtain them either by telephoning (0345 161514) or by writing to Self Assessment, PO Box 555, Bristol BS99 5UJ.

CAPITAL GAINS TAX

Capital gains tax (CGT) tends to be a subject of intense anxiety to investors. Yet comparatively few people ever pay the tax and there is considerable scope for organising your affairs to make full use of your annual CGT exemption.

The basic ground rules for CGT are relatively simple, although the same can hardly be said for the calculations needed to work out any CGT bill!

CGT is a tax on the profits made when you sell, or otherwise dispose of, an asset. However, you do not have to pay any tax if your total profits from all disposals of assets in any one tax year are within your annual CGT exemption. Both marriage partners are now able to offset their gains against their own individual CGT allowance. In the tax year 1996/7 the CGT exemption is worth £6,300. Indexation relief is also given (see the next page).

You make a capital gain whenever you sell something you own at a profit, and you can also realise a capital gain if you dispose of an asset, perhaps by giving it away. Any capital losses that you make by disposing of assets can be offset against these gains. Losses on gifts can only be offset against gains on gifts to the same person.

Some assets do not attract a CGT bill, however – including your main home and any private cars you own – and there is no CGT to pay on your estate when you die. For future CGT calculations, your beneficiaries acquire your investments at their market value (which is the probate value) at the date of your death. There is also no capital gains tax liability on gifts made between husbands and wives.

Whilst the overwhelming majority of unit trust and investment trust investors will be liable to income tax, only a minority are likely to be required to pay a tax on their profits. According to the Inland Revenue, just 85,000 investors pay CGT.

Authorised unit trusts and investment trusts also provide investors with an in-built CGT advantage. Since 31 March 1980, these trusts have been exempt from CGT on the profits they make on investment transactions within the fund. This gives unit trusts and investment trusts a proven performance edge over the collective investment funds offered by the life insurance companies.

Nevertheless, it would be unwise to be complacent about CGT, particularly during periods of generally buoyant stockmarkets. For instance in 1995, investors with portfolios of around £50,000 could have shown gains that would have pushed them close to, if not over, the CGT threshold.

If your profits exceed the exemption limit for the tax year, the excess gains will be added to your income and taxed as if they are the top slice of your income. A 24 per cent taxpayer, for instance, could partly suffer 24 per cent tax and partly 40 per cent tax on capital gains.

■ Indexation relief

There is a somewhat complicated but worthwhile concession, however. The amount of any chargeable gain will be reduced by indexation relief, which was introduced in March 1982. This relief will increase the original cost of the asset by indexation, so that investors do not have to pay tax on purely inflationary gains.

Any tax on gains will be based on the value of your shares or units when you sell them, less their original value when you bought them, adjusted for the rise in inflation over the period that you owned them! If you have any losses from other sale transactions these can usually be set against your gains.

Broadly speaking, the CGT rules are only concerned with

gains and losses notched up since 31 March 1982. Gains on shares or units bought before 31 March 1982 are usually based on the market value of the securities at that date, increased in line with the retail prices index (RPI) up to the day they are sold.

The cost of shares and units that have been bought after 31 March 1982 are increased in line with the RPI from the month of the purchase to the month of disposal. Monthly indexation tables are published in some newspapers, and are always available at tax offices.

Example

It is worth bearing in mind that the annual CGT exemption applies after allowing for indexation relief on your profits. So, if you put £100,000 into a unit trust or investment trust, you could sell the investment in five years' time for £128,000, without any liability to tax if inflation had averaged 4 per cent over the period, and the full CGT exemption of £6,300 is available.

OCCASIONAL PURCHASES AND REGULAR SAVINGS PLANS

Life sometimes becomes complicated if you have built up a shareholding or unit-holding over a period of years.

■ INVESTMENT SNAPSHOT

If you have bought shares or units in the same company or in the same trust, but at different times, it is important to keep accurate records of the dates of purchase. If you then sell part of your holding, there are rules to determine which shares or units you have actually disposed of, their initial price, and what the indexation allowance is based on.

With unit trust and investment trust regular monthly savings schemes there is the potential complication of having to index each purchase and re-investment of income separately. However, it is usually possible to opt for a simpler 'concessionary' basis for calculating any capital gain when you come to sell all, or part, of your accumulated holding.

Under this concessionary method, all monthly investments and re-invested income for the fund's financial year (less any small withdrawals) can be treated as if they had been a single purchase, with all the units and shares bought in the seventh month of the fund's financial year. The seventh month would be May, for instance, if the trust's accounting year-end was 31 October.

Your tax office will give advice on this if you do not have an accountant. Remember to keep records of all your share and unit purchase transactions.

ZERO DIVIDEND PREFERENCE SHARES

There is no income tax liability on zeros because these split capital investment trust shares have no entitlement to income. Instead zeros offer a fixed capital return at redemption and they are therefore chargeable to capital gains tax not income tax.

Zeros are very useful for investors who do not make full use of their CGT exemption, and they are particularly tax-effective for higher-rate income tax payers (the 40 per cent brigade). Providing the gains fall within their annual CGT exemption, investors are able to take tax-free returns from zeros by buying a series of shares which mature at yearly intervals. (For more about zeros, and their role in financial planning, see Chapter Ten, page 223.)

WARRANTS

Holders of the warrants issued by investment trusts do not receive dividends so they have no income tax to pay. Any profits they make will be subject to capital gains tax unless they fall below the

£6,300 annual CGT exemption. (Recently, new 'subscription shares' have been introduced. These are like conventional warrants except that they *do* pay dividends.)

BED AND BREAKFASTING

'Bed and breakfasting' is an unexpectedly homely term for an investment transaction that is designed to save you a CGT bill, and to get round the fact that the Inland Revenue does not allow you to carry forward any unused CGT exemption and set this against profits you might make in later years. In contrast you are allowed to carry forward losses.

When you 'bed and breakfast' you sell a holding before 5 April, and repurchase it on the following day, to realise a capital gain or loss and to make full use of your annual CGT exemption (see Table 8.3).

Table 8.3

Capital gains tax for individuals: 1996/7	
As top slice of income	20/24/40 per cent
Annual exemption	£6,300

For example, if you sell enough unit trust units or investment trust shares to bring your gains for the 1996/7 tax year up to the £6,300 limit, and then repurchase, you will have achieved a tax-saving double. You will not only have made full use of your CGT exemption; you will also have created a higher acquisition or base cost for your units or shares. This will reduce taxable gains when you want to sell at a later date.

There is another situation in which bed and breakfasting can be helpful. If your annual investment profits are likely to exceed £6,300, but at the same time you have units or shares that are standing at a loss, it may be sensible to sell and repurchase enough of these loss-makers to crystallise losses for tax purposes and to bring your gains down to the tax-free limit.

For instance, if investments show £2,000-worth of losses, and you sell these shares or units, you could have £8,300 of gains on other investments without having any liability to CGT. One draw-back, of course, is that when you 'bed and breakfast' loss-making shares or units, you reduce their

> **■ DEFINITION**
>
> **Bed and breakfasting** is the transaction of selling shares or units on one day and buying them back on the next, in order to realise either a capital gain or a capital loss. Bed and breakfasting establishes a new base, or acquisition cost for future disposals.

acquisition cost. This means that you could be storing up a higher CGT bill, and also lowering indexation relief in the future.

'Bed and breakfasting' will inevitably involve some dealing costs, although many discount brokers and some investment management companies charge special low rates for the transaction. There is an additional cost in that there is a difference between the buying and selling price of your shares and units.

In order to convince the Inland Revenue that you are not simply trying to avoid tax, the 'bed and breakfast' transaction must also be properly carried out, with the sale and repurchase taking place on different days. In other words, investors must take the investment risk that market prices will move against them in the course of the transaction.

You will need to calculate whether your gains are going to be handsome enough to merit the cost of 'bed and breakfasting' and of taking a chance on the market. It is unlikely to be worthwhile to 'bed and breakfast' very small profits.

WHERE TO GO FOR HELP ON POTENTIAL CGT LIABILITIES

Inland Revenue leaflets CGT 13 and CGT 16 will provide more details on indexation allowance, and leaflet CGT 14 (an introduction to capital gains tax) and leaflet CGT 15 (which deals with the position between married couples) may also be helpful. All these are available at tax offices.

CGT can be complicated fiscal territory, however, and

investors who regularly face a potential or actual liability would do well to take advice from a professional adviser, unless they are very confident of their D-I-Y tax skills.

INDEPENDENT TAXATION

Husbands and wives with very different tax liabilities may be able to cut the total partnership tax bill by transferring assets such as investment trust shares and unit trust holdings from the higher- to the lower-taxpaying partner.

Since 6 April 1990, husbands and wives have been taxed separately on their earned and unearned income, and on any capital gains that they make on their investments.

Each partner is entitled to a personal allowance in their own right, and each has their own capital gains tax exemption. Where there are income or profits from jointly owned assets these will be taxed according to the exact proportion of ownership, although in practice the Inland Revenue will usually assume that an asset is jointly owned in equal shares. If this is not the case you should make a declaration to the Inland Revenue so that each partner can be taxed on their proper share.

There is no capital gains tax or inheritance tax to pay when husbands and wives gift assets to each other, and there is therefore considerable scope to shuffle the marital assets in order to save tax.

For example, if one spouse has no earned or investment income, they are clearly unable to receive any benefit from their personal tax allowance. But if their partner has investment income, and pays tax, some of the income-producing assets could be transferred unconditionally to the non-taxpayer, to mop up the unused allowance.

There is a similar opportunity to save tax by moving assets around if one partner pays higher-rate income tax, and the other is taxed at the lower 20 per cent or the basic 24 per cent rate of tax.

Moreover if you transfer, say, unit trust units or investment trust shares from one partner to another, you split the capital gains tax liability two ways and can therefore take advantage of the two CGT annual exemptions.

Cynics – or realists – might spot one weak link in this domestic financial planning. What happens if the married pair subsequently part? What indeed? Any major transfer of assets for tax purposes should be undertaken only by couples who are either very confident that they will stay together, or equally confident that both would behave with financial decency if the marriage foundered.

INVESTING FOR CHILDREN

Babies do not only come into the world with a red face and a well-developed pair of lungs. They are also entitled to the single personal tax allowance and a CGT exemption from the moment of their birth.

There will be no inheritance tax liability on any money that has been put into an investment trust or unit trust as a gift to the child, providing that either the gift falls within the annual exemptions or else the generous donor lives for the next seven years.

However, the position regarding any income arising from the child's unit trust or investment trust holding is slightly more complicated.

If the gift of money came from one of the child's parents the investment may earn up to £100 a year tax-free. But if the child's investment income from all a parent's gifts exceeds £100, all the income payments will in general be taxed as if they belonged to the parent.

If anyone else (a grandparent, say) gives money to a child, the income earned on the gift will be taxed as the child's and it can therefore be set against the child's full personal allowance.

The allowance is worth £3,765 in the 1996/7 tax year, and comparatively few children are likely to have investment income that exceeds this figure. So their parents will be able to reclaim the tax deducted from the distributions or dividends of any unit trust or investment trust holdings their children may have. (See *Non-taxpayers*, above.)

Children are also entitled to the £6,300 annual capital gains exemption, so CGT is unlikely to be a problem for young investors. Investments that are liable to CGT rather than income tax, such as zero dividend preference shares, may well be suitable for juvenile investors, especially when the parent makes the gift.

(See Chapter Ten, pages 221–225, for more about investing in a unit trust or investment trust on behalf of children.)

FURTHER READING

The Which? Tax Saving Guide 1996 (contact the Consumers' Association about subscriptions to *Which?* or look in a local public library)

Which? Way to Save Tax 1996-1997 (£14.99, from book shops)

'Unit Trusts and Tax' (free leaflet from The Unit Trust Information Service, 65 Kingsway, London WC2B 6TD; telephone: 0181-207 1361)

Inland Revenue leaflet IR 110, 'A Guide for People with Savings: How to stop paying tax on your interest and how to claim tax back' (from tax offices)

> *Peps should form the backbone of every investor's unit trust and investment trust portfolio*

PEPPING UP YOUR INVESTMENT

9

■ THE FUNDAMENTALS

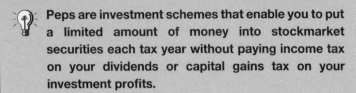 Peps are investment schemes that enable you to put a limited amount of money into stockmarket securities each tax year without paying income tax on your dividends or capital gains tax on your investment profits.

The shares and fixed interest securities of UK and EU companies all qualify as Pep investments.

Some 760 unit trusts and 170 investment trusts invest in these companies, and are therefore eligible Pep investments.

£1,500 of the £6,000 general Pep annual allowance can also be placed in a unit trust or investment trust that invests in other recognised overseas stock-markets.

Once capital is invested in a Pep, it is completely sheltered from tax. You don't have to include any income or investment profits on your tax return.

■ TERMINOLOGY

'Qualifying' trust: For Pep purposes, an investment trust or unit trust that has at least 50 per cent of its portfolio invested in the shares or fixed-interest securities of UK or EU companies.

'Non-qualifying' trust: An investment trust or unit trust that has at least 50 per cent of its portfolio in shares that are quoted on a stock exchange that is recognised by Inland Revenue, but which does not meet the 50 per cent UK/EU rule.

Corporate bond Pep: A Pep that invests at least 50 per cent of its portfolio in the fixed-interest securities issued by UK and EU companies. UK Government securities (gilts) are not eligible investments for a corporate bond Pep.

Gross redemption yield: The return on a fund that takes into account the gross income after charges and the likely capital gains or losses on the underlying investments if these are held until maturity.

9

Are you a taxpayer? If so, do you want to accumulate wealth? Maximise investment income? Find a flexible vehicle to repay a mortgage?

Your financial doctor is unlikely to be at a loss to suggest a remedy. The purchase of an investment trust or unit trust personal equity plan, or Pep, should help you to realise all these ambitions.

Peps are the most tax-efficient way to invest in the stockmarket and if you are a taxpayer the plans should form the backbone of your unit trust and investment trust portfolios.

WHAT IS A PEP?

Peps are savings plans that enable you to invest in the shares and corporate bonds of UK or European Union companies – or in unit trusts and investment trusts that invest in these companies – without paying any income tax on your dividends and interest, and without paying any capital gains tax on your investment profits.

The birth of Peps was announced in the March 1986 Budget by Nigel Lawson, who was at that time Chancellor of the Exchequer. The Government's aim was to persuade more investors to take a stake in the British economy by investing in British companies. In particular, it wanted to encourage savers who had not previously bought shares. The lure was a new tax shelter which offered the opportunity to put a limited amount of money either directly into shares, or into unit trusts and investment trusts, without paying tax on any of the investment returns.

The first plans were launched in January 1987 but in the early years Peps showed little sign that they were to become the popular investment success that had attracted some £22 billion of investments by 1995.

The initial annual contribution limit was relatively low (£2,400) and, significantly, investment in unit trusts and investment trusts, which would have provided a spread of risk for new investors, was restricted to £420 a year. The bureaucratic administration was also a nightmare for Pep providers, one or two of whom retired wounded from the market.

Slowly, however, the Pep scheme was improved and streamlined. In 1992 a second type of plan was added, the single company Pep, which provided a further tax-free savings opportunity, and the investment parameters for the mainstream general Peps were progressively widened.

Example

Today, someone who came in on the ground-floor of the scheme, and has contributed the maximum possible amount each year to a Pep (including the 1996/7 tax year) would by now have ring-fenced £73,200 of investments from tax. And as each marriage partner has their own Pep allowance, a married couple could have amassed £146,400 of tax-free capital.

THE CONTRIBUTION LIMITS

9

There are two types of Pep, the general Pep, which can invest in a range of investments, including unit trusts and investment trusts, and the single company Pep, which allows you to put a further contribution into the shares of just one UK or European Union company.

The maximum contribution to a general Pep is currently £6,000 each tax year and the maximum investment in a single company Pep £3,000 each tax year. Unfortunately an investment trust does not qualify as a single company Pep investment, although all investment trusts are publicly quoted companies. The argument is that, in tax terms, investment trusts are the same as unit trusts – both forms of collective fund are exempt from capital gains tax on investment dealings within the fund.

Anyone who is aged at least 18, and is resident in the UK for tax purposes, may invest in a Pep, but they must not put money into more than one general plan and one single company plan each year (for more details see below for an outline of the Pep ground rules).

■ PEPs: THE GROUND RULES

- You must be at least 18 years old, and resident in the UK for tax purposes to invest in a Pep.

- You must buy your investments through an approved Pep plan manager.

- You may invest up to £6,000 in one tax year into a general Pep but you must not invest with more than one plan manager in any one tax year.

- You may invest up to £3,000 in a single company Pep in any one tax year. The plan manager for this Pep does not have to be the manager of your general Pep. An investment trust is not eligible for a single company Pep.

- Each marriage partner has their own general and single company Pep allowance but couples cannot have a Pep in their joint names.

- The full £6,000 general Pep allowance may be invested in qualifying investment trusts or unit trusts. These are funds that have at least 50 per cent of their assets invested in the shares or bonds of UK or EU companies.

- £1,500 of the general Pep allowance may be invested in non-qualifying investment trusts or unit trusts. These are funds which have at least 50 per cent of their assets in shares of companies that are listed on stockmarkets that are recognised by the Inland Revenue.

- There is no time limit to qualify for the Pep tax benefits, and you can sell your Pep investments whenever you want.

- You can transfer Peps from previous tax years to a different plan manager without sacrificing the tax benefits.

- You cannot buy a Pep for your under-age children and trusts set up for children cannot invest in Peps.

- You cannot contribute to a Pep if you go to live or work abroad, unless you are a Crown employee, but money invested in Peps before you go overseas will continue to accumulate free of all taxes.

- You cannot transfer the ownership of your Pep to someone else or pass it on to someone else in your will.

- Peps lose their tax-free benefits when an investor dies. From the date of death all future capital gains and dividends become taxable.

If investors do not take up their annual Pep contribution in any one tax year it is lost forever; the unused allowance cannot be carried forward to the next tax year.

This chapter concentrates on general Peps, because these are the vehicles that provide the mechanism to invest in investment trusts and unit trusts without paying tax on investment returns. However, the tax position with regard to general and single company Peps is precisely the same. Income and capital gains do not have to be declared on tax returns; indeed, investors do not need to have any personal contact with Inland Revenue as far as their general and single company Peps are concerned.

ELIGIBLE PEP INVESTMENTS

Peps are very nearly a free lunch, but not quite. You will receive the tax benefits only if you invest within the range of permitted Pep investments. These favoured investments are the shares of quoted UK companies or European Union companies that are listed on an EU stock exchange; and the fixed-interest bonds and securities issued by UK and EU companies.

Unit trusts and investment trusts that have at least 50 per cent of their assets in these investments are known as 'qualifying' trusts and are able to provide investors with Peps linked to their funds.

It is also possible to put up to £1,500 of your £6,000 annual general Pep allowance into 'non-qualifying' unit trusts and investment trusts. These funds have most of their assets invested in recognised overseas stockmarkets but they do not meet the 50 per cent UK/EU rule.

THE PEP PROVIDERS

You cannot just decide to designate some shares or units as Pep investments. The Pep has to be run by an authorised plan manager. This requirement is unlikely to clip your selection wings. Investors who are trying to choose a suitable Pep may even feel that there is rather too much choice for comfort. There are more than 200 Pep providers, and something like 1,200 different plans.

Some stockbrokers and investment advisers either manage

portfolios of shares or unit trusts in a Pep for their clients or they offer advice on purchases and sales. These arrangements are known as discretionary managed Peps and advisory Peps.

A minority of confident and experienced investors also prefer to manage their Pep shares themselves in what is known as a self select Pep. These plans are best suited to more substantial investors, who are able to contain the risks of investing money directly in shares.

For the majority of investors, a collective investment fund, which both limits stockmarket risks by offering a spread of holdings and a wide choice of investment sectors, and provides professional fund management at a reasonable cost, is the most effective home for Pep money

At the beginning of 1996, the full £6,000 general Pep contribution could be invested in a choice of 760 unit trusts and 176 investment trusts. The unit trust industry had some £17.8 billion of its £117.8 billion funds under management invested in its Peps, giving it control of something like 60 per cent of all Pep money.

The investment trust industry does not keep a global figure and although it is now attracting a healthy inflow of new Pep money – £204.5 million was invested in packaged investment trust Peps in 1995 – investment trusts manage significantly less Pep money than unit trusts. In total they probably account for something like 15 per cent of the Pep market.

There are a number of reasons for this. Unit trust companies tend to have closer contacts with independent financial advisers. They also pay commission to any adviser who recommends one of their funds, whereas comparatively few investment trust companies as yet make commission payments. As more advisers start to charge their clients fees, rather than relying on commission payments for a living, however, they may well become readier to recommend investment trusts.

Investment trusts also face another obstacle. The investment strategies of some of the most successful and largest investment trusts, which concentrate on a widely dispersed portfolio of international shares, preclude them from qualifying for full Pep status. Investors are therefore confined to the £1,500 'non-qualifying trust' Pep contribution.

This has prompted many managers of big international invest-ment trusts to consider whether to adjust their portfolios, to become fully 'Pepable'. However, the boards of investment trust companies such as Foreign & Colonial trust, Henderson Touche Remnant's Bankers trust, and the Dundee-based Alliance and Second Alliance trusts have decided to continue with the strate-gies that have served them so well in the past, even if this means that investors cannot invest the whole of their £6,000 allowance into the funds.

Investment trusts are also somewhat handicapped by the fact that many make an additional charge for Pep management, while unit trusts manage to absorb the additional administrative costs (see the section on charges pages 197–199).

Although most Peps tend to be linked to just one investment fund, there is scope for investors who want to use collective funds, but to diversify beyond a single trust. Some investment managers offer 'Mixed Peps' to enable them to do this.

For example there are Peps that allow investors to put money in a spread of unit trusts and investment trusts, or in a portfolio of shares and unit trusts, or in a portfolio of shares and investment trusts. And there is a handful of investment trust managers who provide Peps that enable you to add a direct exposure to shares to your core collective fund Pep holding.

The Pep managed by the Alliance Trust is particularly flexible. It permits satellite portfolios of other UK shares and it also allows investors to put £1,500 into either of the two Alliance trusts and the balance of the annual contribution into one or more of a selec-tion of 88 other investment trusts.

THE INVESTMENT SCOPE OF UNIT TRUST AND INVESTMENT TRUST PEPS

Over the years there has been a slow but steady increase in the range of investments that qualify to receive Pep money.

Initially investors were confined to the shares of British com-panies. Today they may also place part or the whole of their

Over the years there has been a slow but steady increase in the range of investments that qualify to receive Pep money.

£6,000 general Pep allowance in companies based in the 12 countries within the EU; they may put up to 25 per cent of the allowance in other overseas stockmarkets; and they can invest in UK and EU corporate bonds, convertibles and preference shares.

The expanded list of eligible securities has provided Pep investors with much more elbow-room to diversify their investment risks, and to spread their assets over a number of stockmarkets and investment sectors.

The range of investment trusts and unit trusts that are now 'Pepable' means that there is scope within the Pep rules to accommodate every kind of investor: the income-seeker as well as the capital growth enthusiast; and the risk-averse and the more adventurous.

■ Equity income Peps

For most people the chief advantage of a Pep is the freedom it provides to receive all dividends and income distributions free of income tax. This is of far more universal benefit than the ability to receive profits free of capital gains tax. Some 27.5 million of us pay income tax. Fewer than 1 per cent of the income tax payers receive a bill for capital gains tax (see Chapter Eight, pages 170–173).

A well-managed equity income Pep will deliver an increasing income over the years. What it cannot do is offer the highest immediate income. Initially your payments may well be only around one-half of what you would receive from a corporate bond Pep (Figure 9.1 on page 195 illustrates this).

Even within the equity income sector itself there is a yield trade-off. This point has already been discussed (see Chapter Five, pages 104–107) but it is worth emphasising again. The higher the yield on a unit trust or investment trust the more modest the prospects of income and capital growth will be.

To secure a very high initial yield managers of an equity income trust must either take some risks with the companies in which the fund invests, or they must add some fixed interest securities such as convertibles or preference shares to the portfolio. Both tactics are likely to restrict future growth.

■ Growth Peps

Many Pep investors point out that they are looking for growth not income, however, because they are accumulating tax-free funds for the future. At 60 or 65 they may want to start to take an income from these investments but at the moment they just want to achieve the greatest possible growth, consistent with the amount of risk they are prepared to take.

Peps concentrating on capital growth invest in both UK and EU companies. You can also give your Pep portfolio a more international exposure, either by investing in an international general fund that meets the UK/EU 50 per cent asset qualifying rule, or by making use of the freedom to invest £1,500 of your allowance in a non-qualifying trust (see page 197).

Growth seekers are presented with a wide spectrum of risk. There are funds that concentrate on relatively stable blue-chip companies, with a record of steady growth over the years. There are others which invest in more speculative recovery stocks, special situations and smaller companies, which mean that investors need a long-term time frame. The longer you are prepared to leave money invested in volatile markets, the more you will limit the investment risks.

9

■ INVESTMENT SNAPSHOT

Growth investors should bear in mind two words: 'total return'. The combination of a growth in share price, and a growing dividend record, will best help you to achieve your ambitions to maximise returns on your Pep portfolios. So even if your priority is capital growth, don't ignore yield considerations.

At the end of the day, dividends are likely to comprise a very considerable part of the total return you will receive from equities over the years.

■ Index or tracker Peps

Peps linked to funds that 'track' – that is, mirror – the performance of specific stockmarket index are becoming increasingly popular. For good reason.

Tracker funds limit some of the risk of investing in shares, because you start off by knowing exactly where you stand. You will never do worse – or better – than a known index.

Tracker fund Peps (with one or two exceptions) are also very cheap, thanks to the outbreak of a competitive price war by unit trust Pep providers. Typically there is now no initial charge on most tracker Peps, while the annual management fee is 0.5 to 1 per cent.

Clearly the more investors can contain the costs of managing their Pep portfolios, the greater their growth prospects will be. Growth investors with tracker funds can opt to have their dividends and income distributions re-invested.

The mainline tracker Peps follow either the FT-SE 100 Index (the Footsie), or the FT Actuaries All-Share Index and the measure of the success of each fund is the fidelity with which it mirrors the movements of its chosen index.

Naturally investors must recognise that they will never do better than the average with a tracker fund Pep. If they want to try to beat the index they will have to invest in an actively managed fund. This fund may outperform a tracker fund (and cushion the effects of falling share prices), but there is certainly no guarantee that it will do so. Indeed, some 90 per cent of actively managed UK general funds fail to beat their chosen stockmarket index. (For more about tracker funds, see Chapter Five, pages 110–114.)

■ Corporate bond Peps

Until recently Pep investors could not put their money into the fixed-interest securities issued by UK and EU companies, but in

July 1995 the legislation was changed. As a result unit trust companies and some other Pep managers are now able to offer Peps that invest in fixed-interest bonds.

However, the vast majority of investment trusts do not hold bonds for tax reasons, so investment trusts are largely excluded from the corporate bond Pep market.

The Government relaxed the Pep rules to embrace fixed-interest securities primarily to provide companies with more access to finance not to give investors more investment choice and a means of maximising their tax-free income.

It comes as no surprise, therefore, that Government stocks ('gilts') are not eligible as corporate bond Pep investments. Do not be confused by corporate bond Peps that are linked to funds that are described as 'gilt and fixed-interest' trusts. The under-

> ### ■ DEFINITION
>
> **A corporate bond Pep** is one that invests at least 50 per cent of its portfolio in the fixed-interest securities issued by UK and EC companies.

lying portfolio will have less than 50 per cent of its holdings in gilts.

The main permitted assets in corporate bond Peps are: bonds which are issued by UK companies and which have a life of at least five years; Eurosterling bonds, which are denominated in sterling and similar to domestic corporate bonds but issued outside the UK market and which must also have a life of at least five years; convertible shares; and preference shares.

As far as risk to capital and income is concerned, corporate bonds come somewhere between bank and building deposits and equities. Capital values are not guaranteed, but bond fund prices are unlikely to be spectacularly volatile. And while a bond is only as secure as its issuing company, bond-holders are that much safer than shareholders. If a company goes into liquidation corporate bond-holders have first rights to its assets.

The great selling point of corporate bond Peps is that they offer a high immediate income from their portfolio of fixed-interest securities. This income is often greater than that obtainable from the savings accounts offered by banks or building societies, and certainly higher than the initial yields on equity income unit trusts and investment trusts.

Unlike equity income Peps, corporate bond Peps will provide little if any growth of income over the years. I make no apology for harping on about this because it is important. The following table makes the point. It compares the ten-year income record of a corporate bond unit trust Pep, a UK equity income unit trust Pep and a gross-paying building society account. The figures are based on average unit trust sector performances over this period.

While the corporate bond Pep starts with a considerable income advantage, by the tenth year the UK equity income Pep has become the most efficient income producer.

Income from a corporate bond Pep will fluctuate and the value of the capital you have invested will be determined by what is happening to interest rates. If interest rates rise, the value of your corporate bond Pep will fall; if interest rates fall, corporate bond Pep prices will rise.

However, while the value of an investment in a corporate bond Pep will not be stable, unlike money in a building society savings account, prices should not be as volatile as the unit prices and share prices of funds that invest in ordinary shares.

Corporate bond Peps will therefore suit the investor who is in need of a very high level of immediate income – or who appreciates the argument for rolling up income from fixed-interest securities under a tax-free Pep umbrella – and who is prepared to take some risk in order to get a higher return than that available on a cash deposit. Bond Peps are also useful for those who want to add an exposure to fixed-interest securities in their portfolio.

But bear in mind that as the prospects of any income or capital growth over the years are modest, corporate bond Peps are a decidedly better bet in periods of low inflation than in times of steeply rising prices.

The low growth potential of these Peps also means that investors must look carefully at the management charges. You do not want to pay a high initial charge when there is likely to be little increase in capital values over the years. Any unit trust company that levies the same charges on its corporate bond funds as on its equity funds needs to have very strong grounds to justify this. Frankly it is hard to think what these grounds could possibly be.

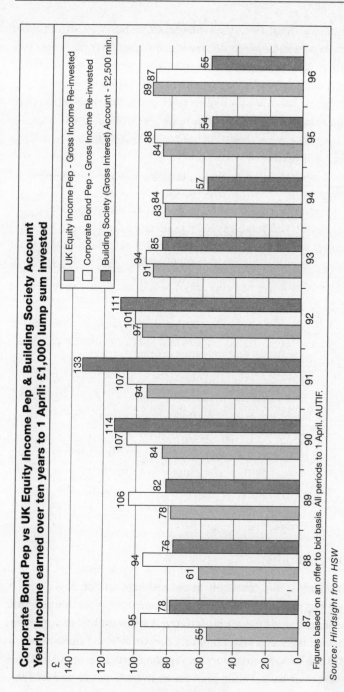

Corporate Bond Pep vs UK Equity Income Pep & Building Society Account
Yearly Income earned over ten years to 1 April: £1,000 lump sum invested

Figures based on an offer to bid basis. All periods to 1 April. AUTIF.

Source: Hindsight from HSW

Figure 9.1

Unit trusts offer two types of corporate bond Pep fund. One invests in a broad spread of fixed interest stocks; the other is a specialist vehicle concentrating on one type of fixed-interest security, such as preference shares or convertibles.

In order to boost yields, some fund managers may follow two strategies, both of which are likely to lead to some capital loss in the future, although they will put more initial income into the pockets of investors.

First, managers may decide to take management expenses out of capital rather than income. Second, they may secure higher yields by buying bonds for the trust's portfolio above their original price. This means that there will be an inevitable loss of value in the future.

It is of course for individual investors to decide whether they are prepared to accept some capital loss in the future in return for a very high immediate income.

Bond funds quote two interest rates: the current yield on the fund and the gross redemption yield (also known as the 'estimated total yield').

The current yield is the income that you are likely to receive this year. The estimated gross redemption yield does not tell you anything about your annual income, but it gives a fairer view of the long-term returns from the fund.

It takes into account likely capital growth or losses on the underlying investments if they are held to maturity, and it is the best yardstick to use when you are comparing the relative prospects of the different corporate bond funds. (For more about bonds, see Chapter Five, page 96.)

■ European Peps

More than 90 European unit trusts and investment trusts qualify for full Pep status because they have at least 50 per cent of their assets invested in companies based in European Union countries.

Under the general sobriquet of 'Europe', these funds provide a wide range of investments. The general trusts that invest in more than one continental European economy offer a choice of large and small companies while two investment trusts (managed by Kleinwort Benson Investment Management and Mercury Asset Management) concentrate on the shares of European privatisation issues. There are also single company trusts, investing in Ireland, Spain, Germany and France. Investors must recognise that as these trusts concentrate on a single economy they are likely to be more high risk.

■ Non-qualifying unit trusts and investment trusts

Up to £1,500 of the annual £6,000 general Pep allowance may be invested in a 'non-qualifying' fund, with the balance placed in a qualifying trust, as long as all trusts are managed by the same Pep manager.

A non-qualifying investment trust or unit trust does not have at least 50 per cent of its assets in UK or EU securities, but it does have to have at least 50 per cent in 'qualifying shares'. 'Qualifying shares' are ordinary shares that are quoted on a recognised stock exchange. The Inland Revenue decides whether or not a stock exchange is recognised, and some of the emerging markets are not on its list.

The £1,500 facility is a useful bonus to established Pep investors who want to diversify their assets and to add a rather wider international flavour to their portfolios. For instance, some of the most successful international investment trusts are non-qualifying trusts. The £1,500 rule gives investors a chance to take some tax-free returns from these funds.

WHAT IT COSTS TO 'PEP' YOUR INVESTMENTS

■ Unit trusts

One bonus of investing in a unit trust Pep is that management groups very seldom make any additional charge for the Pep facility. In general, investors pay exactly the same, whether they are investing directly in a unit trust or via a Pep. Indeed competition for business has recently prompted unit trust managers to cut charges on their Peps so that with some funds it is actually cheaper now to invest via a Pep.

Typically, unit trust managers levy an initial charge of between 5 and 6 per cent, and have an annual management fee of 0.75 to 1.5 per cent. There are a number of 'Pepable' funds that make no initial charge, however, although where there is no entry fee, one or two companies levy a range of exit charges if investors cash in their Pep within five years.

Charges on tracker fund Peps and corporate bond Peps are usually particularly competitive and so they should be. The tracker funds do not involve as much active management participation (see Chapter Five, pages 110–114) and many management groups have decided to reduce and sometimes scrap front-end charges on corporate bond Peps, accepting that a 5 or 6 per cent fixed initial charge is too big a bite to take out of a low-growth investment.

Some income fund managers are now taking their annual management charge from the invested capital, rather than the earned income, in order to enhance yields for investors. However, if you are considering a corporate bond Pep with this charging structure, you need to make sure that you understand what is happening.

Taking annual management fees from capital will boost income returns. But while this method of charging may be helpful if the highest possible immediate income is a priority, it is a somewhat dangerous long-term charging structure for investments such as corporate bonds, which have very modest capital growth prospects. Over the years, you risk reducing your capital – the very asset that is generating your income, as the figures in Table 9.1 show.

■ Investment trusts

Investment trust charges are usually lower (sometimes considerably lower) than the comparative unit trust charges for straightforward investments. However, these low management fees mean that investment trusts' profit margins are pretty tight. Unlike unit trust companies, they cannot afford to subsidise Pep investors by effectively bearing the costs of running the plan. As a result many investment trust managers levy an additional charge to cover the cost of administering a Pep.

Table 9.1

Corporate bond funds: a comparison of fees charged to income and capital		
Assuming a £6,000 investment; an initial charge of 3.25 per cent; an annual gross yield of 8.35 per cent; and an annual charge of 0.75 per cent		
	Fees charged to	
	Income	Capital
Year 1		
Interest paid	£485	£529
Capital value	£5,805	£5,761
Year 5		
Interest paid	£485	£509
Capital value	£5,805	£5,591
Year 10		
Interest paid	£485	£491
Capital value	£5,805	£5,385
Figures based on the Barclays Unicorn Gilt & Fixed Interest Income fund's quoted yield at 14 March 1996		

Source: Barclays Unicorn.

9

Even with the added fee, investment trust Peps are sometimes cheaper than similar unit trust investments. Indeed, despite razor-thin profit margins, ten investment trust managers have no initial Pep charge, and six levy no annual fee.

However, where there is an additional charge, this may influence whether you invest in an investment trust through a Pep, or through a straightforward investment trust savings scheme. The latter may be a better buy than the Pep version of the trust for those paying lower rates of income tax, because the tax benefits of the Pep may not be enough to compensate for the additional charges.

THE PEP PLAN MANAGERS

Authorised Pep plan managers are companies that have been approved by Inland Revenue to set up the Pep umbrella over your investments. The plan manager is almost invariably the organisation that is also managing your investments for you. Pep plan managers are often unit trust and investment trust companies. They may also be banks, building societies, stockbrokers, insurance companies and investment managers and advisers.

Plan managers have to make sure that the Pep is run according to the rules of the scheme. They buy the investments; do the administration; and organise the recovery of tax from Inland Revenue.

Contact numbers for unit trust and investment trust management companies, which will set up a £6,000 Pep for you on one or more of the funds that they manage, are listed in Appendix 3.

HOW TO BUY AND SELL PEPs

Inland Revenue is understandably keen to ensure that investors do not abuse the Pep tax exemptions by sneakily investing in more than one plan in each tax year. Every tax year when you invest in a Pep, therefore, you will be asked for your National Insurance number, so that the Revenue can make the necessary cross-checks. If you have forgotten, or never knew, this number you will find it either on your form P60, or on the front cover of your pension book.

The provision of a National Insurance number is the only additional formality attached to a Pep application. In every other respect it is a very simple procedure, although you must apply for a Pep in writing. You cannot deal by telephone.

Money can be invested in a unit trust or investment trust Pep either in a lump sum or through a regular savings scheme. In the latter case, plan managers will ask investors to fill in a direct debit mandate.

The minimum lump sum accepted is usually £500 to £1,000, although some companies have a higher figure. The minimum monthly subscription will be anything from £20 to £50. The maximum investment is the annual general Pep contribution, £6,000 or £500 a month. Many schemes allow investors to top up plans with one-off payments, provided they keep within the contribution limits.

When you send money off for a Pep, it is prudent to ensure that the cheque is signed by you, as the applicant. It is a small detail, but under Inland Revenue rules, you must invest your own money in a Pep, and a cheque signed by another person may be queried and returned.

Units and shares within your Pep are held on your behalf by your plan manager, and you will not receive any certificate as proof of your investment. However you should have regular – probably half-yearly – statements about the progress of your plan, and it is quite likely that you will also be sent a stream of further information designed to interest you in other investment opportunities!

Pep contributions must be made in cash. If you want to 'Pep' existing unitholdings and shareholdings you will have to sell them and then re-invest the proceeds through an approved plan manager. The only exceptions to this are new issue shares (including privatisation shares), and shares acquired through an employee share option or profit-sharing scheme. These can be transferred directly into a Pep.

Many unit trust and investment trust plan managers offer a share exchange facility, which can be used either to set up a new Pep or to top up an existing plan. This may well prove to be the most cost-effective way to sell and re-invest existing holdings (see Chapter Four, pages 79–81).

There is no minimum investment period with a Pep; you may cash in your investment at any time. However, to get the best out of the tax benefits – particularly the ability to earn a growing tax-free income – you should aim at an investment time frame of not less than five years.

You may also cash in part of your Pep at any time, but make sure you really need to raise the money from this source. Once you have cashed a Pep investment, the tax benefits are gone for ever.

9

DELAYING A PEP PURCHASE

Shrewd readers will by now have spotted one potential weakness with the Pep scheme from an investor's point of view. Money must be invested in Stock Exchange securities, and the permitted annual contribution must be used by the end of the relevant tax year. But what if time is ticking away, yet you think this is the wrong time to go into the market, perhaps because it looks over-priced? Do you have to accept that you have missed out on one year's Pep allowance?

Happily, no. There is no need to plunge into the market if this is against your better judgement. Investments may be held in cash within a general Pep, and there is no time limit controlling how long this money remains uninvested, provided the intention is to buy qualifying Pep investments eventually (with single company Peps, investments must be made within 42 days, however). Interest earned on the cash will be tax-free if not more than £180 of interest is withdrawn in a tax year.

A handful of unit trust and investment trust companies, and some financial advisers, offer another facility to investors who want to shelter their Pep allowance without committing themselves immediately to the stockmarket: the phased investment option.

Phased investment schemes enable you to open a Pep with a lump sum, which is then placed on deposit to earn tax-free interest. Over the next year – usually at quarterly intervals – cash is stripped out and invested in the fund of your choice, with the final payment including all accrued interest. At any time during the year, you may abandon the phasing device, and invest all the outstanding cash in your Pep.

Of course, phasing does not always benefit investors. With hindsight, they may well discover that they would have earned better returns if they had invested their £6,000 from the word 'go'. For example, one financial institution, Legal & General, conducted research which suggested that in the majority of cases, phasing an investment in 12 monthly instalments gives a better overall return only when the yield on the FT-SE All-Share Index is around or below 3.6 per cent at the time of the investment.

MOVING PEP MONEY TO ANOTHER PEP MANAGER

It is possible to take Pep money accumulated over the years and to transfer this to a different manager without affecting your Pep contributions for the current year by the transaction.

You will not lose the tax benefits on the transferred Pep, providing you follow the correct procedures and do not handle any of the sale proceeds. This means that you must on no account cash in your old Pep yourself.

To effect the transfer, you will first need to check with your chosen new managers to make sure that they are willing to accept a transfer; they are under no obligation to do so. If they are willing, get a transfer form from them and fill it in. The new managers will then contact your existing managers and complete the transaction on your behalf. The whole process may take a few weeks.

There are a number of perfectly good reasons why you should wish to transfer your Pep to a different fund manager, and with the increase in the amount of accumulated Pep money, and the proliferation of new plans, the Pep transfer market is growing rapidly.

■ You may want to change your investment emphasis, particularly if you have just retired and would like to increase your retirement income.

■ You may feel that the time has come to do a bit of financial spring-cleaning and to reduce paperwork and correspondence by consolidating a number of different Pep holdings within one management company.

■ You may be dissatisfied with the performance or the charging structure of the unit trust or investment trust Pep that you originally selected. It is entirely proper to consider your Pep investment as a medium- to long-term one, but if a trust persistently underperforms the other funds investing in its market sector, it is time to move your money.

In any of these circumstances, transferring your Pep may well be the sensible thing to do. But it is important to remember that a transfer inevitably involves selling and buying costs, because the

This is the bottom-line question. How on earth do you select a Pep fund from the hundreds on offer?

old Pep will usually have to be liquidated in order to buy shares or units in the new fund.

Your existing plan manager may also impose a transfer fee, and there could be an initial charge to go into the new plan, although around a dozen unit trust groups waive these on transfer business.

If you are quite happy with your existing Pep manager, but you want to secure a different investment strategy, look at what other funds the manager offers. If one of these meets your needs it will often be cheaper to switch to this than to move to another investment house. Many fund managers will offer discounts on their initial charge when investors switch (see Chapter Four page 73).

HOW TO CHOOSE A PEP

This is the bottom-line question. How on earth do you select a Pep fund from the hundreds on offer?

As always, the first step is to define your investment objectives and to be absolutely honest with yourself as to the amount of risk you are comfortable with. If you are an income-seeker, decide whether you can afford to buy a growing income, or whether you must maximise returns now. If you are a long-term capital growth seeker, remember that the longer you can invest, the more chance there is that a high growth/high-risk strategy will come off.

Peps should be the core holdings in any stockmarket portfolio, and it is sensible to start by building up a mainstream exposure to the UK stockmarket. You can then consider adding other satellites to the core, first bringing an international element to your portfolio and then perhaps moving into more specialised UK and overseas investment sectors.

Remember, there is no need to keep to the same Pep manager, year in and year out. It can limit investment risk to spread your Pep money among a number of managers, even if this strategy adds to the paperwork.

Choosing a Pep fund involves exactly the same criteria as choosing an investment trust or unit trust for a direct investment (see Chapter Seven). Once you have established the type of fund you want compare the *long-term* performance records of managers in this sector.

You can largely ignore flash-in-the pan brilliance. Look for the funds that have performed consistently well over the years when measured against the stockmarket index that is the yardstick for their sector. Then check whether there have been any managerial or ownership changes that could affect future performance, and whether the funds are run by management companies that have produced an above average performance across their range of trusts.

Management charges are of particular relevance when choosing a Pep. All management fees impact on performance, but there is a double impact if there is an additional charge for administering the Pep. In a few cases, a Pep administration charge can virtually wipe out the tax advantages of the plan.

The charging structure is absolutely fundamental to a choice of tracker fund. These trusts are not competing with actively managed funds or even with each other. Their aim is simply to mimic the performance of their chosen index. It makes no sense whatsoever to choose a more expensive trust, because charges erode tracking performance.

WHO SHOULD HAVE A PEP?

It is a mug's game to be categoric on investment planning matters, but there is little argument that a Pep should be the first stockmarket investment for taxpayers.

If you have decided that you can afford to invest in the stockmarket – having assessed your personal financial needs, your investment time frame and your tolerance of risk – take that first step through a Pep, and choose a unit trust or investment trust plan. That way you will buy yourself professional fund management and a decent spread of risk.

What if you are a non-taxpayer? There are two perspectives here. If you are a non-taxpayer who expects to pay tax in the future, consider using the Pep tax shelter. If you are likely to remain a non-taxpayer there is no advantage or disadvantage in investing through a Pep, unless the Pep plan manager charges *more* for a Pep than for a direct investment.

This will be the case with a number of investment trust Peps, for instance. Non-taxpayers should invest directly in an investment trust that has an additional Pep charge, and those who pay only modest amounts of tax must make sure that any extra charges levied do not negate the Pep's tax benefits.

With some unit trusts, on the other hand, it is actually cheaper to invest via a Pep than directly. Little wonder that Peps now account for something like three-quarters of all unit trust sales to private investors.

PEPs *versus* TESSAs

'Should I put money into a Tessa or a Pep?' people sometimes ask. It is rather like pondering whether it would be better to eat an apple or an orange. Certainly there is no 'right' answer.

Tessas and Peps are the Government's two mainstream tax-free savings vehicles and they complement rather than compete with each other.

■ INVESTMENT SNAPSHOT

Tessas are bank and building society savings accounts that pay tax-free interest if you leave your money untouched for five years. You can have only one Tessa over any one five-year period and the maximum investment into the account is £9,000. You can withdraw income from a Tessa during the savings term, but this will be paid net of tax, with the tax relief component returned to you at the end of five years.

> ■ **INVESTMENT SNAPSHOT**
>
> *Peps are Stock Exchange investments that provide tax-free capital growth and tax-free dividends. You can take tax-free income from year one, and you can withdraw your money at any time without losing the tax benefits. The maximum investment into a Pep (if both general and single company plans are used) is £9,000 a year, five times as generous as the Tessa maximum contribution.*

Tessas guarantee security of capital; Peps don't; you could get back less than you have invested. If you need to be assured of being able to put your hands on a known amount of money in five years' time, stick to a Tessa.

If you want a plan with the potential for your capital and income to grow, Tessas will not meet your requirements. Use a Pep. If you are somewhat nervous of stockmarket fluctuations, but need to withdraw a high tax-free income straightaway, consider investing in a corporate bond Pep.

PEPs AND FINANCIAL PLANNING

Peps not only enable you to build a ring-fence around your investments, to keep them permanently protected from tax. Their flexibility makes them versatile financial planning tools.

In particular Peps may be used in the two most important financial exercises most of us will ever undertake: buying a house, and amassing income for our retirement.

■ Pep mortgages

Not so long ago most mortgage lenders adopted a robust 'take it or leave it' policy with regard to their loans. Borrowers were offered either a repayment mortgage or an endowment mortgage, and generally speaking, that was that.

But then pension mortgages started to grow in popularity, and managers of collective funds began to point out rather more loudly the considerable advantages of repaying a mortgage with the proceeds of a unit trust or investment trust savings scheme, rather than an inflexible endowment policy.

With the arrival of tax-free Peps, this argument became even more forceful and today most lenders will not only accept a Pep as a mortgage repayment vehicle, many will actually recommend it.

For instance, the Halifax, the largest building society in the country, now has a Pep mortgage (the Tax Free Home Plan) as its flagship mortgage repayment plan.

In structure, a Pep mortgage is simply a variant of the endowment or pension loan. Housebuyers pay interest only on the money they have borrowed, while at the same time they contribute to a Pep. At the end of the mortgage term, the proceeds from this plan will be used to clear the mortgage debt.

Although there is a ceiling on annual Pep contributions, this should be no restriction, even to housebuyers living in areas of high property prices. Over a 25-year period, a maximum investment into a Pep of £500 a month should produce sufficient funds to cover a mortgage of around £300,000.

The advantages of using a Pep to repay a mortgage loan are unambiguous. A Pep mortgage is likely to be cheaper to buy than an endowment or pension mortgage, as Pep charges tend to be lower than charges on life insurance policies; a Pep mortgage is completely portable when you move; a Pep mortgage is tax efficient; and above all a Pep mortgage is flexible.

Flexibility is one of the most persuasive arguments in favour of Pep mortgages. Contributions to a Pep can be increased or decreased without penalty, and part of your plan can be sold at any time, without sacrificing the tax benefits. You can therefore crystallise your investment profits when stockmarkets are booming and share prices are high, and take money out of the Pep to pay off part of your mortgage debt.

Of course Pep mortgages have potential disadvantages and housebuyers must recognise what they are doing. They are repaying their mortgage with a vehicle that carries the risk of stockmarket volatility. Over the past 25 years, shares have provided better returns than building society savings, houses or gilts, and over the term of a mortgage share price, fluctuations should even out.

Nevertheless you cannot ignore the inherent risk. If the end of the mortgage term coincides with a slump in share prices there may well not be enough money in your plan to repay the loan.

So, defensive strategies are necessary if you choose a Pep mortgage. One essential is to conduct regular reviews of your plan's performance, to see if you are on target to repay the mortgage or whether it would be prudent to increase monthly contributions.

Pep mortgages

Flora and Toby Pound-Sign have felt like battery hens in their starter home since the birth of their twin sons and have decided to move.

Flora believes that they should take the opportunity to change from a repayment mortgage to a Pep mortgage that offers tax breaks and investment potential. They discover that their lender will accept any Pep as a repayment vehicle but that it also offers its own packaged Pep mortgage, linked to its in-house UK Income & Growth unit trust.

Working on a 7.25 per cent mortgage rate, the Pound-Signs discover that the monthly cost of a £50,000 loan with this package – including life cover, interest payments and the Pep contribution – will be £355.52. This is slightly more than the comparable £352.18 monthly cost of a repayment loan and Toby begins to think it is not worth the hassle.

Flora disagrees. She likes the flexibility of a Pep mortgage and as they can use any investment profits to pay off part of their loan at any time there should be opportunities to decrease monthly costs in the future.

If the Pound-Signs maintain their initial Pep payments they will pay £20,764.72 into their plan over 25 years. They will get back £62,400 tax free, if their investments grow by 9 per cent a year and £98,200 if they grow by 12 per cent.

Toby, a professional pessimist, asks what happens if their Pep only manages a 6 per cent growth rate. Flora admits that in that case there would not be enough money to repay the mortgage as

9

▶

▶

their plan would only be worth £40,000. The Pound-Signs need a yearly growth rate of 7.50 per cent to cover their £50,000 mortgage.

Toby is alarmed at the prospect of a shortfall. Flora is not. Under the packaged scheme their lender will carry out automatic reviews to see if the Pound-Signs are on target. If they are not they have plenty of scope, within the Pep contribution limits, to top up their plan. As usual, Flora wins the argument.

When building up capital within a Pep to repay a mortgage, it is also sensible to stick to conservative funds that invest in mainstream blue-chip investments rather than slightly more adventurous securities. And two or three years before the end of the mortgage term, you should consider safeguarding your accumulated profits by moving them into a low-risk investment fund.

If you have dependants, you will also need to take out a separate low-cost life insurance policy to cover the mortgage, but there is the same need if you have a repayment mortgage or a pension mortgage.

The other potential downside of a Pep mortgage is political uncertainty. No-one knows for sure the likely shelf-life of this tax-free scheme. Certainly there is no guarantee that future Governments will continue the Pep tax benefits.

However, the possibility that there might be a change in the Pep rules in the future is no good reason for not taking advantage of the tax breaks while these are available. It is unlikely that any moves to restrict the scheme would be accompanied by retrospective action that would affect the tax exemption of investments already sheltered in a Pep.

If Peps were to be scrapped, or the scheme was to be so radically altered that the plans were no longer sensible mortgage repayment vehicles, housebuyers would simply need to look for another way of building up funds. For instance they could move to a straightforward unit trust or investment trust savings scheme.

■ Retirement planning

A pension scheme is the financial cornerstone of retirement planning, and the personal pension plans that are now available from some unit trust and investment trust companies are discussed later (see Chapter Ten, pages 227–232).

However, many people who are eligible to contribute to a pension tend to fall into the 'too little, too late', trap. Too many don't start thinking seriously about how they are going to cope in retirement until they are in their 40s and 50s, and then they tend to underestimate just how much money they will need to contribute to buy themselves a decent income when they are in their 60s.

Changes in employment patterns also militate against people's ability to build up the maximum possible pension benefits. Pension contributions can be made out of earned income only, and two groups of people suffer pension shortfalls because of this.

There are those who choose to take career breaks, and to leave paid work for a period of years in order to bring up their families. And there are a significant number of people who are forced to take involuntary breaks from work, because of unemployment and redundancy. The days of a 40-year career with one company are over.

For all their many benefits, pensions are also somewhat inflexible vehicles. Your investments are locked into the scheme until retirement, and at that point most of the fund must be taken as annuity income. If you are a high earner you run up against the earnings cap, the salary point – currently £82,200 – when earnings are no longer pensionable.

A Pep is the ideal complementary long-term planning vehicle to fill any gaps in a pension contribution record. Your investments roll-up in a tax shelter during your working life, and can be converted to produce a stream of tax-free income after you retire. Pep income is not taken into consideration when the tax man calculates your eligibility for age allowance.

In many respects, indeed, Peps and pensions are virtual mirror images of each other. With a pension all eligible contributions receive tax relief, and are invested in funds that pay no tax on the income or profits that they earn. The pension income is subject to tax, however.

With a Pep, money goes into tax-free investments but there is no tax relief on the contributions themselves. On the other hand, the income taken from the Pep fund is tax free and the capital is not tied up. If you need to spend some of your Pep investments, whether this is to fund a world cruise or to meet health or nursing care costs, you are free to do so.

During their working lives, many financial planners choose a Pep fund that invests for capital growth and re-invests its dividend income. When they retire they can then adjust their investment strategy, and move their accumulated fund to an income-producing Pep.

Obviously your personal circumstances will dictate whether you opt for an equity income fund, that offers prospects of growing your income during retirement, or a corporate bond Pep that provides a much higher immediate income, but little scope for future capital and income growth. It does not have to be a 'do or die' decision, however. The beauty of Peps is that you can always finetune your investment strategy as the years go by.

■ Using Peps to meet school fees

School fees planning is discussed in greater detail in Chapter Ten, pages 225–227. Clearly an equity-based investment plan, where capital values will fluctuate, is suitable only for those who have time on their side to amass funds before they need to pay the fees.

The tax advantages of Peps give an extra kicker to any equity-based educational plan. At least one firm of specialist school fees advisers has designed a Pep education package based on a range of investment trusts and unit trusts – underpinned by insurance to protect contributors against life's disasters – and there is obvious scope for the development of other Pep school fees packages, or D-I-Y versions.

FURTHER READING

Five leaflets – 'Peps', 'Bond Fund Peps', 'Pep Mortgages','Peps and Pensions' and 'Peps and Tessas' – are available free from The Unit Trust Information Service, 65 Kingsway, London, WC2B 6TD (telephone: 0181–207 1361)

'Investment Trust Peps' is available free from the AITC, Durrant House, 8–13 Chiswell Street, London EC1 4YY (telephone: 0171-588 5347)

9

*Investment trusts and unit trusts
provide an almost unlimited
scope to build up a portfolio of
funds, tailor-made to fit your
financial figure*

PLANNING FOR THE FUTURE

10

■ THE FUNDAMENTALS

 The progressive privatisation of pensions and welfare benefits will force everyone to take more responsibility for their financial futures.

 Investments trusts and unit trusts provide a means to accumulate capital and income through lump sum investments or through regular savings.

 The wide choice of funds available enables planners to tailor their investments to their changing circumstances.

 Investment trusts and unit trusts are well suited to the long-term investment needs of children and of those saving for future school fees bills.

 There are increasing opportunities to link personal pension plans and FSAVCs to investment trusts and unit trusts.

■ TERMINOLOGY

Inheritance tax: A tax on chargeable lifetime gifts and on the value of an estate when one dies.

Personal pension schemes: Pension arrangements for employees who are not members of an occupational pension scheme and for the self-employed.

Free-standing AVCs: Top-up pensions for members of occupational pension schemes which are arranged independently by the employee.

10

Increasing attention is being focused on the need for people to take personal action to ensure their financial security at retirement and into their old age.

The demographic figures underline the urgency. Since 1951, the number of people in the UK who are over 85 has quintupled to more than one million, and over the next 35 years the number will double again.

The vital statistics to consider are risk profile, time frame and investment needs and targets.

Virtually every Western economy with a developed social security system is facing the same problem. Declining birth rates and increased life expectancy mean that there will be progressively fewer workers to support the growing number of pensioners in future years. The consequent contraction of State pensions and other State benefits seems inevitable.

Governments of all colours are likely to continue to shift more responsibility for the provision of pensions and welfare benefits off public shoulders and on to the backs of individuals. As a result, those who have not managed to invest for their old age may face an uncomfortably uncertain financial future in the 21st century.

Equity-based investments, with their potential for generating capital profits and income growth over the years, are valuable long-term financial planning tools. Investment trusts and unit trusts are particularly flexible in that they provide a stockmarket vehicle both for those with capital and for those who need to accumulate wealth through regular savings.

BUILDING A PORTFOLIO OF FUNDS

The available collective investment funds provide almost unlimited scope to build up a portfolio of trusts, tailor-made to fit your particular financial figure. The vital statistics to consider are risk profile, time frame and investment needs and targets.

The construction of a portfolio of investment funds should be as methodical as the building of a house. You need to lay the foundations (the core holdings) and to decide how many rooms you want (your exposure to other mainstream international markets and investment sectors). After that you can choose whether to put in some fancy brickwork round the chimney (highly geared investment trust capital shares, perhaps, or a stake in an emerging markets fund).

As a cautious portfolio construction worker, you will want to wear a safety helmet. You can lose money with any investment trust or unit trust, but there are ground rules to help you to limit the risks:

- Don't put all your money into one market sector.

- Reduce the risk of picking an incompetent fund manager by spreading your money among the funds of more than one investment management company or by having a tracker fund as your core investment.

- Never invest short-term money in an investment trust or unit trust. You need to be able to take a three-year view or longer.

- Don't be distracted by fashion. A new fund, or a specific market sector, may be attracting column inches of comment in the financial Press, but do the investments actually meet your requirements?

- Don't churn your unit trust and investment trust holdings. The more you trade, the more dealing costs will eat into your investment returns. All fund managers should be given the chance to demonstrate their competence through at least two market cycles.

- However, be prepared to sell a trust that persistently underperforms other funds in its sector, and its benchmark index.

10

ADJUSTING TO CHANGING CIRCUMSTANCES

The sheer number and variety of the available unit trusts and investment trusts may make selection a testing task, but the compensation is that there is plenty of scope to alter the balance of your investments to adapt to changing needs.

For instance, redundancy or an inheritance are both likely to prompt a rethink of the way your assets are invested, while retirement is tremendous financial planning upheaval, and a watershed in the life of most investors.

Up to that point you may well have been a growth investor. Even if you have been investing in a fund with a reasonable yield it is more than likely that you have opted for accumulation units or for the re-investment of your dividends or income distributions.

After you retire, your investment priorities will almost certainly change. There may be a need to generate more income from your investments and with no earnings, and limited scope to accumulate further capital, you may well want to contain or reduce your investment risks.

The days when you were happy to have warrants in your portfolio or an exposure to commodity shares could well be over. Indeed, if virtually all your capital is tied up in equities, this will be the time to redress the risk balance of your portfolio by adding some fixed-interest securities and easily realisable bank, building society or National Savings assets to the mix.

This restructuring will not necessarily involve selling existing holdings. Many people have some additional capital to invest when they retire, because they choose to take the maximum tax-free lump sum from their pension fund.

Retirement will prompt some hard decisions about future income requirements. It is one thing to accept the need to generate more income from investments but not all income funds come dressed in the same suit of clothes (see Chapters Five, pages 104–107 and Nine, pages 190–191 and 192–196).

Think carefully before selecting a trust with a currently high yield but limited potential to grow its dividends over the years. Is this really what you want? You may well have a third of your life ahead of you at the age of 60 or 65.

Retirement is also a time when you may have an understandable urge to take some of the investment profits you have accumulated over the years and do some serious spending. Don't resist it. Those liable to excessive guilt feelings should not regard spending capital on a conservatory, or a world cruise, or whatever, as a form of theft, but as just reward for sensible financial planning providing their remaining capital is adequate to keep them secure.

INVESTING FOR CHILDREN

Younger children are in many respects the perfect equity investors. They have time on their side and can sit unmoved through economic cycles and bull and bear markets.

Indeed, apart from their need to earn or be given some money in the first place, their only weakness as potential shareholders is their inevitable reliance on other people to make the investment decisions on their behalf.

10

A unit trust or investment trust solves at least half this problem. Of course the adult who is looking after the child's interests must get the initial asset selection right, but after that the child's money will be run by professional investment managers and some of the risk of stockmarket investment will be limited by an exposure to a broad spread of companies.

■ The legal position

Children under 18 may hold shares in their own name but there are legal barriers to prevent them exercising voting rights and buying and selling securities.

A 'bare trust' (or 'absolute trust') is one straightforward way for an adult to invest in shares or unit trust units for a child, and some investment trust savings scheme managers will supply a simple trust deed.

The trustee or trustees register the shares or units in their own name, adding the child's name or initials to show that the investment is not for the beneficial ownership of the adult. The shares can be registered in the child's name at the age of 18 (16 in Scotland) without any capital gains tax complications.

(There are a number of other types of trust that can be used for the benefit of children. It is important to take professional advice on these.)

Although some unit trusts will allow children of 14 years to invest in their own names, 18 years is the more common age limit. Unit trusts have designated accounts for children's investments. The adult buys units in his or her name – adding the child's initials to show who owns them – and acts as a nominee for the holding, buying and selling units on the child's behalf.

When the child is old enough the units can be transferred to the child's name by filling in a 'stock transfer form'; the likely cost will only be the 50p stamp duty charge.

■ The tax position

Even babies still in the delivery room are potential taxpayers and are entitled to a personal tax allowance (see Chapter Eight, pages 177–178) For the 1996/7 tax year this allowance is worth £3,765. As most children are likely to be non-taxpayers they can make full use of funds that provide a reasonable and growing yield, because they are are able to reclaim the tax deducted from unit trust distributions and investment trust dividends.

For example, if a child's net total income for the 1996/7 tax year is £400 of dividends, and this income has been generated on investments that have not been given by a parent, all the tax credits can be reclaimed. In other words, the child will get £100 back from the Inland Revenue (20/80 x £400). The tax can be reclaimed by filling in Inland Revenue form R40 (see Chapter Eight, pages 166–167).

If parents have given money to their children, however, the position is not quite so rosy. Children may earn up to £100 a year tax-free from a parental gift, but income in excess of this will be taxed as if it belonged to the parent. Each parent may give their child investments that produce up to a total of £100 of income. (There may be tax advantages if a bare trust or accumulation trust is used but professional advice is essential.)

Gifts for grandchildren

Ivor Pound-Sign has given £20,000 to each of his two-year old grandsons, the children of Toby and Flora.

He and his wife Sally want the twins, Archie and Alistair, to have the money when they are 18, by which time they hope that the infant wonders will have stopped trashing their toys and will be ready for university.

The money is transferred to a bare trust for the twins' benefit, with Ivor and Sally as trustees, retaining legal ownership and control. In view of the long investment time frame, Ivor and Sally want asset-backed investments, and they construct two portfolios of unit trusts and investment trust shares on behalf of the boys.

Any income will be taxed as Archie's and Alistair's and can be set against their personal allowances. Any capital gains will also be taxed as the children's, which gives Ivor and Sally scope, if appropriate, to 'bed and breakfast' holdings to make use of the twins' £6,300 annual capital gains tax exemptions.

The money gifted by Ivor is a potentially exempt transfer (PET) for inheritance tax purposes. This means that it will be free of this tax after seven years if he survives.

10

Many parents will decide to use investment funds that concentrate on growth rather than the delivery of income for their gifts.

For instance both warrants and the zero dividend preference shares of split capital investment trusts are taxed under the CGT regime. One strategy for children's investments might be to buy a small quantity of high risk/high reward warrants, and to invest the balance in a selection of low-risk zeros to protect the capital value of the investment.

All children are entitled to the full £6,300 annual CGT allowance in their own right, and gains from their investments can be periodically 'bed and breakfasted' to make use of this, providing the investments are of a sufficient size to warrant the costs of the transaction (see Chapter Eight, pages 174–175). Although the adult runs the investment, for tax purposes it will be treated as the child's.

Whatever investment arrangements you decide to make for your child, grandchild, nephew, niece or godchild, do let the taxman into the secret to avoid any possible confusion in the future. All children's gifts should be notified to Inland Revenue. Simply write to a local tax office, telling them that you intend to make an investment on behalf of the child. If you are planning significant gifts to children it may be wise to consult a solicitor or accountant.

■ Inheritance tax

If your estate is likely to be liable to inheritance tax (IHT), lavish gifting may have potential IHT implications.

Under the rules anyone can give away up to £3,000 a year free of IHT; they can also give as many gifts of £250 to different people as they want and there are special concessions for wedding presents.

If annual gifts exceed the IHT exemptions they become what are known as 'potentially exempt transfers' (or PETs). You don't have to pay IHT on a PET when you make it, and if you survive for seven years the gift will be completely free of tax. However, if you die within seven years of making the gift, and your estate is larger than the nil rate band (currently the first £200,000 of an estate is taxed at a nil rate) the gift may be taxed, although there is some tapering relief.

■ Getting the child involved

Children may have unit trust or investment trusts holdings for a number of reasons. They may have inherited money; or earned it; or been given it by a generous adult.

Whatever the circumstances, try to get your children interested, and progressively more involved, in what is happening to their money.

A good start is to show them where to look up the prices of their unit trust units or investment trust shares in a newspaper, and to explain what the various bits of information given in each entry actually mean. This should help them to understand, for example, the difference between putting money in a building society account and in the shares of a company, and the sort of factors that cause stockmarket prices to rise and fall.

Show them the annual reports and accounts of their funds so that they can see the sort of companies their unit trust or investment trust invests in. There may well be one or two companies in the portfolio whose activities will excite their interest. And as they get older, discuss with them what sort of companies they would like to invest in and why. If the answers are not too outlandish, take some notice of their preferences if you can.

In general, schools do not appear to spend much time or show much enthusiasm in teaching their charges about money management and investment matters. Interesting a child in what is happening to their money is one way of filling the knowledge gap, and of making them more informed investors when the time comes for them to take control.

SCHOOL FEES PLANNING

If you are holding a gurgling baby on your knee at this moment, and you plan to give the little cherub 10 years of boarding school education, you could face a bill of as much as £200,000 over the next 18 years. If you intend your prodigy to go through university, the costs will not stop there. Clearly it is sensible to start saving now.

'School fees planning' is often presented as if it was a separate investment activity, quite unconnected with mainstream investing. In fact, there is nothing singular about parents and others looking for ways to pay school bills as efficiently as possible, either through a savings and investment programme or, if needs must, by borrowing. In general, companies that describe themselves as 'school fees specialists' are simply selling services and packages to help these parents.

Equity-based investments are not the place for school fee planners who are going to need money relatively quickly. In these circumstances you should stick to a savings vehicle where capital values will not fluctuate.

However, if you are one of the forward planners, who is starting to organise for school fees virtually before the child has been conceived, and you have time to work through at least two or three stockmarket cycles, it is sensible to use some investments where there is potential to grow the income and the capital.

Unit trusts and investment trusts enable the investment to be tailored to parents' resources. The funds will accept lump sums or regular savings and they are also more flexible – although more volatile – than with-profit endowment policies, which are the traditional favoured investment vehicle for school fee planners.

With a unit trust or investment trust you can vary payments, you can add any unexpected windfalls on an irregular basis and as you can stop investing at any time without penalty and sell your holding. Moreover, if you shelter your shares or units in a Pep, you will pay no tax on your dividends or profits.

What an investment trust or unit trust cannot promise is that share prices will be booming in September 2004, when little Julian starts at his prep school.

To an extent this problem can be overcome, in that the range of securities offered by unit trusts and investment trusts enables investment strategies to be geared to the time frame in which school fee planners are working. For instance, money can be moved from volatile trusts to a fixed-interest or cash fund some months before the fees are needed.

In contrast, a with-profits endowment policy has the advantage of smoothing out stockmarket fluctuations through the payment of regular bonuses, and of maturing at a fixed point of time, although there is no certainty about the extra bonus often due on maturity. It also provides a small amount of life cover.

The policy has less potential than an investment trust or unit trust to produce capital growth, however, and it is not adaptable to changing circumstances. You cannot suspend payments for a period if you fall on hard times, and surrender values are often poor and may mean that if you cash in early you will lose money.

The zero dividend preference shares of split capital investment trusts, which do not pay dividends and therefore carry no liability for income tax, are particularly useful school fees planning instruments. Zeros are low risk because, providing there are sufficient assets in the trust, they give a predetermined capital return, at a specific time – a most useful characteristic for those facing a quantifiable school fees bill a few years hence.

For instance, parents could invest in a series of zeros, which mature in, say, five, six and seven years time, to meet educational costs. Zeros can either be sheltered in a Pep or parents can protect themselves from tax by using their joint capital gains tax exemptions.

There are more than 40 issues of zeros with various maturity dates, and some school fees planners may consider it prudent to take professional advice before making a judgement on how fully a specific trust's current assets cover the zeros. Each stock-broking house is likely to have a senior executive who specialises in investment trusts (a list of stockbrokers can be obtained from the Association of Private Client Investment Managers and Stockbrokers, telephone: 0891 335521).

10

PERSONAL PENSIONS

A pension is essentially a tax-efficient savings plan, whose purpose is to help people amass as much money as they can before they retire.

■ INVESTMENT SNAPSHOT

In all important essentials therefore, a pension is trying to do exactly the same job as a unit trust or investment trust savings plan. The key differences are that the pension is more tax-efficient and that most of the ultimate investment benefits must be taken in the form of pension income, between the ages of 50 and 75.

Pension contributions qualify for tax relief at your highest rate of income tax and are invested in tax-exempt funds. So, if you invest in a unit trust or investment trust through a personal pension plan, you are effectively able to make payments out of gross income.

Table 10.1

Personal pension contributions 1996/7	
Age on 6 April	% of net relevant earnings
35 years or less	17.5
36–45 years	20.0
46–50 years	25.0
51–55 years	30.0
56–60 years	35.0
61–74 years	40.0
75 years and over	Nil
Earnings cap	£82,200

Net relevant earnings are earnings from an employer which are not subject to any company pension scheme or, if you are self-employed, are roughly equivalent to your annual profits.

When personal pensions were launched to a great fanfare on 1 July 1988, there were hopes that the unit trust companies, in particular, would take on the life insurance industry at its own game and introduce a range of easy-to-understand and competitively priced personal pensions.

Eight years on, however, some 95 per cent of personal pensions continue to be sold by the life insurance companies. In part, this can probably be attributed to the fact that personal pensions were launched less than a year after the great stockmarket crash of October 1987, which understandably dented consumer enthusiasm for equity-based unit trust pension schemes.

Leading unit trust groups such as M & G, Save & Prosper and Mercury have opted to provide personal pensions through a subsidiary life company but a minority of companies – notably Gartmore and Rothschild – do offer simple and cost-effective personal pensions that invest directly in their unit trusts. The funds can be used for personal pensions or for free-standing additional voluntary contribution schemes (FSAVCs).

Unit trust personal pensions can score over some of the life insurance company personal pensions by having simpler and more cost-effective charging structures and by offering greater flexibility on premium payments. However, competition for personal pension business among the life companies, and the new disclosure rules, may whittle away some of these inherent advantages.

The rules require providers to set up separate personal pension unit trusts, which then invest in the group's equivalent mainstream trusts. Past performance statistics are therefore highly visible.

Unlike unit trusts, investment trust companies and their managers are not allowed to be pension providers. The 1989 Finance Act permits them to supply the pension investment vehicle, but they must link with an approved provider for the administration of the scheme.

This restriction delayed the arrival of investment trusts into the personal pension market. Although insurance companies and investment management firms offered investment trust funds as an option to their personal pension clients, it was not until the beginning of 1994 that the first investment trust personal pension plan was launched (in tandem with an approved provider) by Foreign & Colonial. Since then Edinburgh Fund Managers and Flemings have also entered the market and more companies have plans to follow.

Investment trust companies have concentrated on stripping pension investment back to the fundamentals, and concentrating on simplicity, flexibility and low management charges. They offer few frills and furbelows, designing pension plans whose framework is based on that of their existing and highly successful savings schemes.

Those unit trust and investment trust companies that are in the personal pension market offer a wide choice of investment funds, covering a considerable diversity of market risk. Because of its price volatility, however, it is unlikely that any equity-based fund will be an appropriate place for your pension fund a few years before you retire.

10

Unless you are prepared to accept the risk that your planned retirement may coincide with a slump in share prices and that you may have to defer taking your pension, you will need to take measures to stabilise capital values on your accumulated fund. The general advice is to switch from an equity into cash or a fixed-interest fund, two or three years ahead of retirement.

Case Study   ## Planning for a pension

Victoria Pound-Sign, a self-employed caterer, has been deterred from buying a personal pension by headlines about mis-selling and high charges. However, she is pleased with the performance of her two investment trust holdings and when she discovers that she can effectively have a simple investment trust savings plan, with all the benefits of the personal pension tax breaks, she wants to know more.

The information sent by Foreign & Colonial Management, Edinburgh Fund Managers and Fleming Investment Trust Management is a revelation. She can actually understand the plans and the charges are unambiguous, with no hidden extras and no loading for the payment of commission. For instance, Edinburgh Fund Managers' tariff is a set-up charge of £100; a £50 a year administration fee; an 0.5 per cent annual management charge; and a £15 fee if Victoria wants to switch between trusts in the future.

Victoria appreciates that a fund's future performance will be even more important than its charges, but the three managers all have proven pedigrees and offer a wide choice of investments. The minimum monthly contribution of either £50 or £100 is also within Victoria's pocket.

Even so she is slightly worried about placing her pension savings entirely at the mercy of stockmarket volatility. She is therefore reassured to find that with all three plans it is possible to ring-fence accumulated profits by switching to cash ahead of retirement.

FREE-STANDING ADDITIONAL VOLUNTARY CONTRIBUTIONS

Virtually every unit trust and investment trust company in the personal pension market also provides a free-standing additional voluntary contribution (FSAVC) plan.

Additional voluntary contributions (AVCs) are a facility whereby members of company pension schemes can top up their pensions by making extra payments out of their own pockets (employers *can't* contribute to an AVC).

> ■ **DEFINITION**
>
> **Free-standing AVCs** are top-up pensions for members of occupational pension schemes which are arranged independently by the employee

You have a choice of either using the AVC scheme offered to staff by your employer, or of setting up your own arrangement (a free-standing AVC or FSAVC) with a pension provider of your choice.

The first option will be more cost-effective. Administration charges are bound to be lower on any AVC scheme organised on a group basis and it is quite likely that your employer will pay the bill anyway.

However, the advantage of an FSAVC is that it puts you, a member of a company scheme, in personal control of a small part of your pension planning and it can continue if you change employers. It also offers more investment choice. All FSAVC providers manage a wide variety of investment funds.

Members of company pension schemes are allowed to invest up to 15 per cent of salary (up to the £82,200 earnings cap) in a pension arrangement, and this 15 per cent covers contributions to the main scheme and AVCs or FSAVCs. So, if the mandatory employee contribution to the company scheme is 6 per cent you could contribute up to 9 per cent to an AVC or FSAVC. The contributions will qualify for full tax relief.

You will need to ensure that you do not build up so much benefit in your FSAVC fund that you exceed the limits set by Inland Revenue for company pension benefits, however. If you do, your contributions will be returned to you, after a tax deduction.

10

When choosing an investment fund for FSAVCs, some people are happy to take more investment risk with this 'top up' part of their pension, and choose a specialist unit trust or investment trust. They argue that they already have the basic security of membership of a mainstream company pension, which will either provide them with defined benefits or will be invested in a conservatively run investment fund.

That is a reasonable argument for younger FSAVC contributors but it is likely to be too high-risk a strategy for those near retirement. The pension from your FSAVCs must be taken at the same time as you retire and start to draw the pension from your company scheme.

If stockmarkets are depressed at this point, therefore, you do not have the flexibility to wait until prices recover before taking the benefits from your FSAVC fund.

YOU HAVE ACHIEVED YOUR INVESTMENT GOALS: WHAT NEXT?

You have built up a well-diversified portfolio of investment funds, suited to your income or capital requirements and to the degree of risk with which you are comfortable.

... try to steer a middle way between fussy and costly activity, and punchdrunk inertia.

A professional investment manager is overseeing the stock picking and asset allocation within each fund on your behalf. Really, there seems little left for you to do, other than to bank your dividends and income distributions, and to cast an occasional eye over the progress of the price of the shares or units.

It is a reasonable conclusion, but try to steer a middle way between fussy and costly activity, and punchdrunk inertia.

Your own circumstances may change, and so may the environment in which you made your investment selections. Genuinely new and profitable investment opportunities may present themselves; or action may be needed in response to a new fiscal, political or economic situation.

So while you don't want to be a slave to prevailing investment fashion, and to waste money selling perfectly good investments in order to buy the latest newspaper tip, you should not fall asleep over your portfolio.

■ INVESTMENT SNAPSHOT

Spare time to read your annual reports to check whether your money is still being invested in the way you intended, and that your chosen fund is performing at least in line with its sector index.

And – most important – conduct a periodic audit of your investments, to make sure they are still appropriate both to you and to the times in which you are living.

FURTHER READING

'Investing for Children', 'Planning for School Fees' and 'Investing for Income', free leaflets from the Association of Investment Trust Companies, Durrant House, 8-13 Chiswell Street, London EC1Y 4YY (Tel: 0171-588 5347)

'Saving for Children' and 'Education Costs: Planning ahead with unit trusts', free leaflets from the Unit Trust Information Service, 65 Kingsway, London WC2B (Tel: 0181-207 1361)

10

APPENDIX 1

Members of the Association of Unit Trusts and Investment Funds (AUTIF)

ABBEY UNIT TRUST MANAGERS LTD
100 Holdenhurst Road, Bournemouth BH8 8AL (Tel: 01202 292373)

ABTRUST UNIT TRUST MANAGERS LTD
10 Queen's Terrace, Aberdeen, AB9 1QJ (Tel: 01224 631999)

AIB UNIT TRUST MANAGERS LTD
Young James House, 51 Belmont Road, Uxbridge, Middlesex UB8 1RZ
(Tel: 01895 259783)

AIRWAYS UNIT TRUST MANAGERS LTD
1 Douglas Road, Stanwell, Staines, Middlesex, TW19 9QS
(Tel: 01784 247311)

ALBERT E SHARP FUND MANAGERS LTD
Temple Court, 35 Bull Street, Birmingham B4 6ES (Tel: 0121-200 2244)

ALLCHURCHES INVESTMENT MANAGEMENT SERVICES LTD
Beaufort House, Brunswick Road, Gloucester GL1 1JZ (Tel: 01452 305958)

ALLIANCE & LEICESTER LIFE AND UNIT TRUSTS
Insurance House, 125–129 Vaughan Way, Leicester LE1 4ZX
(Tel: 0116-242 6234)

ALLIED DUNBAR UNIT TRUSTS PLC
Allied Dunbar Centre, Station Road, Swindon, Wiltshire SN1 1EL
(Tel: 01793 514514)

AXA EQUITY & LAW UNIT TRUST MANAGERS LTD
AXA Equity & Law House, Corporation Street, Coventry CV1 1GD
(Tel: 01203 555424)

BAILLIE GIFFORD & CO LTD
1 Rutland Court, Edinburgh EH3 8EY (Tel: 0131-222 4244)

B & CE UNIT TRUST MANAGEMENT COMPANY LTD
Manor Royal, Crawley, West Sussex RH10 2QP (Tel: 01293 526911)

BANK OF IRELAND FUND MANAGERS LTD
36 Queen Street, London EC4R 1BN (Tel: 0171-489 8673)

BARCLAYS UNICORN LTD
Gredley House, 11 Broadway, Stratford, London E15 4BJ
(Tel: 0800 374373)

BARING FUND MANAGERS LTD
155 Bishopsgate, London EC2M 3XY (Tel: 0171-628 6000)

BRITANNIA FUND MANAGERS LTD
50 Bothwell Street, Glasgow G2 6HR (Tel: 0141-248 2000)

BSI-THORNHILL UNIT TRUST MANAGERS LTD
77 South Audley Street, London W1Y 6DX (Tel: 0171-629 0662)

BURRAGE UNIT TRUST MANAGEMENT LTD
117 Fenchurch Street, London EC3M 5AL (Tel: 0171-480 7216)

BWD RENSBURG UNIT TRUST MANAGERS LTD
Woodsome House, Woodsome Park, Fenay Bridge, Huddersfield,
West Yorkshire HD8 OJG (Tel: 01484 602250)

CANADA LIFE UNIT TRUST MANAGERS LTD
Canada Life Place, High Street, Potters Bar, Hertfordshire EN6 5BA
(Tel: 01707 651122)

CAPEL CURE MYERS UNIT TRUST MANAGEMENT LTD
The Registry, Royal Mint Court, London EC3N 4EY (Tel: 0171-488 4000)

CAZENOVE UNIT TRUST MANAGEMENT LTD
3 Copthall Avenue, London EC2R 7BH (Tel: 0171-606 0708)

CIS UNIT MANAGERS LTD
CIS Buildings, Miller Street, Manchester M60 0AL (Tel: 0161-837 5060)

CITY FINANCIAL UNIT TRUST MANAGERS LTD
1 White Hart Yard, London Bridge, London SE1 1NX (Tel: 0171-407 5966)

CITY OF LONDON UNIT TRUST MANAGERS LTD
10 Eastcheap, London EC3M 1AJ (Tel: 0171-711 0771)

CLERICAL MEDICAL UNIT TRUST MANAGERS LTD
Narrow Plain, Bristol BS2 OJH (Tel: 0800 373369)

CLOSE FUND MANAGEMENT LTD
12 Appold Street, London EC2A 2AA (Tel: 0171-426 4000)

COLONIAL MUTUAL UNIT TRUST MANAGERS LTD
Colonial Mutual House, Quayside, Chatham Maritime, Gillingham,
Kent ME4 4YY (Tel: 01634 890000)

COMMERCIAL UNION FUND MANAGEMENT INTERNATIONAL LTD
Exchange Court, 3 Bedford Park, Croydon CR9 2ZL (Tel: 0181-686 9818)

CONSISTENT UNIT TRUST MANAGEMENT COMPANY LTD
111 Cannon Street, London EC4N 5AR (Tel: 0171-283 0114)

CREDIT SUISSE INVESTMENT FUNDS (UK) LTD
Beaufort House, 15 St Botolph Street, London EC3A 7JJ
(Tel: 0171-426 2929)

DISCRETIONARY UNIT FUND MANAGERS LTD
40 Clifton Street, London EC2A 4AY (Tel: 0171-377 8819)

DUNEDIN UNIT TRUST MANAGERS LTD
See Edinburgh Unit Trust Managers Ltd (Tel: 0800 378486)

EAGLE STAR UNIT MANAGERS LTD
Eagle Star Centre, Montpellier Drive, Cheltenham, Gloucester GL53 7LQ
(Tel: 01242 577555)

EDINBURGH UNIT TRUST MANAGERS LTD
Donaldson House, 97 Haymarket Terrace, Edinburgh EH12 5HD
(Tel: 0131-313 1000)

ELY PLACE UNIT TRUST MANAGERS
28 Ely Place, London EC1N 6RL (Tel: 0171-242 0242)

EQUITABLE UNIT TRUST MANAGERS LTD
Walton Street, Aylesbury, Buckinghamshire HP21 7QW
(Tel: 01296 431480)

EVERMORE INVESTMENT MANAGERS LTD
1 White Hart Yard, London Bridge, London SE1 1NX (Tel: 0171-407 5966)

EXETER FUND MANAGERS LTD
23 Cathedral Yard, Exeter EX1 1HB (Tel: 01392 412144)

FAMILY INVESTMENT MANAGEMENT LTD
16 West Street, Brighton, East Sussex BN1 2RE (Tel: 01273 724570)

FIDELITY INVESTMENT SERVICES LTD
Oakhill House, 130 Tonbridge Road, Hildenborough, Tonbridge,
Kent TN11 9DZ (Tel: 0800 414161)

FLEMING PRIVATE FUND MANAGEMENT LTD
20 Finsbury Street, London EC2Y 9AQ (Tel: 0171-814 2762)

FLEMING UNIT TRUST MANAGEMENT LTD
25 Copthall Avenue, London EC2R 7DR (Tel: 0171-638 5858)

FOREIGN & COLONIAL UNIT MANAGERS LTD
8th Floor, Exchange House, Primrose Street, London EC2A 2NY
(Tel: 0171-628 8000)

FOSTER & BRAITHWAITE FUND MANAGEMENT LTD
3 London Wall Buildings, London EC2M 5RB (Tel: 0171-588 6111)

FRAMLINGTON UNIT MANAGEMENT LTD
155 Bishopsgate, London EC2M 3FT (Tel: 0171-374 4100)

FRIENDS PROVIDENT UNIT TRUST MANAGERS LTD
Enterprise House, Isambard Brunel Road, Portsmouth, Hampshire PO1 2AW
(Tel: 01705 881340)

GA UNIT TRUST MANAGERS LTD
2 Rougier Street, York YO1 1HR (Tel: 01904 628982)

GAM STERLING MANAGEMENT LTD
GAM House, 12 St James's Place, London SW1A 1NX (Tel: 0171-493 9990)

GAN UNIT TRUST MANAGEMENT LTD
Gan House, Harlow, Essex CM20 2EW (Tel: 01279 626262)

GARTMORE FUND MANAGERS LTD
Gartmore House, 16–18 Monument Street, London EC3R 8AJ
(Tel: 0800 289336)

GEM DOLPHIN INVESTMENT MANAGERS LTD
5 Giltspur Street, London EC1A 9BD (Tel: 0171-236 6441)

GRANVILLE UNIT TRUST MANAGEMENT LTD
Mint House, 77 Mansell Street, London E1 8AF (Tel: 0171-488 1212)

GT GLOBAL FUND MANAGEMENT LTD
Alban Gate, 14th Floor, 125 London Wall, London EC2Y 5AS
(Tel: 0171-710 4567)

GUINNESS FLIGHT UNIT TRUST MANAGERS LTD
Lighterman's Court, 5 Gainsford Street, London SE1 2NE
(Tel: 0171-522 2109)

HALIFAX UNIT TRUST MANAGEMENT LTD
Trinity Road, Halifax, West Yorkshire HX1 2RG (Tel: 0171-220 5050)

HAMBROS UNIT TRUST MANAGERS LTD
One America Square, 17 Crosswall, London EC3N 2EB (Tel: 0800 289895)

HENDERSON TOUCHE REMNANT UNIT TRUST MANAGEMENT LTD
3 Finsbury Avenue, London EC2M 2PA (Tel: 0171-638 5757)

HENRY COOKE INVESTMENT FUNDS LTD
1 King Street, Manchester M2 6AW (Tel: 0800 526358)

HIGH PEAK FUND MANAGEMENT LTD
Alberton House, St Mary's Parsonage, Manchester M3 2WS
(Tel: 0161-831 7433)

HILL SAMUEL UNIT TRUST MANAGERS LTD
10 Fleet Place, London EC4M 7RH (Tel: 0171-203 3000)

HSBC UNIT TRUST MANAGEMENT LTD
6 Bevis Marks, London EC3A 7QP (Tel: 0171-955 5050)

INVESCO FUND MANAGERS LTD
11 Devonshire Square, London EC2M 4YR (Tel: 0800 010733)

JOHN GOVETT UNIT TRUST MANAGEMENT LTD
Shackleton House, 4 Battle Bridge Lane, London SE1 2HR
(Tel: 0171-378 7979)

JOHNSON FRY UNIT TRUST MANAGERS LTD
20 Regent Street, London SW1Y 4PZ (Tel: 01277 227300)

JUPITER UNIT TRUST MANAGERS LTD
Knightsbridge House, 197 Knightsbridge, London SW7 1RB
(Tel: 0171-581 3020)

KLEINWORT BENSON UNIT TRUSTS LTD
10 Fenchurch Street, London EC3M 3LB (Tel: 0171-956 6600)

LAURENCE KEEN UNIT TRUST MANAGEMENT LTD
49–51 Bow Lane, London EC4M 9LX (Tel: 0171-489 9493)

LAURENTIAN UNIT TRUST MANAGEMENT LTD
Barnett Way, Barnwood, Gloucester GL4 7RZ (Tel: 01452 371500)

LAZARD UNIT TRUST MANAGERS LTD
21 Moorfields, London EC2P 2HT (Tel: 0171-588 2721)

LINCOLN FUND MANAGERS LTD
Barnett Way, Barnwood, Gloucester GL4 7RZ (Tel: 01452 371500)

LLOYDS BANK UNIT TRUST MANAGERS LTD
Mountbatten House, Chatham, Kent ME4 4JF (Tel: 01634 834000)

M & G SECURITIES LTD
7th Floor, 3 Minister Court, Great Tower Street, London EC3R 7XH
(Tel: 0171-626 4588)

MALDON UNIT TRUST MANAGERS LTD
Beaufort House, 15 St Botolph Street, London EC3A 7EE (Tel: 0171-247 6555)

MARKS & SPENCER UNIT TRUST MANAGEMENT LTD
Marks & Spencer Financial Services, Kings Meadow, Chester Business Park,
Chester CH99 9UT (Tel: 0800 363432)

MARTIN CURRIE UNIT TRUSTS LTD
Saltire Court, 20 Castle Terrace, Edinburgh EH1 2ES (Tel: 0131-229 5252)

MATHESON UNIT TRUSTS LTD
63 St Mary Axe, London EC3A 8AA (Tel: 0171-369 4800)

MAYFLOWER MANAGEMENT COMPANY LTD
122 Leadenhall Street, London EC3V 4QH (Tel: 0171-303 1234)

MERCURY FUND MANAGERS LTD
33 King William Street, London EC4R 9AS (Tel: 0171-280 2800)

METROPOLITAN UNIT TRUST MANAGERS LTD
Metropolitan House, Darkes Lane, Potters Bar, Hertfordshire EN6 1AJ
(Tel: 01707 662233)

MGM UNIT MANAGERS LTD
MGM House, Heene Road, Worthing, West Sussex BN11 2DY
(Tel: 01903 204631)

MIDLAND UNIT TRUST MANAGEMENT LTD
Norwich House, Nelson Gate, Commercial Road, Southampton,
Hampshire SO15 1GX (Tel: 0345 456123)

MORGAN GRENFELL UNIT TRUST MANAGERS LTD
20 Finsbury Circus, London EC2M 1UT (Tel: 0171-588 7171)

MURRAY JOHNSTONE UNIT TRUST MANAGEMENT LTD
7 West Nile Street, Glasgow G1 2PX (Tel: 0141-226 3131)

MW JOINT INVESTORS LTD
46 Court Street, Haddington, East Lothian EH41 3NP (Tel: 01620-825 867)

N & P UNIT TRUST MANAGEMENT LTD
Alberton House, St Mary's Parsonage, Manchester M3 2WJ
(Tel: 0161-839 8277)

NATIONAL AUSTRALIA TRUST MANAGEMENT COMPANY LTD
PO Box 3004, Glasgow G81 2NS (Tel: 0141-951 2501)

NATIONAL PROVIDENT INVESTMENT MANAGERS LTD
48 Gracechurch Street, London EC3P 3HH (Tel: 0171-623 4200)

NATIONWIDE UNIT TRUST MANAGERS
Kingsbridge Point, Princes Street, Swindon, Wiltshire SN38 8NL
(Tel: 01793 482300)

NATWEST UNIT TRUST MANAGERS LTD
PO Box 886, Trinity Quay, Avon Street, Bristol BS99 5LJ
(Tel: 0117 940 4040)

NEWTON FUND MANAGERS LTD
71 Queen Victoria Street, London EC4V 4DR (Tel: 0500-550 000)

NFU MUTUAL UNIT MANAGERS LTD
Tiddington Road, Stratford-upon-Avon, Warwickshire CV37 7BJ
(Tel: 01789 204211)

NORTHERN ROCK UNIT TRUSTS LTD
Bulman House, Regent Centre, Gosforth, Newcastle-upon-Tyne NE3 3NG
(Tel: 0191-285 2555)

NORWICH UNION TRUST MANAGERS LTD
PO Box 124, Discovery House, Whiting Road, Norwich NR4 6EB
(Tel: 01603 680231)

OLD MUTUAL FUND MANAGERS LTD
Providence House, 2 Bartley Way, Hook, Basingstoke, Hampshire RG27 9XA
(Tel: 01256 768888)

PEARL UNIT TRUSTS LTD
The Pearl Centre, Lynch Wood, Peterborough PE2 6FY (Tel: 01733 470470)

PEMBROKE ADMINISTRATION LTD
37–41 Bedford Row, London WC1R 4JH (Tel: 0171-813 2244)

PENNINE UNIT TRUST MANAGERS LTD
Martins Building, 4 Water Street, Liverpool L2 3UF (Tel: 0151-236 0232)

PERPETUAL UNIT TRUST MANAGEMENT LTD
47–49 Station Road, Henley-on-Thames, Oxfordshire RG9 1AF
(Tel: 01491 417000)

PHILLIPS & DREW UNIT MANAGERS LTD
Triton Court, 14 Finsbury Square, London EC2A 1PD
(Tel: 0171-901 5050)

PILGRIM UNIT TRUST MANAGEMENT LTD
Commercial Union House, 39 Pilgrim Street,
Newcastle-Upon-Tyne NE1 6RQ (Tel: 0191-201 3927)

PORTFOLIO FUND MANAGEMENT LTD
64 London Wall, London EC2M 5TP (Tel: 0171-638 0808)

PREMIUM LIFE UNIT TRUST MANAGERS LTD
37–39 Perrymount Road, Haywards Heath, West Sussex RH16 3BN
(Tel: 01444 416871)

PROLIFIC UNIT TRUST MANAGERS LTD
Walbrook House, 23 Walbrook, London EC4N 8LD (Tel: 0171-280 3700)

PROVIDENT MUTUAL UNIT TRUST MANAGERS LTD
PO Box 568, 25–31 Moorgate, London EC2R 6BA (Tel: 0171-628 3232)

PRUDENTIAL UNIT TRUSTS LTD
Valentines House, 51–69 Ilford Hill, Ilford, Essex 1G1 2DL
(Tel: 0181-478 3377)

REFUGE UNIT TRUST MANAGERS LTD
Refuge House, Alderley Road, Wilmslow, Cheshire SK9 1PF
(Tel: 01625 535959)

RIVER & MERCANTILE INVESTMENT FUNDS LTD
7 Lincoln's Inn Fields, London WC2A 3BP (Tel: 0171-405 3240)

ROTHSCHILD FUND MANAGEMENT LTD
PO Box 528, Five Arrows House, St Swithin's Lane, London EC4N 8NR
(Tel: 0171-623 1000)

ROYAL BANK OF SCOTLAND UNIT TRUST MANAGEMENT LTD
2 Festival Square, Edinburgh EH3 9SU (Tel: 0800 716749)

ROYAL LIFE FUND MANAGEMENT LTD
Royal Insurance House, Peterborough Business Park, Peterborough PE2 6GG
(Tel: 01733 390000)

ST JAMES'S PLACE UNIT TRUST GROUP LTD
PO Box 14963, Craigforth, Stirling FK9 4ZE (Tel: 01786 448844)

SANWA INTERNATIONAL INVESTMENT SERVICES LTD
City Place House, PO Box 245, 55 Basinghall Street, London EC2V 5DJ
(Tel: 0171-330 0572)

SAVE & PROSPER SECURITIES LTD
Finsbury Dials, 20 Finsbury Street, London EC2Y 9AY (Tel: 0171-417 2200)

SCHRODER UNIT TRUSTS LTD
Senator House, 85 Queen Victoria Street, London EC4V 4EJ
(Tel: 0800 526535)

SCOTTISH AMICABLE UNIT TRUST MANAGERS LTD
Grosvenor Building, 72 Gordon Street, Glasgow G1 3RS
(Tel: 0141-248 2323)

SCOTTISH EQUITABLE FUND MANAGERS LTD
Edinburgh Park, Edinburgh EH12 9SE (Tel: 0800 454422)

SCOTTISH LIFE INVESTMENT MANAGEMENT COMPANY LTD
19 St Andrews Square, Edinburgh EH2 1YE (Tel: 0131-225 2211)

SCOTTISH MUTUAL INVESTMENT MANAGERS LTD
Abbey National House, 301 St Vincent Street, Glasgow G2 5HN
(Tel: 0141-248 6321)

SCOTTISH WIDOWS FUND MANAGEMENT LTD
15 Dalkeith Road, Edinburgh EH16 5BU (Tel: 0131-655 6000)

SINGER & FRIEDLANDER UNIT TRUST MANAGEMENT LTD
199 Bishopsgate, London EC2M 3XP (Tel: 0171-638 7541)

SOVEREIGN UNIT TRUST MANAGERS LTD
Tringham House, Wessex Fields, Deansleigh Road, Bournemouth, Dorset
BH7 7DT (Tel: 01202 435400)

STANDARD LIFE FUND MANAGEMENT LTD
PO Box 41, 1 Tanfield, Edinburgh EH3 5RG (Tel: 0800 393777)

STANDARD LIFE TRUST MANAGEMENT LTD
PO Box 41, Tanfield, Edinburgh EH3 5RG (Tel: 0800 393777)

STATE STREET UNIT TRUST MANAGEMENT LTD
One Canada Square, London E14 5AF (Tel: 0171-416 2641)

STEWART IVORY UNIT TRUST MANAGERS LTD
45 Charlotte Square, Edinburgh EH2 4HW (Tel: 0131-226 3271)

SUN ALLIANCE UNIT TRUST MANAGEMENT LTD
St Mark's Court, Chart Way, Horsham, West Sussex RH12 1XL
(Tel: 01403 230230)

SUN LIFE OF CANADA UNIT MANAGERS LTD
Basing View, Basingstoke, Hampshire RG21 4DZ (Tel: 01256 841414)

SUN LIFE TRUST MANAGEMENT LTD
Granite House, 101 Cannon Street, London EC4N 5AD (Tel: 0171-606 4044)

TEMPLETON UNIT TRUST MANAGERS LTD
Saltire Court, 20 Castle Terrace, Edinburgh EH1 2EH (Tel: 0131-469 4000)

THORNTON UNIT MANAGERS LTD
Swan House, 33 Queen Street, London EC4R 1AX (Tel: 0171-246 3000)

TILNEY UNIT TRUST MANAGEMENT LTD
Royal Liver Building, Pier Head, Liverpool L3 1NY (Tel: 0151-236 6000)

TSB UNIT TRUSTS LTD
Charlton House, Andover, Hampshire SP10 1RE (Tel: 01264 346794)

TU FUND MANAGERS LTD
Congress House, Great Russell Street, London WC1B 3LQ
(Tel: 0171-637 7116)

UNITED FRIENDLY UNIT TRUST MANAGERS LTD
42 Southwark Bridge Road, London SE1 9HE (Tel: 0171-800 8000)

WAVERLEY UNIT TRUST MANAGEMENT LTD
13 Charlotte Square, Edinburgh EH2 4DJ (Tel: 0131-225 1551)

WESLEYAN UNIT TRUST MANAGERS LTD
Colmore Circus, Birmingham B4 6AR (Tel: 0121-200 3003)

WHITTINGDALE UNIT TRUST MANAGEMENT LTD
75 Leadenhall Market, London EC3V 1LR (Tel: 0171-623 2444)

WOOLWICH UNIT TRUST MANAGERS LTD
1 White Oak Square, Swanley, Kent BR8 7AG (Tel: 0181-298 4000)

Source: AUTIF

APPENDIX 2

Investment trusts: management companies

The Association of Investment Trust Companies (AITC) has 317 member trusts which are managed by the following companies:

3I ASSET MANAGEMENT
91 Waterloo Road, London SE1 8XP (Tel: 0171-928 3131)

3I PLC
91 Waterloo Road, London SE1 8XP (Tel: 0171-928 3131)

ABERFORTH PARTNERS
14 Melville Street, Edinburgh EH3 7NS (Tel: 0131-220 0733)

ABTRUST FUND MANAGERS
99 Charterhouse Street, London EC1M 6AB (Tel: 0171-490 4466)

AIB INVESTMENT MANAGERS (UK)
Bankcentre – Britain, Belmont Road, Uxbridge, Middlesex UB8 1SA
(Tel: 01895 259783)

ALBANY INVESTMENT TRUST
Port of Liverpool Building, Pier Head, Liverpool L3 1NW
(Tel: 0151-236 8674)

ALLIANCE TRUST PLC
Meadow House, Reform Street, Dundee DD1 1TJ (Tel: 01382 201900)

ASSET MANAGEMENT INVESTMENT COMPANY PLC
6th Floor, Burne House, 88 High Holborn, London WC1V 6LS
(Tel: 0171-831 0066)

BAILLIE GIFFORD & CO
1 Rutland Court, Edinburgh EH3 8EY (Tel: 0131-222 4244)

BARING INTERNATIONAL INVESTMENT MANAGEMENT
155 Bishopsgate, London EC2M 3XY (Tel: 0171-628 6000)

BARING INVESTMENT MANAGEMENT
155 Bishopsgate, London EC2M 3XY (Tel: 0171-628 6000)

BARING PRIVATE INVESTMENT MANAGEMENT
155 Bishopsgate, London EC2M 3XY (Tel: 0171-628 6000)

BETA FUNDS
3 Bolt Court, Fleet Street, London EC4A 3DQ (Tel: 0171-353 2066)

BROADGATE INVESTMENT MANAGEMENT LIMITED
4 Broadgate, London EC2M 7LE (Tel: 0171-374 1942)

BROKER FINANCIAL SERVICES
Whitelodge Farm, Goose Rye Road, Worplesden, Surrey GU3 3RQ
(Tel: 01483 237773)

BZW INVESTMENT MANAGEMENT LIMITED
c/o Ivory & Sime plc, One Charlotte Square, Edinburgh EH2 4DZ
(Tel: 0131-225 1357)

CANDOVER INVESTMENTS
20 Old Bailey, London EC4M 7LN (Tel: 0171-489 9848)

CAZENOVE FUND MANAGEMENT
12 Tokenhouse Yard, London EC2R 7AN (Tel: 0171-588 2828)

CITY OF LONDON INVESTMENT MANAGEMENT CO
10 Eastcheap, London EC3M 1AJ (Tel: 0171-374 0191)

COMMERCIAL UNION INVESTMENT MANAGEMENT
St Helen's, 1 Undershaft, London EC3P 3DQ (Tel: 0171-662 6000)

CROSBY ASSET MANAGEMENT LIMITED
27/F Two Pacific Place, 88 Queensway, Hong Kong
(Tel: 00 852 2844 4238)

CW ASSET MANAGEMENT
12th Floor, Moor House, 119 London Wall, London EC2Y 5ET
(Tel: 0171-256 8388)

DISCRETIONARY UNIT FUND MANAGERS
40 Clifton Street, London EC2A 4AY (Tel: 0171-377 8819)

DUNEDIN FUND MANAGERS
Donaldson House, 97 Haymarket Terrace, Edinburgh EH12 5HD
(Tel: 0800 838993)

EDINBURGH FUND MANAGERS
Donaldson House, 97 Haymarket Terrace, Edinburgh EH12 5HD
(Tel: 0800 838993)

ELECTRA FLEMING
65 Kingsway, London EC2B 6QT (Tel: 0171-831 6464)

ERMGASSEN & CO
c/o Henderson Secretarial Services, 3 Finsbury Avenue, London EC2M 2PA
(Tel: 0171-638 5757)

EXETER ASSET MANAGEMENT
23 Cathedral Yard, Exeter EX1 1HB (Tel: 01392 412122)

FIDELITY INVESTMENTS INTERNATIONAL
Oakhill House, 130 Tonbridge Road, Hildenborough, Kent TN11 9DZ
(Tel: 01732 361144)

FINSBURY ASSET MANAGEMENT
Alderman's House, Alderman's Walk, London EC2M 3XR
(Tel: 0171-623 1363)

FLEMING INVESTMENT TRUST MANAGEMENT
25 Copthall Avenue, London EC2R 7DR (Tel: 0171-638 5858)

FOREIGN & COLONIAL EMERGING MARKETS
Exchange House, 8th Floor, Primrose Street, London EC2A 2NY
(Tel: 0171-454 1415)

FOREIGN & COLONIAL MANAGEMENT
Exchange House, 8th Floor, Primrose Street, London EC2A 2NY
(Tel: 0171-454 1415)

FOREIGN & COLONIAL VENTURES LTD
Exchange House, 8th Floor, Primrose Street, London EC2A 2NY
(Tel: 0171-782 9829)

FRAMLINGTON INVESTMENT MANAGEMENT
155 Bishopsgate, London EC2M 3XJ (Tel: 0171-374 4100)

FRIENDS PROVIDENT ASSET MANAGEMENT
c/o Sinclair Henderson Limited, 23 Cathedral Yard, Exeter EX1 1HB
(Tel: 01392 412122)

GARTMORE
Gartmore House, 16–18 Monument Street, London EC3R 8AJ
(Tel: 0171-782 2655)

GENESIS FUND MANAGERS
21 Knightsbridge, London SW1X 7LY (Tel: 0171-235 5040)

GLASGOW INVESTMENT MANAGERS
29 St Vincent Place, Glasgow G1 2DR (Tel: 0141-226 4585)

GORDON HOUSE ASSET MANAGEMENT
5 Half Moon Street, London W1Y 7RA (Tel: 0171-409 3185)

JOHN GOVETT & CO
Shackleton House, 4 Battle Bridge Lane, London SE1 2HR
(Tel: 0171-378 7979)

JOHN GOVETT MANAGEMENT (JERSEY)
AIB House, PO Box 335, Grenville Street, St Helier, Jersey JE4 8WT
(Tel: 01534 873220)

GRAHAM INVESTMENT MANAGERS
PO Box 641, 1 Seaton Place, St Helier, Jersey JE4 8YJ (Tel: 01534 58847)

GUILDHALL INVESTMENT MANAGEMENT
Merchants House, 5/7 Southwark Street, London SE1 1RQ
(Tel: 0171-403 7572)

GUINNESS FLIGHT INVESTMENT TRUST MANAGERS
Lighterman's Court, 5 Gainsford Street, Tower Bridge, London SE1 2NE
(Tel: 0171-522 2100)

HAMBRECH & QUIST ASSET MANAGEMENT
c/o Hambros Fund Management, 30 Queen Anne's Gate, London SW1H 9AL
(Tel: 0171-222 2020)

HAMBROS FUND MANAGEMENT
41 Tower Hill, London EC3N 4HA (Tel: 0171-480 5000)

HAMBRO PACIFIC FUND MANAGEMENT
c/o Hambros Bank, 41 Tower Hill, London EC3N 4HA (Tel: 0171-480 5000)

J O HAMBRO & PARTNERS
10 Park Place, London SW1A 1ZP (Tel: 0171-222 2020)

HENDERSON TOUCHE REMNANT IT MANAGEMENT
3 Finsbury Avenue, London EC2M 2PA (Tel: 0171-638 5757)

HILL SAMUEL INVESTMENT MANAGEMENT
10 Fleet Place, London EC4M 7RH (Tel: 0171-203 3485)

ICE MANAGEMENT
9 Devonshire Square, London EC2M 4YL (Tel: 0171-929 5269)

INGOT CAPITAL MANAGEMENT
c/o Hambros Fund Management, 10 Park Place, London SW1A 1LP
(Tel: 0171-222 2020)

INVESCO ASSET MANAGEMENT
11 Devonshire Square, London EC2M 4YR (Tel: 0171-626 3434)

INVESCO PRIVATE PORTFOLIO MANAGEMENT
9 Devonshire Square, London EC2M 4YL (Tel: 0171-929 5269)

IVORY & SIME
One Charlotte Square, Edinburgh EH2 4DZ (Tel: 0131-220 4239)

IVORY & SIME ASSET MANAGEMENT
14th Floor, 1 Angel Court, London EC2R 7HR (Tel: 0171-600 6655)

JARDINE FLEMING INVESTMENT MANAGEMENT
47th Floor, Jardine House, 1 Connaught Place, Central, Hong Kong
(Tel: 00 852 2978 7450)

JOHNSON FRY ASSET MANAGERS
20 Regent Street, London SW1Y 4PZ (Tel: 0171-451 1000)

JORDAN ZALAZNICK ADVISORS
c/o Gartmore Investment Limited, Gartmore House, 16–18 Monument Street,
London EC3R 8AJ (Tel: 0171-782 2000)

JUPITER ASSET MANAGEMENT
11th Floor, Knightsbridge House, 197 Knightsbridge, London SW7 1RB
(Tel: 0171-412 0703)

KLEINWORT BENSON DEVELOPMENT CAPITAL
10 Fenchurch Street, London EC3M 3LB (Tel: 0171-956 6600)

KLEINWORT BENSON INVESTMENT MANAGEMENT
10 Fenchurch Street, London EC3M 3LB (Tel: 0171-956 6151)

THE LAW DEBENTURE CORPORATION
Princes House, 95 Gresham Street, London EC2V 7LY (Tel: 0171-606 5451)

LAZARD FRERES ASSET MANAGEMENT
30 Rockefeller Plaza, New York, NY 10020 USA (Tel: 001 212 632 6000)

LEGAL & GENERAL INVESTMENT MANAGEMENT
Bucklesbury House, 3 Queen Victoria Street, London EC4N 8EL
(Tel: 0171-528 6883)

LEGAL & GENERAL VENTURES LIMITED
9th Floor, Temple Court, 11 Queen Victoria Street, London EC4N 4TP
(Tel: 0171-489 1888)

LGT ASSET MANAGEMENT PLC
14th Floor, Alban Gate, 125 London Wall, London EC2Y 5AS
(Tel: 0171-710 4567)

LLOYD GEORGE INVESTMENT MANAGEMENT
c/o Raphael Zorn Hemsley, 10 Throgmorton Avenue, London EC2N 2DP
(Tel: 0171-628 4000)

LOMBARD ODIER INTL PORTFOLIO MANAGEMENT
Norfolk House, 13 Southampton Place, London WC1A 2AJ
(Tel: 0171-831 2350)

MAJEDIE INVESTMENTS
1 Minster Court, Mincing Lane, London EC3R 7ZZ (Tel: 0171-626 1243)

MANAGEMENT INTERNATIONAL (GUERNSEY)
Bermuda House, St Julian's Avenue, St Peter Port, Guernsey,
Channel Islands GY1 3NF (Tel: 01481 726268)

MARTIN CURRIE INVESTMENT MANAGEMENT
Saltire Court, 20 Castle Terrace, Edinburgh, EH1 2ES (Tel: 0131-229 5252)

MAXWELL MEIGHEN & ASSOCIATES
110 Yonge Street, Suite 1601, Toronto, Ontario, Canada M5C 1T4
(Tel: 001 416 366 2931)

MERCURY ASSET MANAGEMENT
33 King William Street, London EC4R 9AS (Tel: 0171-280 2800)

MONTANARO INVESTMENT MANAGERS
c/o Sinclair Henderson Ltd, 23 Cathedral Yard, Exeter EX1 1HB
(Tel: 01392 412122)

MOORGATE INVESTMENT MANAGEMENT
49 Hay's Mews, London W1X 8NS (Tel: 0171-409 3419)

MORGAN GRENFELL TRUST MANAGERS
20 Finsbury Circus, London EC2M 1NB (Tel: 0171-256 7500)

MURRAY JOHNSTONE
7 West Nile Street, Glasgow G1 2PX (Tel: 0141-226 3131)

NATWEST INVESTMENT MANAGEMENT
Fenchurch Exchange, 8 Fenchurch Place, London EC3M 4TE
(Tel: 0171-374 3000)

NEW GUERNSEY SECURITIES
c/o Carey Langlois & Co, PO Box 98, 7 New Street, St Peter Port,
Guernsey GY1 4BZ (Tel: 01481 700300)

NORTHERN VENTURE MANAGERS
Northumberland House, Princess Square, Newcastle Upon Tyne, NE1 8ER
(Tel: 0191-232 7068)

OLD MUTUAL PORTFOLIO MANAGERS
Providence House, 2 Bartley Way, Hook, Basingstoke, Hants RG27 9XA
(Tel: 01256 743361)

OLD MUTUAL INTERNATIONAL ASSET MANAGEMENT (GUERNSEY)
Fairbairn House, Rohais, St Peter Port, Guernsey, Channel Islands
(Tel: 01481 726726)

OLIM
Pollen House, 10–12 Cork Street, London W1X 1PD (Tel: 0171-439 4400)

PANTHEON VENTURES
43–44 Albermarle Street, Mayfair, London W1X 3FE (Tel: 0171-493 5685)

PARIBAS ASSET MANAGEMENT LIMITED
2–3 Philpot Lane, London EC3M 8AQ (Tel: 0171-621 1161)

PERPETUAL PORTFOLIO MANAGEMENT
48 Hart Street, Henley-on-Thames, Oxon RG9 2AZ (Tel: 01491 417280)

PERSONAL ASSETS TRUST
One Charlotte Square, Edinburgh EH2 4DZ (Tel: 0131-225 1357)

PICTET ASSET MANAGEMENT UK LTD
Cutlers Gardens, 5 Devonshire Square, London EC2M 4LD
(Tel: 0171-972 6800)

PROLIFIC ASSET MANAGEMENT
Walbrook House, 23 Walbrook, London EC4N 8LD (Tel: 0171-280 3700)

REA BROTHERS (INVESTMENT MANAGEMENT)
Alderman's House, Alderman's Walk, London EC2M 3XR
(Tel: 0171-623 1155)

J ROTHSCHILD CAPITAL MANAGEMENT
27 St James's Place, London SW1A 1NR (Tel: 0171-493 8111)

ROTHSCHILD ASSET MANAGEMENT LTD
Five Arrows House, St Swithin's Lane, London EC4N 8NR
(Tel: 0171-623 1000)

RUTHERFORD ASSET MANAGEMENT LIMITED
99 Charterhouse Street, London EC1M 6HR (Tel: 0171-490 3882)

SCHRODER INVESTMENT MANAGEMENT
Senator House, 85 Queen Victoria Street, London EC4V 4EJ
(Tel: 0171-382 6000)

SCOTTISH AMICABLE INVESTMENT MANAGERS
The Grosvenor Building, 72 Gordon Street, Glasgow G1 3RS
(Tel: 0141-303 0000)

SCOTTISH INVESTMENT TRUST
6 Albyn Place, Edinburgh EH2 4NL (Tel: 0131-225 7781)

SCOTTISH VALUE MANAGEMENT
2 Canning Street Lane, Edinburgh EH3 8ER (Tel: 0131-229 1100)

SCUDDER, STEVENS & CLARK
New London House, 6 London Street, London EC3R 7BE
(Tel: 0171-264 5000)

SECOND ALLIANCE TRUST
Meadow House, Reform Street, Dundee DD1 1TJ (Tel: 01382 201900)

SFM INVESTMENT MANAGEMENT LIMITED
16 Newton Place, Glasgow G3 7PY (Tel: 0141-332 2334)

SLOANE ROBINSON INVESTMENT MANAGEMENT
Den Norske (Bank Building), 20 St Dunstan's Hill, London EC3R 8HY
(Tel: 0171-929 2771)

STEWART IVORY
45 Charlotte Square, Edinburgh EH2 4HW (Tel: 0131-226 3271)

SUN LIFE INVESTMENT MANAGEMENT SERVICES
107 Cheapside, London EC2V 6DU (Tel: 0171-606 7788)

TEMPLETON INVESTMENT MANAGEMENT
Saltire Court, 20 Castle Terrace, Edinburgh EH1 2EH (Tel: 0131-469 4000)

THORNTON INVESTMENT MANAGEMENT
Swan House, 33 Queen Street, London EC4R 1AX (Tel: 0171-246 3000)

TRUST OF PROPERTY SHARES
Fifth Floor, 77 South Audley Street, London W1Y 6EE (Tel: 0171-486 4684)

VENTURI INVESTMENT MANAGEMENT
Burne House, 88 High Holborn, London WC1V 6LS (Tel: 0171-831 8883)

VOYAGEUR INTERNATIONAL ASSET MANAGERS
133 Rose Street Lane South, Edinburgh EH2 4BB (Tel: 0131-226 6985)

WELLINGTON MANAGEMENT INTERNATIONAL
c/o Aberforth Partners, 14 Melville Street, Edinburgh EH3 7NS
(Tel: 0131-220 0733)

Source: AITC

APPENDIX 3

Unit trust and investment trust
PEP providers

Unit Trust Managers

Abbey National Unit Trust Managers	(Tel: 0141-275 8500)
Abbey Unit Trust Managers Ltd	(Tel: 01202 292373)
Abtrust Unit Trust Managers Ltd	(Tel: 01224 631999)
AIB Unit Trust Managers Ltd	(Tel: 01895 259783)
Albert E Sharp Fund Managers Ltd	(Tel: 0121-200 2244)
Allchurches Investment Management Services Ltd	(Tel: 01452 305958)
Allied Dunbar Unit Trusts Plc	(Tel: 01793 514514)
AXA Equity & Law Unit Trust Managers Ltd	(Tel: 01203 553231)
Baillie Gifford & Co Ltd	(Tel: 0131-222 4244)
Barclays Unicorn Ltd	(Tel: 0800 374373)
Britannia Fund Managers Ltd	(Tel: 0141-248 2000)
BWD Rensburg Unit Trust Managers Ltd	(Tel: 01484 602250)
Canada Life Management (UK) Ltd	(Tel: 01707 651122)
Capel Cure Myers Unit Trust Management Ltd	(Tel: 0171-488 4000)
Cazenove Unit Trust Management Ltd	(Tel: 0171-606 0708)
CIS Unit Managers Ltd	(Tel: 0161-837 5060)
City Financial Unit Trust Managers Ltd	(Tel: 0171-407 5966)
Clerical Medical Unit Trust Managers Ltd	(Tel: 0800 373369)
Colonial Mutual Unit Trust Managers Ltd	(Tel: 01634 890000)
Commercial Union Financial Management International Ltd	(Tel: 0181-686 9818)
Consistent Unit Trust Management Company Ltd	(Tel: 0171-283 0114)
Credit Suisse Investment Funds (UK) Ltd	(Tel: 0171-426 2929)
Direct Line Unit Trusts Ltd	(Tel: 0181-253 7738)
Discretionary Unit Fund Managers Ltd	(Tel: 0171-377 8819)
Dunedin Unit Trust Managers Ltd	(Tel: 0800 378486)

Eagle Star Unit Managers Ltd (Tel: 01242 577555)
Edinburgh Unit Trust Managers Ltd (Tel: 0800 378486)
Ely Place Unit Trust Managers Ltd (Tel: 0171-242 0242)
Equitable Unit Trust Managers Ltd (Tel: 01296 431480)
Exeter Fund Managers Ltd (Tel: 01392 412144)

Family Investment Management Ltd (Tel: 01273 724570)
Fidelity Investment Services Ltd (Tel: 0800 414171)
Fleming Private Fund Management Ltd (Tel: 0171-814 2762)
Foreign & Colonial Unit Managers Ltd (Tel: 0171-628 8000)
Foster & Braithwaite Fund Management Ltd (Tel: 0171-588 6111)
Framlington Unit Management Ltd (Tel: 0171-374 4100)
Friends Provident Unit Trust Managers Ltd (Tel: 01705 881340)

GA Unit Trust Managers Ltd (Tel: 01904 628982)
GAN Unit Trust Management Ltd (Tel: 01279 626262)
Gartmore Fund Managers Ltd (Tel: 0800 289336)
GEM Dolphin Investment Managers Ltd (Tel: 0171-236 6441)
Granville Unit Trust Management Ltd (Tel: 0171-488 1212)
GT Global Fund Management Ltd (Tel: 0171-710 4567)
Guardian Financial Services (Tel: 01473 212422)
Guinness Flight Unit Trust Managers Ltd (Tel: 0171-522 2109)

Halifax Unit Trust Management Ltd (Tel: 0171-220 5055)
Hambros Unit Trust Managers Ltd (Tel: 0800 289895)
Hargreaves Lansdown Fund Managers Ltd (Tel: 0117-988 9880)
Henderson Touche Remnant Unit Trust
    Management Ltd (Tel: 0171-638 5757)
Henry Cooke Investment Funds Ltd (Tel: 0800 526358)
Hill Samuel Unit Trust Managers Ltd (Tel: 0171-203 3000)
HSBC Unit Trust Management Ltd (Tel: 0171-955 5050)

INVESCO Fund Managers Ltd (Tel: 0800 010733)

John Govett Unit Trust Management Ltd (Tel: 0171-378 7979)
Jupiter Unit Trust Managers Ltd (Tel: 0171-581 3020)

Kleinwort Benson Unit Trusts Ltd (Tel: 0171-956 6600)

Laurence Keen Unit Trust Management Ltd (Tel: 0171-407 5966)
Laurentian Unit Trust Management Ltd (Tel: 01452 371500)

Lazard Unit Trust Managers Ltd   (Tel: 0171-588 2721)
Legal & General Unit Trust Managers Ltd   (Tel: 0171-528 6740)
Lincoln Fund Managers Ltd   (Tel: 01452 371500)
Lloyds Bank Unit Trust Managers Ltd   (Tel: 01634 834000)
London & Manchester Trust Management   (Tel: 01392 282676)

M & G Securities Ltd   (Tel: 0171-626 4588)
Marks & Spencer Unit Trust Management Ltd   (Tel: 0800 363432)
Martin Currie Unit Trusts Ltd   (Tel: 0131-229 5252)
Mercury Fund Managers Ltd   (Tel: 0800-244 400)
Metropolitan Unit Trust Managers Ltd   (Tel: 01707 662233)
MGM Unit Managers Ltd   (Tel: 01903 204631)
Midland Unit Trust Management Ltd   (Tel: 0345 456123)
Morgan Grenfell Unit Trust Managers Ltd   (Tel: 0171-588 7171)
Murray Johnstone Unit Trust Management Ltd   (Tel: 0141-226 3131)
MW Joint Investors Ltd   (Tel: 01620-825 867)

N & P Unit Trust Management Ltd   (Tel: 0161-839 8277)
National Australia Trust Management
  Company Ltd   (Tel: 0141-951 2501)
National Provident Investment Managers Ltd   (Tel: 0171-623 4200)
Nationwide Unit Trust Managers   (Tel: 01793 482300)
NatWest Unit Trust Managers Ltd   (Tel: 0117-940 4040)
Newton Fund Managers Ltd   (Tel: 0500-550 000)
NFU Mutual Unit Managers Ltd   (Tel: 01789 204211)
Northern Rock Unit Trusts Ltd   (Tel: 0191-285 2555)
Norwich Union Trust Managers Ltd   (Tel: 01603 680231)
Old Mutual Managers Ltd   (Tel: 01256 768888)

Pearl Unit Trusts Ltd   (Tel: 01733 470470)
Pembroke Administration Ltd   (Tel: 0171-813 2244)
Pennine Unit Trust Managers Ltd   (Tel: 0151-236 0232)
Perpetual Unit Trust Management Ltd   (Tel: 01491 417000)
Portfolio Fund Management Ltd   (Tel: 0171-638 0808)
Premium Life Unit Trust Managers Ltd   (Tel: 01444 416871)
Principal Unit Trust Management   (Tel: 01732 740700)
Prolific Unit Trust Managers Ltd   (Tel: 0171-280 3700)
Provident Mutual Unit Trust Managers Ltd   (Tel: 0171-628 3232)
Prudential Unit Trusts Ltd   (Tel: 0171-911 4490)

Refuge Unit Trust Managers Ltd (Tel: 01625 535959)
River & Mercantile Investment Funds Ltd (Tel: 0171-405 3240)
Rothschild Fund Management Ltd (Tel: 0171-623 1000)
Royal Bank of Scotland Unit Trust
    Management Ltd (Tel: 0800 716749)
Royal Life Fund Management Ltd (Tel: 01733 390000)

St James's Place Unit Trust Group Ltd (Tel: 0141-307 6500)
Save & Prosper Securities Ltd (Tel: 0171-417 2200)
Schroder Unit Trusts Ltd (Tel: 0800 526535)
Scottish Amicable Unit Trust Managers Ltd (Tel: 0141-248 2323)
Scottish Equitable Fund Managers Ltd (Tel: 0800 454422)
Scottish Mutual Investment Managers Ltd (Tel: 0141-248 6321)
Scottish Widows Fund Management Ltd (Tel: 0131-655 6000)
Singer & Friedlander Unit Trust
    Management Ltd (Tel: 0171-638 7541)
Skandia Life Pep Managers Ltd (Tel: 01703 334411)
Sovereign Unit Trust Managers Ltd (Tel: 01202 435400)
Standard Life Fund Management Ltd (Tel: 0800 393777)
Stewart Ivory Unit Trust Managers Ltd (Tel: 0131-226 3271)
Sun Alliance Unit Trust Management Ltd (Tel: 01403 230230)
Sun Life of Canada Unit Managers Ltd (Tel: 01256 841414)
Sun Life Trust Management Ltd (Tel: 0171-606 4044)

Templeton Unit Trust Managers Ltd (Tel: 0131-469 4000)
Thornton Unit Managers Ltd (Tel: 0171-246 3000)
Tilney Unit Trust Management Ltd (Tel: 0151-236 6000)
TSB Unit Trusts Ltd (Tel: 01264 346794)
TU Fund Managers Ltd (Tel: 0171-637 7116)

United Friendly Unit Trust Managers Ltd (Tel: 0171-800 8000)

Virgin Direct Personal Financial Service (Tel: 0345 959595)

Waverley Unit Trust Management Ltd (Tel: 0131-225 1551)
Wesleyan Unit Trust Managers Ltd (Tel: 0121-200 3003)
Whittingdale Unit Trust Management Ltd (Tel: 0171-623 2444)
Woolwich Unit Trust Managers Ltd (Tel: 0181-298 4000)

Investment Trust Managers

3i (administered by the Royal Bank of Scotland, Helpline	(Tel: 0131-523 6116)
Abtrust Fund Managers Ltd	(Tel: 0171-490 4466)
Albany Investment Trust	(Tel: 0151-236 8674)
Alliance Trust Savings Ltd	(Tel: 01382 201900)
Baillie Gifford Savings Management Ltd	(Tel: 0131-222 4244)
Broker Financial Services Ltd	(Tel: 01483 237773)
Dunedin Fund Managers Ltd	(Tel: 0800 838993)
Fidelity Investment Services Ltd	(Tel: 0800 414171)
Finsbury Asset Management Ltd	(Tel: 0171-623 1363)
Fleming Investment Trust Management Ltd	(Tel: 0171-638 5858)
Foreign & Colonial Management Ltd	(Tel: 0171-454 1415)
Gartmore Investment Management Plc	(Tel: 0171-623 1212)
Glasgow Investment Managers	(Tel: 0141-226 4585)
John Govett & Co Ltd	(Tel: 0171-378 7979)
Guinness Flight Fund Managers Ltd	(Tel: 0171-522 2100)
Henderson Touche Remnant Investment Trust Management Ltd	(Tel: 0171-638 5757)
INVESCO Asset Management Ltd	(Tel: 0171-626 3434)
Ivory & Sime Plc	(Tel: 0131-225 1357)
Kleinwort Benson Investment Management Ltd	(Tel: 0171-956 6151)
The Law Debenture Corporation (administered by NatWest)	(Tel: 0171-895 5600)
LGT Asset Management plc	(Tel: 0171-710 4567)
Lloyds Investment Managers	(Tel: 0345 418418)
M & G Group	(Tel: 0171-626 4588)
Majedie Investments (administered by Royal Bank of Scotland,	(Tel: 0131-523 6101)
Martin Currie Investment Management Ltd	(Tel: 0131-229 5252)
Mercury Asset Management Plc	(Tel: 0800-244 400)
Moorgate Investment Management Ltd	(Tel: 0171-409 3419)
Morgan Grenfell Trust Managers Ltd	(Tel: 0171-256 7500)

Murray Johnstone Ltd   (Tel: 0141-226 3131 or 0800 289978)

Perpetual Portfolio Management Ltd   (Tel: 01491 417000)
Personal Assets Trust (administered by
Ivory & Sime,   (Tel: 0131-225 1357)
Pilot IT (administered by Sharelink)   (Tel: 0121-200 4545)

Schroder Investment Management Ltd   (Tel: 0171-382 6000)
Scottish Amicable   (Tel: 0141-303 0000)
SIT Savings Ltd   (Tel: 0800 424422)
Stewart Ivory & Co Ltd   (Tel: 0131-226 3271).

GLOSSARY

Accumulation units: Unit trust units that provide for any net income earned to be automatically re-invested so that the value of the units is increased. Accumulation units are taxable in the same way as income units.

Additional voluntary contributions: A tax-efficient top-up pension facility, available to members of company pension schemes.

AITC: The Association of Investment Trust Companies, the industry's collective voice or trade body. The AITC was formed in 1932 to promote and protect the interests of investment trust companies and their shareholders. It has 317 member trusts.

Annuity income shares: The shares of a split capital investment trust that offer a very high income, but which repay only a negligible amount of capital.

AUTIF: The Association of Unit Trusts and Investment Funds, the trade body of the unit trust industry. AUTIF was founded in 1958 (as the Unit Trust Association) to lobby for regulatory and fiscal improvements for the unit trust industry and to communicate the benefits of collective investment to the general public.

Back-to-back loan: A transaction that hedges the currency exposure on overseas investments.

Bear market: A market when share prices fall consistently over a period of time, and investors are more likely to sell than to buy shares.

Bed and breakfasting: The transaction of selling shares or units on one day and buying them back on the next, in order to realise either a capital gain or a capital loss. 'Bed and breakfasting' establishes a new base, or acquisition, cost for future disposals.

Bid price: The price at which investors sell their unit trust units and investment trust shares.

Blue-chip shares: The shares of 'household name' companies that have substantial assets, solid and stable managements and a consistent track record for growth. Ironically, the name comes from a highest denomination poker chip.

Bonds: Fixed interest securities which are issued by governments, local authorities and companies to raise money. Repayment of this form of debt is guaranteed by the government or the company, so a bond is as secure as the issuer. UK Government bonds are known as gilt-edged securities or gilts.

Bottom-up investment: An investment approach that concentrates on stock selection, and an analysis of the balance sheet strength and prospects of individual companies, rather than on broad economic and political factors, or the outlook for any particular market sector.

Bull market: A market where share prices are rising and more investors are buying than selling shares.

Bulldog bonds: Fixed-interest bonds issued in sterling by foreign governments and corporations.

Cancellation rights: A right to cancel some unit trust purchases.

Capital gains tax (CGT): A tax on the gains or profits made when an asset is sold or otherwise disposed of. There is no CGT to pay on a main or only home, household goods or assets when someone dies.

Capital shares: Shares issued by split capital investment trusts which receive no income during the life of the trust, but offer the potential of large capital gains when the trust is wound up, because they are entitled to all or most of the capital appreciation on the portfolio.

Capital structure: The ordinary shares and preference shares that make up an investment trust's structure.

Certificated savings scheme/investment: An investment where the investor receives a certificate as proof of individual ownership.

Closed-end fund: An investment vehicle like an investment trust that has a fixed capital structure with a fixed number of shares. The share price of a closed-end fund will reflect investor demand for the shares.

Concentration: The number of holdings in a fund's portfolio. The fewer the holdings, the more concentrated the portfolio is.

Contract note: The printed confirmation of an investment deal.

Convertible loan stock: A fixed-interest security that gives holders the right to convert into the ordinary shares of the company that has issued the stock at a future date.

Corporate bond Pep: A personal equity plan (Pep) that invests at least 50 per cent of its portfolio in the fixed-interest securities issued by UK and EU companies. UK Government securities (gilts) are not eligible investments for a corporate bond Pep.

Coupon: The quoted interest rate on a fixed interest security, based on its par value.

CREST: The new computerised settlement system for UK equities.

Debenture: Loan capital which is secured on a company's assets. Debentures pay a fixed rate of interest and have a fixed repayment value. If an investment trust is wound up, debenture stockholders take precedence over preference shareholders and ordinary shareholders.

Designated account: A unit trust investment held by an adult for a child.

Discount: In the world of investment trusts, a trust is described as trading at a discount, when its share price is lower than the trust's net asset value (NAV) per share.

Distribution: The term used for the income paid out to investors by a unit trust.

Dividend: The income paid from an investment in the shares of companies. Dividends are usually paid twice a year, with the mid-year payment known as the 'interim dividend' and the end-of-year payment as the 'final dividend'. Dividends are paid to shareholders after the deduction of tax at 20 per cent.

Dog funds: Investment funds that consistently underperform the benchmark index for their sector.

Dow Jones industrial average index: A narrowly based index of shares listed on the New York Stock Exchange.

Emerging markets: The stockmarkets of young or immature economies which have the potential to grow much faster than the markets of more mature economies.

Equalisation payment: A refund, made with a unit trust investor's first income payment, of that part of the buying price of the unit that reflects income accumulated in the fund, but not yet distributed. The equalisation payment is refunded to the investor as a return of capital, and it is not subject to income tax.

Equities: A general term for the ordinary shares of companies listed on the Stock Exchange. Shareholders own the 'equity' of a company.

Ethical funds: Funds that invest in accordance with a set of specific ethical or environmental criteria (funds with an environmental emphasis are often known as 'green funds'). Typically such funds will exclude companies with interests in oppressive regimes; armaments; nuclear power; tobacco; vivisection and gambling. Positive criteria will include companies providing products and services that are of benefit to the community, and companies with good environmental records.

Eurobonds: International bonds issued outside the domestic market of the issuer.

Execution-only dealing: A facility to buy and sell shares without the provision of any investment advice.

Exercise price: The price at which warrant-holders are entitled to buy shares in an investment trust company.

Financial Services Act (FSA): The 1986 legislation which established a protective framework for investors, and introduced the current regulation of investment businesses. Under the FSA all companies or businesses that deal with, or give advice on, investment must be authorised.

Foreign income dividends (FIDs): Dividends issued by companies or unit trusts when they have received income from overseas sources.

Forward pricing: The pricing of unit trust units after the sale and purchase orders of the day have been received and the fund has been revalued. With forward pricing, investors do not know what price they are dealing at.

FT-SE Actuaries All-Share Index: A broadly based index and the one most widely used to assess the performance of a portfolio. It covers some 900 companies and represents more than 95 per cent of the UK stockmarket capitalisation.

FT-SE 100 Index: Familiarly known as the 'Footsie'. An index comprising the shares of the 100 largest companies by market capitalisation. It represents 70 per cent of the UK stock market.

FT-SE Mid 250 Index: The index consisting of the next 250 companies, below those represented by the FT-SE 100. The companies are capitalised at £150 million to £1 billion and represent slightly over 20 per cent of UK stockmarket capitalisation.

Flotation: The issue of shares for subscription by the public when a new company is launched.

Fund of funds: A unit trust that invests not in individual shares and securities, but in a portfolio of other unit trusts. Also known as a 'Mastertrust'.

Gearing: The effect on the capital growth and income of an investment trust of borrowing money on fixed terms to buy more assets. If the total assets of a trust grow in value, the net assets will grow even more, proportionately, because the debt remains the same. The converse is true if the total assets of a trust fall.

General Pep (personal equity plan): The mainstream Pep that enables investors to tax-shelter £6,000 a year in UK and EU shares and bonds.

Gilts/gilt-edged securities: The everyday name for British Government securities, the bonds issued by the UK Government to finance its borrowing. The bonds were given the name 'gilt-edged securities' ('gilts' for short) because the first certificates issued had gilded edges.

Gross redemption yield: The return on a fixed-interest fund (or security) that takes into account both the gross income after charges and the likely capital gains or losses on the underlying fixed-interest investments if these are held until maturity.

Hang Seng Index: A weighted index of shares on the Hong Kong Stock Exchange.

Hedging: Protecting the purchase or sale of currencies or shares or commodities against fluctuating prices by the use of financial instruments such as futures (agreements to buy or sell on a fixed date at a fixed price), options (which give the right but not the obligation to buy or sell on a fixed date at a fixed price) and back-to-back loans.

Highly geared ordinary shares: Shares that are entitled to a split capital investment trust's income, and any surplus capital left when the trust is wound up, and payment has been made to the holders of zero dividend preference shares and other prior charges. Also known as 'income and residual capital' shares.

Historic pricing: The pricing of unit trust units according to the last valuation of the fund. With historic pricing, investors know what price they are dealing at.

Hurdle rate: The annual rate of growth in the assets of an investment trust that is needed if a class of shareholder is to be repaid at redemption.

IMRO: Investment Management Regulatory Organisation. IMRO is responsible for regulating investment managers, such as investment trust and unit trust fund managers.

Income and residual capital shares: See **highly geared ordinary shares**.

Income shares: Shares in a split capital investment trust that are entitled to all or most of the income, and provide a known capital sum when the trust is wound up.

Income units: Units in a unit trust that entitle the investor to regular payments of income.

Index funds: See **tracker funds**.

Initial charge: The charge made when money is first invested, to cover expenses, such as commission to intermediaries and advertising, which have been incurred by the investment managers.

Investment trust: A publicly quoted company with a fixed number of shares that are traded on the London Stock Exchange. The business of an investment trust is to invest in the shares and fixed-interest securities of other companies.

Liquidity: The amount of cash, or assets that can be easily turned into cash, that investment managers keep in a managed portfolio.

Market capitalisation: A measure of the value of a company, calculated by multiplying the number of shares in issue by the share price.

Mastertrust: See **fund of funds**.

National Savings: The savings arm of the Government, which raises money from the public to help fund the National Debt. National Savings is the only savings institution that can provide investors with complete security from the risk of default.

Net asset value (NAV) The total value of the assets of an investment trust at current market values, after all debts and prior charges have been deducted. The NAV is usually quoted in pence per ordinary share. This figure is calculated by dividing these assets by the number of ordinary shares in issue.

Net relevant earnings: The earnings used as a basis to calculate permitted contributions to personal pension plans.

New issues: Shares that are issued on the Stock Exchange for the first time. There is a regular stream of new investment trust flotations.

Nikkei Dow Index: An index of a basket of blue-chip shares on the Tokyo Stock Exchange.

Nominee company: A company that holds shares and securities on behalf of their beneficial owners.

Nominee savings scheme/investment: Scheme or investment where all investments are held in a nominee account to reduce paperwork and simplify administration.

Non-qualifying trust: For Pep purposes, an investment trust or unit trust that has at least 50 per cent of its assets in shares that are quoted on a stock exchange that is recognised by Inland Revenue, but which does not meet the 50 per cent UK/EU Pep rule. Up to £1,500 of the annual £6,000 general Pep allowance may be invested in non-qualifying trusts. See **qualifying trust**.

Offer price: The price at which investors buy units. The offer price of a unit trust includes initial management charges and any commission payments to advisers.

Open-ended funds: Funds such as unit trusts that increase or decrease in size, depending on the buying and selling demands of investors.

Open-ended investment companies (OEICS): A type of collective investment fund that is widely available in the rest of Europe but new to the UK. It is very similar to a unit trust, but it has a company structure, and there is a single price at which its shares are bought and sold.

Optimisation: An investment technique used by managers of index or tracker funds. A statistical model of the index is produced, defining it by criteria such as the size of company, growth, share price and earnings.

Ordinary shares: The main type of share capital of a company. Ordinary shares are the risk capital of a company. They are traded on the Stock Exchange and earn a proportion of the profits of a company in the form of dividends.

Personal equity plans: Investment schemes that enable investors to put a limited amount of money into the shares and corporate bonds of UK and European Union companies, without paying any tax on the income or capital growth from their investment.

Pep plan managers: Managers approved by Inland Revenue to administer Peps. With an investment trust or unit trust Pep, the plan manager is usually also the investment manager.

Personal Investment Authority (PIA): The regulator responsible for overseeing financial advisers and all authorised investment businesses which market investment products to the public.

Personal pension plans: Pension plans for the self-employed and employees who are not members of company pension schemes.

Pound-cost averaging: Investing a fixed sum on a regular basis which results in acquiring shares or units at a lower average price than the average of the prices on the days when the purchases were made.

Preference shares: Part of the share capital of the company. Preference shares pay dividends at a fixed rate, and holders come after creditors, but before ordinary shareholders in the queue, if there is a liquidation.

Premium: An investment trust is said to trade at a premium when its share price is higher than its net asset value (NAV) per share.

Qualifying trust: For Pep purposes an investment trust or unit trust that has at least 50 per cent of its portfolio invested in the shares or fixed-interest securities of listed UK or European Union companies.

Redemption price: The repayment price of gilts and other fixed-interest stocks.

Re-investment of dividends/distributions: The use of a net income distribution to purchase more units or shares.

Replication: An investment technique used by managers of index or tracker funds. The managers buy all the stocks that make up the relevant index, in proportion to their index weighting.

Retail prices index (RPI): An index of a basket of consumer goods and services in retail shops which is calculated each month to determine the movement of prices. It is the main measure of the rate of inflation.

Rights issue: The issue of new shares by a company, in order to raise additional capital.

Sampling: An investment technique used by the managers of index or tracker funds. The managers buy a representative sample of companies within each sector of the index.

Scrip dividends: The issue of shares rather than cash dividends to help conserve a company's cash flow, and to enable shareholders to accumulate more shares.

Securities: General term used for financial assets such as shares, government bonds, corporate bonds and other forms of company debt, and unit trusts.

Securities and Investments Board: The overlord regulator responsible for monitoring the working of the Financial Services Act.

Share exchange scheme: Scheme to enable investors with existing shareholdings to convert these at modest cost into unit trust units or investment trust shares.

Shareholder: The owner of shares in a limited company, and therefore a member or proprietor of the company.

Special situations trust: A fund investing in companies whose share prices may be depressed, but which the fund managers believe have above average growth prospects, because they are likely to have a change of fortune.

Split capital investment trust: An investment trust with a fixed life that has more than one class of share to meet the different investment priorities of its shareholders.

Stepped preference share: A share with a fixed redemption value which provides dividends that rise each year by a known amount.

Switching discount: A reduction in the offer price of units which is given to investors if they move their money from one trust to another within the same management company.

Tax credit: The credit on a tax voucher showing the amount of tax that has been deducted from the dividend or income distribution.

Top-down investment approach: An investment approach that assesses investments by taking into account broad macro-economic and political circumstances and market trends, rather than concentrating on the balance sheet strengths of individual companies.

Total return: The return from a fund taking into account both dividends and interest received, and any capital gains or losses. With an investment trust, total return may be calculated either on the NAV performance of the trust or on the share price performance.

Tracker funds: Or 'index funds'. Funds that mirror the performance of a specific stockmarket index, either by investing in all its shares, or in a representative sample or in futures and options. Both unit trust companies and investment trust companies run tracker funds.

Trust deed: In the context of unit trusts, the legal arrangement between the company that manages the unit trust and the independent financial institution that acts as trustee, holds all the fund's investments and supervises the managers to ensure that they act in accordance with the deed's provisions.

Trustees: The trustee of a unit trust is usually a major bank or insurance company. The trustee holds the unit trust's investments on behalf of its investors.

UCITS: Undertakings for Collective Investment in Transferable Securities. UCITs are collective funds that can be marketed in any EU country.

Unit trust: A legal trust that manages a fund of stockmarket securities on behalf of a number of investors. The pool of investments in the trust is divided into equal portions, called 'units'.

Unitholder: An investor in a unit trust and therefore the owner of units.

Units: The equal portions into which the assets of a unit trust are divided. Investors' units are the measure of their share in the fund.

Unlisted or unquoted investments: Investments in companies which do not have a stockmarket listing.

Venture capital: Capital invested by individuals or companies in new or developing companies. Investors receive shares in the company.

Venture capital trusts: Companies similar to investment trusts, that invest in unquoted companies and provide generous tax incentives for investors.

Warrants: A type of stockmarket security that gives holders the right to purchase shares at a specified price at a specified date or dates in the future. There is no obligation to buy the shares.

Winding-up date: The date for winding up an investment trust company and distributing its assets to shareholders, unless these shareholders vote to extend the trust's life.

XD: When share prices and unit prices are marked 'XD' this means that the fund or company has gone ex-dividend (or ex-distribution) ahead of the income payment to investors. The XD price no longer includes the dividend or income distribution and is likely to fall slightly.

Yield: The size of the prospective annual income paid by an investment in relation to its price. The yield shows the income return as a percentage of the current share price or unit offer price. It is calculated by dividing the share price by the annual gross dividend.

Zero dividend preference shares: Shares that provide no income, but offer a fixed-capital return, which is paid to investors when a split-capital investment trust is wound up. Usually simply called 'zeros'.

INDEX

THE BUCK STARTS HERE!

Do you know how to invest in a Pep?

Are you a charting sceptic?

Do you understand what your advisers are talking about?

How do you choose the right unit trust and investment trust when there are so many on the market?

What's the best way to start planning my investment strategy?

How do I know whether my stockbroker is providing the right level of service?

If you are interested in how your money is working for you, then these are the kind of questions you should want answered.

The *Investors Chronicle* series of investment guides are accessible to those who know nothing about investment services, tactics and techniques. This, balanced by the technical information featured for the more sophisticated, experienced investor, makes them essential for every investor's bookshelf.

Written with the private investor's view-point in mind, by experts who are close to the market.

Titles in this series:

GUIDE TO INVESTMENT TRUSTS & UNIT TRUSTS
GOOD PEPS GUIDE
GUIDE TO CHARTING
A-Z OF INVESTMENT
DIRECTORY OF STOCKBROKER SERVICES
PERSONAL FINANCE PLANNER

Investors Chronicle: **the Authoritative Voice in Investment – providing independent, objective and reliable advice.**

Call Pitman Publishing on 0171 447 2000 for information on titles in this series.

SAVE 10%
on your subscription to Investors Chronicle.
Simply complete this tear-out form and post it to our FREEPOST address.

Mr/Mrs/Miss ....

Job Title ....

Business ....

☐ Company   ☐ Private Address

Address ....

....

Postcode ....

Tel ....

Fax ....

Signed ....

Date........../.........../..........

☐ Please accept my subscription to
INVESTORS CHRONICLE

☐ 1 Year £89.00 (normally £99.00)
☐ 2 Years £160.00 (normally £178.00)
☐ 3 Years £213.00 (normally £237.00)
UK Prices only

☐ I enclose a cheque payable to
FT Magazines

Please debit my: ☐ Access
☐ Amex   ☐ Diners   ☐ Visa

Card No.: ....

Expiry Date ..../..........

☐ Please invoice me/my company

SUBSCRIPTION HOTLINE 01622 778866
Please quote reference 13085H/D085H

Offer applies to new subscribers only. Valid until 31st October 1997.
Please allow up to 14 days for your subscription to be processed.

FT MAGAZINES
Subscription Department
FREEPOST
SEA 0524
HAYWARDS HEATH
WEST SUSSEX
RH16 3BR